Ideology and Image

MULTILINGUAL MATTERS SERIES
Series Editor: Professor John Edwards, *St. Francis Xavier University, Antigonish, Nova Scotia, Canada*

Please contact us for the latest book information:
Multilingual Matters, Frankfurt Lodge, Clevedon Hall,
Victoria Road, Clevedon, BS21 7HH, England
http://www.multilingual-matters.com

MULTILINGUAL MATTERS 124
Series Editor: John Edwards

Ideology and Image
Britain and Language

Dennis Ager

MULTILINGUAL MATTERS LTD
Clevedon • Buffalo • Toronto • Sydney

Library of Congress Cataloging in Publication Data
Ager, D.E.
Ideology and Image: Britain and Language/Dennis Ager.
1. Language planning–Great Britain. 2. Language policy–Great Britain. 3. Linguistic
minorities–Great Britain. 4. Great Britain–Politics and government. I. Title.
P40.5.L352 G73 2003
306.44'941–dc21   2002154985

British Library Cataloguing in Publication Data
A catalogue entry for this book is available from the British Library.

ISBN 1-85359-660-4 (hbk)
ISBN 1-85359-659-0 (pbk)

Multilingual Matters Ltd
UK: Frankfurt Lodge, Clevedon Hall, Victoria Road, Clevedon BS21 7HH.
USA: UTP, 2250 Military Road, Tonawanda, NY 14150, USA.
Canada: UTP, 5201 Dufferin Street, North York, Ontario M3H 5T8, Canada.
Australia: Footprint Books, PO Box 418, Church Point, NSW 2103, Australia.

Printed and bound in Great Britain by the Cromwell Press Ltd.

Contents

Preface

The contrast between France and Britain could not apparently be greater than in their respective attitudes and policies towards language. The French Academy defends and protects French; the British Academy has no such role. Language is specifically mentioned in the French Constitution and the Toubon Law of 1994 declares that 'French is a fundamental constituent of French identity and heritage'. Yet the British Statute of Pleading confirming English as the official language of the law dates from 1362, nearly two centuries before the French equivalent. The 1611 Authorised Version of the Bible, with its incalculable influence on English culture and language, was commissioned by royal authority. Samuel Johnson's Dictionary, which 'beat forty Frenchmen', resulted in his being awarded a pension from prime minister Lord Bute. While the French government took until 1992 to alter the Constitution and until 1994 to 'defend' French against Americanisms in the Toubon Law, in Britain during the 1980s and 1990s the Secretary of State for Education launched a Better English Campaign and legislated for 'correct' English in the National Curriculum. How true is it therefore that the British state has had no interest in and no influence on English?

In the present study of language planning and policy in Britain I have deliberately sought to identify the effect of, and motivation for, the exercise of political authority, and hence social behaviour, on language and on language behaviour in the recent past. That the British state and governments have an interest in controlling and directing language and language behaviour seems to me undeniable. What is different is how they do it.

Acknowledgements

The author is grateful to a number of people for comments on drafts of this book. Dhruba Biswas helped considerably with issues of language maintenance. Bernard Spolsky has made helpful comments. An anonymous reader for Multilingual Matters, too, pointed out the need to sharpen up the argument and made a number of helpful suggestions. I am particularly grateful to Joseph LoBianco and Tom Bloor, who have confirmed the importance of the connection between language usage and politics, both in the narrow sense of the politics of language and in more general ways. Joseph Lo Bianco has provided much help from an international point of view, from his practical experiences of language planning in a political environment, and from his deep knowledge of research in language planning and policy. Tom Bloor, who read the manuscript at a late stage, has helped me clarify the argument in detail, and has helped greatly with his knowledge of sociolinguistics and experience in English studies. Many unidentified and unidentifiable British civil servants, from a number of government departments, have responded courteously, fully and patiently to requests, telephone calls and emails, giving information and sometimes the background to the facts. Annis Ager, as ever, has been an invaluable help in many ways.

Tables

Figures

Introduction

> The English language has never had a state-registered guardian. English is already such a patchwork language that the Word Police would hardly know where to start. Instead of an academy, we've ruled ourselves and allowed the natural forces of change to be curbed only loosely by general dogma and prejudice. (John Simpson, chief editor of the *Oxford English Dictionary*, in *The Guardian* 27.12.1995)

There has long been a naive and romantic belief that in Britain language, like culture, is, or ought to be, a simple reflection of a mysterious social consensus. We, the robustly individual Yeomen, with our Old Etonian's inbred, effortless superiority and our Little Englander's xenophobia, have democratically rejected 'them', the committees, the centralising academy and the intrusive state. 'Many linguists have held the view that language change is a natural, spontaneous phenomenon, the result of underlying social and/or linguistic forces that it is impossible or undesirable to tamper with' (Crystal, 1987: 364). The history of English has been one of apparently untrammelled development and expansion, without any of the controls and checks imposed by such authorities as the French Academy, which is often represented as the archetype of an oppressive authority. Indeed, many English-speaking countries seem to have adopted the same attitude.

English is in this way supposed to enjoy a unique position among languages, and to be a natural product like rainwater. The 'general dogma and prejudice' of those who speak it may be regrettable, but the end product is cause for pride. So, even for the linguist Jespersen in 1905 (Jespersen 1982: 14), 'English is like an English park, which is laid out seemingly without any definite plan, and in which you are allowed to walk anywhere without having to fear a stern keeper enforcing rigorous regulations'. The result of this aimless and uncontrolled development, for the BBC editor Elmes, introducing a Radio 4 series in 2000 on the *Routes of English* presented by Melvyn Bragg, is a

1

wonderful and marvellous achievement brought about by complete anarchy : 'It is that unfettered freedom to do what we damn well like with our words that is the glory of English' (Elmes, 2000: 106).

The view raises any number of questions. Who are the democratic 'we'? How have 'we' ruled ourselves? How 'natural' are the mysterious 'forces of change'? What is meant by 'dogma and prejudice', or, for that matter, 'unfettered freedom'? What sort of contrasts with France and the French Academy does the absence of an English one imply? Is it true, as Elmes alleges (p. 104) , that 'this country has always resisted the formal establishment of an Academy to legislate on matters of linguistic correctness'? Is it true, as he continues, that 'This seems to bubble up out of the British character'? In essence, and taken to the extreme, what is being suggested is that British English has a life independent of its users and of British society. It is our belief that such reification of language is dubious; that, as in most countries, there has long been control and management of language and particularly of language behaviour; that language control by authority, much of it connected to the state, continues; and that views like Simpson's or Elmes' require us to explore what is meant by 'authority', by 'we' and by 'they' in such matters. In a book about Language Policy and Planning in the United Kingdom, where of course English is also not the only language, we should explore society as much as language.

Society and Language

Many of those who are professionally concerned with language study, including Simpson and Elmes, have long accepted that language change, and language behaviour more generally, are directly affected by social forces. As an aspect of social behaviour, language behaviour is not an abstract or idealised phenomenon but depends on relationships with other people: 'language is a social fact', as Saussure was already saying in 1900 (Saussure, 1916: 33).

Society affects how language is used and how it changes. The main disciplines studying the effects of society on language are sociolinguistics and the sociology of language. Chambers (1995), examining sociolinguistic theory, is convinced that the origin and theoretical core of the discipline is the systematic correlation of dependent linguistic variables, such as the pronunciation of -*ing* in English, with independent social variables such as age, gender or class. Identifying systematic correlation of the choice of a variant (such as -*in'* or -*ing*) of the linguistic variable with a variant (such as upper, middle or lower class) of the independent social variable class, is the origin of sociolinguistics. During the period since Labov's 1966 studies of covariation in New York City, and Trudgill's 1974 work on Norwich, many data-driven sociolinguistic studies have appeared and there remain many who consider that covariation remains at the heart of sociolinguistics. There have also however been interpretative studies of such correlations between social category and language use, investigating the significance of a wide range of language behaviour in social contexts. The linguistic variable has developed from being a very specific item of pronunciation or grammar to such wider examples of language behaviour as the choice of language variety (as between Cockney or standard English in London), the choice of language (as between French and English in Quebec), or the choice of discourse (as in political rhetoric). Kaplan and Baldauf (1997: 271), dealing more specifically with language planning and policy, give a list of variables in language behaviour which includes categories such as language change, language shift, language death, language survival, language revival, and language contact.

The social variable, originally a specific feature of social structure such as age, sex or class, has been modified through the concept of the 'social actor' whose social role it is that determines linguistic behaviour. Thus a person's membership of social networks could determine selection of linguistic variants, as could their role, whether such an actor is a group or an individual, within the power structure of society and particularly within group relations. The social variable can thus represent not merely social structure but also social institutions (the professions, political parties, the state bureaucracy) or social processes (network membership, upward or downward social mobility, social attitudes). Chambers notes that there is a wide range of studies of the language-society relationship, all of them often confusingly called sociolinguistics, which he defines as personal, stylistic, social, sociocultural and sociological according to the degree of attention paid to language behaviour (near to psychology and linguistics) as against social behaviour (near to sociology and other social sciences). Cameron, commenting on the 'correlational fallacy' that 'language reflects society', calls for a 'demythologized sociolinguistics' which would 'deal with such matters as the production and reproduction of linguistic norms by institutions and socializing practices; how these norms are apprehended, accepted, resisted and subverted by individual actors and what their relation is to the construction of identity' (Cameron, 1990; reprinted in Coupland & Jaworski, 1997: 62).

Because sociolinguistics was born - or at least baptised - in the 1960s, its view of how language was affected by society was coloured by the attitudes of the time towards the study of society. Sociology itself, also a new science, was preoccupied with the roles of the socioeconomic categories, with studying social systems but particularly with opposition to the established order and to the elite, and with the battle between capitalism and socialism. The two other main social sciences, economics and political science, were involved only insofar as they affected social variables. Coulmas (1992:30) did indeed point out that the invention of the printing press, and, crucially, the development of the market in printed books that it enabled, meant that in Europe the Reformation could take place and could be taken to the people. It was this economic development that led to the need for language codification, for use of the vernaculars rather than Latin and for the social revolution that followed. But only rarely, and recently, have the specifically political ideologies, parties and personalities been invoked to explain or understand influences on language behaviour, and vice-versa, whether this involves language itself, its users or their attitudes. Thus Critical Discourse Analysis was described by van Dijk in 1993 (Cheshire and Trudgill,1998: 367) as 'focusing on the role of discourse in the (re)production and challenge of dominance ... defined here as the exercise of social power by elites, institutions and groups, that results in social inequality, including political, cultural, class, ethnic, racial and gender inequality'.

Such developments in sociolinguistics accept that socioeconomic structures, institutions and processes, however defined, influence language behaviour. The best evidence of this is diachronic or historical: a change in language is noted and correlated with a change in society. Sometimes, but not always, the social change is alleged to be the cause of the linguistic change. Language change usually requires time, so the change from an agrarian to an industrial society in Britain between 1750 and 1850 was not reflected in improved literacy or greater use of the standard language until the early 1900s or even later. Stylistic changes in the language, such as increased use of Americanisms, first required social changes based on increased communication, the invention of film and radio. But there are at least two much more rapid ways in which the social actors of today can cause change in language and language behaviour. The first is through discourse, the language practices of individual or group social actors. These language practices affect the way other people understand that such social actors see the world, and, if these other people adopt these practices or refuse them, they, consciously or unconsciously, have adopted the politics and the policies of the actors concerned along with their language. When group A refers to group B as *freedom fighters*, while group C calls the same people *terrorists*, attempts are being made to persuade others to adopt a sociopolitical stance through adoption of deliberately biased language. This hegemonic effect, realised eventually in language change, is important in two aspects of social behaviour: consumer behaviour and political behaviour. In both domains language is fundamental, both as a means of influencing others and also as an indication of the extent to which such influence has been successful. In both domains, too, the linguistic consequences of social pressure may well be ephemeral: in modern German, the linguistic differences which had developed between East and West Germany between 1945 and 1989 had all but disappeared by 2002.

The second direct method of social influence over language is through specific planning or policy actions, as when a parent instructs a child not to use a swearword, when a regulatory body attempts to prohibit the use of discriminatory racist or sexist terms, or when a government passes legislation directly affecting a particular language. Perhaps surprisingly, the linguistic consequences can be rapid, as with the disappearance of overtly discriminatory language between 1970 and 1990.

Language Planning and Language Policy

The question then arises as to whether both these methods, and other ways in which social behaviour affects language behaviour, can fairly be called language planning. Language planning and policy, henceforth referred to as LPP, is both a practical activity and an area of study and research (Ricento, 2000). It has generally been recognised as worthy of attention since about the end of World War 2, from the period when major efforts were being made in nation building following the decolonisation of the British, and later the French, empires. At about this time, many aspects of life in new nations and old were thought to be amenable to planning and social organisation. The social sciences, including linguistics, were developing methods to solve practical problems such as the writing of grammars, the development of dictionaries and the writing of textbooks, and generally avoided open statements of political ideas and ideologies. After about 1970, though, with the oil crisis of the mid-1970s, and recognising the effectiveness of such 'practical' planning, LPP was more often considered by commentators to be an activity whose effects did little more than represent and reinforce existing power relationships. Many social scientists, evaluating LPP efforts, adopted a more critical tone, noting continuing (neo)colonialism, the social stratification of societies both developed and developing, and the role of language in perpetuating inequality. Many earlier hopes for the social sciences faded, particularly for their role in progress and linear development. After about 1990 and the breakup of the Soviet Union, growing recognition of the continuing power of psycho-social forces such as ethnicity and nationalism, and the movement towards the recognition of human rights, meant that LPP practice became more concerned with trying to save endangered languages, with multiculturalism and multilingualism, and with fostering diversity. It was at this time, too, that in LPP research new analyses of opposition movements, including terrorist/freedom fighter movements such as the IRA and ETA, saw that language had long had a powerful symbolic role in defining communities and providing a rallying point for attitudinal change, which LPP had to be careful in approaching.

'"Language planning" is an activity ... intended to promote systematic language change in some community of speakers ... Language policy (promulgated by government or other authoritative body or person) is a body of ideas, laws, regulations, rules and practices intended to achieve the planned language change' (Kaplan and Baldauf, 1997: xi). The differences, although they will be followed in this book and are clear to Kaplan and Baldauf, are by no means followed in the literature. Our use of the acronym LPP includes the two ideas of forward planning for language change and the implementation of precise actions of various sorts intended to bring it about.

LPP research investigates society's influence on language, firstly from a linguistic (language-internal) point of view, where LPP affects the ways in which people use the forms of a language and hence linguistic processes like codification (standardisation) and elaboration (terminological expansion). Secondly, from a sociological (language-external) standpoint, LPP research investigates influence on the status in society of particular languages or language varieties, and hence on social processes of the selection of these and the acceptance of norms. It also discusses the acquisition (teaching and learning) of language(s) and language varieties. These three widely recognised areas of application (technically known in LPP as corpus, status, and acquisition) are sometimes complemented by a fourth, concerned with what might be called symbolic or prestige policy, manipulating the image of a language its users, or others, have towards it. So corpus policy may recognise a spelling reform, as with dictionary entries; a particular language may be allowed to enter parliamentary use in order to certify its status, as with Scottish Gaelic; textbooks may be written to encourage its acquisition, as with Cornish; and the prestige of a language may be raised by erecting new road signs in Welsh. Finally, and inevitably, LPP research is also concerned with the structures and processes of policy making and policy implementation: who does it and how. In this area it quickly became apparent that it is not just Language Academies which plan language behaviour: the agents of control are far more widely spread.

LPP practice is seen by some as a mechanism mainly concerned with deciding who in society should have access to power and economic resources. Indeed, the ideology of language planners is often cited as though it were itself a social variable. Thus for Tollefson (1991: 16-7), for example, 'there is a close association between language, power, and privilege'. For Rahman (2002: 289) 'power should be the focal analytical category ... in the US ... freedom of linguistic choice is denied in practice, and non-English speakers learn English ... or remain powerless ... in Australia, nationalist (language policy) ... was supported by powerful elite groups.' Certainly sociolinguists generally would agree with Cooper that 'to plan language is to plan society', that language planning is rarely solely about language. Many social scientists would go as far as to say that to plan society is to plan language, and that social planners inevitably influence both language and language use. This may be done directly, by language legislation, or influence may be subtler, as when the hegemonic discourse of social planners becomes itself a form of LPP. An account of language planning and policy in a particular context hence needs to identify, not solely what is proposed, what behavioural prescriptions are put forward, but 'what actors attempt to influence what behaviours of which people for what ends under what conditions by what means through what decision-making processes with what effect?' (Cooper, 1989: 98).

LPP in practice is carried out by a range of social actors, which we have divided for convenience into three: authoritative individuals; groups, categories and communities which often lack direct political power; and the politically powerful government and state. Individuals certainly have influenced language: Dr Johnson and Shakespeare have both left their mark on English. Communities and groups have also influenced language use: the British elite, particularly, has had a major role in influencing how every member of British society speaks and writes standard English. Territorial groups like the dialect speakers of Yorkshire and east London have ensured the survival and sometimes the dissemination of their own ways of speaking; so have ethnic groups like Jamaican Creole speakers and large-scale social categories like women. Our question, here, is whether and how far British governments and public authorities, too, have influenced and do influence language and language behaviour. Does Britain have a language policy or policies?

Motivation

One of the questions which arises when investigating the planning and policy decisions made in a particular society, is 'Why?' Why do planners make the decisions they do? Cooper's eight-point accounting scheme quoted above lacks the psychological dimension. In a previous book (Ager, 2001:144), we developed a way of presenting planners' motivations for a particular action.

Identity sequence	Attitudinal structure								Purposes
Identity	Excellence	Vitality		Attractiveness		Action			Ideals,
Ideology	L1	L2	L1	L2	L1	L2		L1	L2	Objectives and
Image										Targets
Insecurity										
Maintain identity										
Defend identity										
Maintain inequality										
Correct inequality										
Integrate										
Improve instrument										
Despair										

Figure Intro.1 Identity sequence, attitudinal structure and purposes in motivation.

Figures Intro.1 and 2 portray the three components of motivation that we proposed to explain a particular action by planners. These are identity, attitude and goals. We assume, first, that individuals or organisms construct, develop and defend their own self-identity, and that we can identify eleven different aspects of this process:

- the construction of personal and social identity;
- ideology, or the philosophical, religious or moral underpinning of the identity;
- image, or the manipulation of the way that identity appears to others;
- insecurity, the feeling that the identity is under attack;
- the maintenance of identity;
- its defence against attack;
- the maintenance of inequality between groups living in a host society;
- the correction of such inequality;
- two motives for learning a new language: integration, or the desire to empathise with another country or community;
- and instrumentality, the desire to improve skills;
- and finally, perhaps, feelings of despair at the prospect of the destruction of identity.

So, for example, the stages in British identity construction and defence to which the Education Acts of the 1880s can be related are a mixture of instrumentality, the wish to improve the skills of those being educated, and the correction of the social inequality from which the uneducated suffered.

Figure Intro.1 lists these aspects of identity in the left-hand column. In the central columns we represented the attitudes related to each action. Attitudes are made up of three components: knowledge, emotion, and desire for action. Knowledge, we decided, meant knowledge about a language's history, structure, advantages and value, summarised as its 'excellence', and about its 'vitality', or the number of domains in which it is used. The emotive component is represented by the 'attractiveness' of the language. 'Action' means the desire to pass a specific law, or carry out some specific action in language planning such as writing a dictionary or teaching a foreign language. The right-hand column of Figure Intro.1 represents three levels of 'goal' or purpose for each planning action: the general ideal, a more specific objective and a very precise and definite target.

As an example of how the display portrays motivation we could consider the actions of the Conservative government in the 1980s in developing the National Curriculum, as we discussed the issue in Ager, 2001: 40-55. In this display, attitudes are measured: from 3 for strongly felt ones to 1 for weak or absent ones.

Conservative government policy in the 1980s								
Identity sequence	Attitudinal structure							Purposes
	Excellence		Vitality		Attractiveness		Action	
	L1	L2	L1	L2	L1	L2	L1	L2	
Ideology									**elitism/ ignore diversity**
	3	1	3	1	3	1	3	1	

Here, we felt that the issue was provoked by Conservative ideology, applied to the issue of UK identity (left-hand column). This lay behind a number of policy actions, among them the development of particular instructions within the National Curriculum as to what could be taught and what should not. The attitudes of planners (central columns) at that time showed that they thought of English (L1) as a language of the highest excellence; its vitality, the number of domains in which it is used, was similarly strong; it was highly attractive; and, furthermore, in the specific circumstances of the 1980s, there was a high degree of willingness to plan for it, so '3' appears in all the L1 boxes of the chart above. For other languages in the UK, collectively referred to as L2, the attitudes were different: they were not thought of as excellent and in fact little was known about them at all. They were certainly not used in the public domain and their vitality could thus be questioned. There was little desire to take any action in regard to them, whether to assist in maintaining them or in supporting their teaching more widely. All the L2 boxes display '1'. The overall social purpose (right-hand column) could be regarded as supporting elitism, in that standard English for many party members and supporters of government action was a regional and class variety rather than the general language. More specifically, planners' objectives included a desire to repress social manifestations of diversity, whether regional, social or that represented by the growing multiculturalism of society.

Figure Intro.2 portrays, in one chart, nine policy actions in a number of countries in a similar way. It is taken from a more detailed survey of motivational issues in language planning, to which reference should be made for more details. We identified there such overall ideals as cohesion, mosaicity, elitism, competition and conflict.

Motivation of powerful states									
Identity sequence	Attitudinal structure								Ideal/objective
	Exc'ence		Vitality		Attract		Action		
	L1	L2	L1	L2	L1	L2	L1	L2	
IDENTITY (personal)									
IDENTITY (social) eg Algeria (Arabic/Berber)	1	1	1	1	1	1	1	3	cohesion/ accept L1 spoken Arabic, reject L2 Berber
Algeria (spoken/ Classical Arabic)	1	3	1	1	1	3	1	3	cohesion/ accept L1 spoken, promote L2 Classical Arabic
India	3	3	3	3	3	3	3	3	mosaic/ multiculturalism
IDEOLOGY UK	3	1	3	1	3	1	3	1	elitism/ ignore diversity
IMAGE Germany	3	1	3	1	3	1	3	1	competition/ foster German
Japan	3	1	3	1	3	1	3	1	competition/ seek favourable image
INSECURITY									
Neologism in French	1	3	1	3	2	1	3	3	conflict/ xenophobia
MAINTAIN IDENTITY									
DEFEND IDENTITY									
MAINTAIN INEQUALITY eg anti-Roma (Slovakia)	3	1	3	1	3	1	3	1	conflict/ repress Roma
CORRECT INEQUALITY eg Australia	3	3	3	1	3	3	3	3	mosaic/ multilingualism
INTEGRATE									
IMPROVE INSTRUMENT									
DESPAIR									

Figure Intro. 2 Motivations of powerful states
Source: Ager, 2001: 201

This book

This book has two aims: firstly to investigate a dozen examples of recent action on language or language behaviour in the United Kingdom, in order to see how these fit into the definitions of LPP we have mentioned above. Secondly, to describe and characterise contemporary British LPP against an understanding of British society, to compare it with countries such as France, and to explore issues of motivation and power that it raises.

The book is based on published material, on the declarations of the social actors involved, and on generally available information, and tries to be as balanced as possible when considering the more political statements and opinions involved. It concentrates on authoritative and on governmental actions, on attempts to control language by the leaders and rulers of society. It directs attention particularly to what has happened during the last twenty-five years of the twentieth century, examining the position in the year 2002. It looks at issues of the motivation for language policy to see whether there is a type of motivation which characterises British LPP, in the same way that we found characteristic structures for France. It treats the United Kingdom of England, Wales, Scotland and Northern Ireland, although there is necessarily a brief mention of LPP actions in the Republic of Ireland. Because there is a close link between society and language, because we are investigating social influences on language, and because of the view exemplified above that 'we', rather than 'they', control language, we take the view that we must examine aspects of British society and social behaviour just as much as linguistic behaviour. We also define both social and linguistic behaviour broadly, including language attitudes and language-related behaviour as well as the actual words and expressions used. We thus continue the approach we adopted in Ager 1999, on LPP in France, and in Ager 2001, on motivation in LPP.

The social variables we use include, to start with, the various language communities within the United Kingdom and their interrelationships. We hence discuss in Chapters 1 and 2 the nature of the British language communities, starting with the standard English community itself. Here, we look at such issues as the size of the population which can be said to speak or recognise standard English; the various definitions of the term which have been used, and the social, political and economic characteristics of the community. One of our main concerns here is with issues of identity, and we have noted the extent to which the identity issue has been changing in the United Kingdom in recent years. 'Identity' is often used as a code word for 'nationalism', and we investigate the changing nature of English nationalism. Discussion of such issues often takes us apparently far from language behaviour; it is our contention that without an appropriate understanding of the nature of the society which uses the language, any attempt to understand language behaviour, and particularly language planning and policy, must be incomplete. One cannot remove the 'socio' from 'sociolinguistics', and nor can one remove the 'planning' from 'language planning'. Even less can one begin to understand language policy without realising that it is indeed a policy, and like any other policy, is closely connected with social conditions, with social structures and processes, with the environmental background to decisions, and particularly with politics, political parties, their aims and ideologies. We continue in the same way with the other language communities of Britain: the regional and social communities using varieties of English; the territorial communities, particularly Wales, Scotland and Northern Ireland; and the non-territorial language communities. In Chapter 2 we examine the language attitudes of these communities. Some of these have been specifically studied and measured; others must be deduced from influential published writings or actions. Overall, we devote about a quarter of the book to Chapters 1 and 2, and to such considerations, which are unfortunately often regarded as irrelevant to language planning. In our view they are crucial; although they are often ignored in writing on LPP, they are neither simply background nor inessential. They condition the appearance of language behaviour, as well as of behaviour towards language.

We regard language behaviour as one aspect of social behaviour. Our view of the linguistic variable is that we are interested in the choice of language or variety, where there is the possibility of choice; the existence and role of types of discourse; the nature of language use in certain professions including the state bureaucracy; attempts to 'purify' or 'improve' language use in the general population; attempts to improve literacy; attempts to outlaw the use of certain discriminatory terms; attempts to influence the status of different languages through the educational system; and deliberate attempts to influence the fate of 'minority' languages. These types of language behaviour are not limited to 'corpus' matters, but cover all the areas of possible language planning, including 'status', 'image' and 'acquisition'. As in our discussion of France, we refuse to accept that language planning is just about the forms of language.

In Chapter 3 we briefly review some of the main aspects of the development of LPP in Britain since 880 AD. There have been centuries of careful language planning, much of it official. There are many cogent demonstrations of the nature of this planning on English, such as Bailey (1991) or, in a specific period, Smith (1984). Histories of the language (Baugh and Cable, 2002; Fennell, 2001) give many examples of social pressures including those evidenced in Samuel Johnson's Dictionary of 1755 or in the nineteenth century Public Schools, and indeed of official language policy decisions such as those of Parliament in 1362 or the royal decision to authorise a translation of the Bible, published in 1611 and in use for 250 years. The decision not to have an Academy in Britain in 1714, far from 'bubbling out of the British character', was as political as Richelieu's decision to take over a private group in France in 1635. The ideological, and occasionally political, nature of British LPP up to quite recent times, and the fact of its existence, can be traced in many ways.

In Chapter 4 we examine the influence of individuals, societies and such groups as the publishing industry. But our main aim in this book has been to study recent official planning and policy. Governmental language planning and policy decisions are sometimes regarded as reflecting the _rights_ to use or acquire a language or language variety, which individuals or social groups have or wish to have in society; the _resources_ a society has or wishes to develop among its citizens; or the _problems_ which confront it (Ruiz, 1984). Many LPP decisions fall neatly into such categories, although there remain plenty which do not or which combine them in different ways. A dozen or so examples of recent UK LPP decisions, taken from quite different areas of public life, are organised in successive chapters (5 to 8) according to this basic structure of rights, resources and problems. We feel that these demonstrate, firstly, an increasing concern with language on the part of social planners over the period. There is, secondly, an increasingly political approach to LPP. Then, in Chapter 9, the conclusion assesses and evaluates contemporary LPP in Britain, compares it with LPP elsewhere, shows how significant it actually is, and also how closely our examples have been associated with other types of policy and with political ideologies. We then evaluate the motivations which seem to have provoked policy decisions. We have concluded as a general comment that although planners' motives are often mixed, both ideology, the philosophical, religious or moral underpinning of identity construction, and image construction, the manipulation of the outsiders' view of British identity, seem to have significant roles to play in the history of British LPP.

Chapter 1

Language Communities

In this Chapter we consider the language communities of the United Kingdom. We examine who they are, explore their self-awareness and their attitudes, particularly political ones like nationalism and regionalism. In the next chapter we look at attitudes towards these languages and towards language behaviour, although these often relate closely to political attitudes.

The concept of a 'language community' is at first sight a convenient way of describing the group of people who share a common language and who thus may be expected to share attitudes towards that language and towards other ones. The Sapir-Whorf hypothesis (see e.g. Crystal 1987: 15) proposes that the meanings of languages are unique to their community of users, and that each community hence interprets the world differently through the mask of its language. In the strong version of the hypothesis, all the meanings and relationships expressed by a particular language are specific to it, and its speakers are united in the unique understanding of the world they have. But the idea is not so simple as it at first appears. The first and most obvious difficulty, for English, is that the language itself is not monolithic. The English-language community cannot be sensibly defined as 'those whose first language is English', for the obvious reasons that in such a large group - several hundred million people at least - the 'common' language is likely to vary. American, British, Australian, Canadian, Indian and New Zealand English, to name a few recognisable geographically distinguishable varieties, differ considerably in vocabulary, less so in syntax, identifiably so in pronunciation. Attitudes towards particular linguistic features and variables will themselves vary, so that for example 'in the USA prestige forms are rhotic, whereas in England they are non-rhotic' in words like *car, card, butter* (Milroy and Milroy, 1985: 20). Each country also has within it numerous regional differences of dialect and accent, so *while* in northern England means *until* in the South and *bus* is pronounced quite differently in the two areas. Similarly, even within one geographically-marked variety there are differences between socially-marked varieties: apart from phonetic variables like the pronunciation of the vowel in *rope* or *brooch* (Chambers, 1995: 61), syntactic ones like *the play what I wrote* provoke different reactions as between different social classes. Indeed, the same pronunciation (such as *-ing*) or choice of word (such as *filly*) may attract condemnation in one area and be regarded as elitist in another. Over time, too, linguistic items that are elitist become less so, as with *ain't* or h-dropping. Items that are regarded as socially inferior rise in status, like the British Estuary pronunciation, and attitudes towards such changes vary between parts of the English-speaking community.

The second set of difficulties derives from the differences between the circumstances, history and social conditions of different users of the 'same' language. The history, traditions and feelings of nationhood of Australians are not readily shared even with near neighbours the New Zealanders, let alone with other nations and groups. Both may use English but since Australia was a penal colony and then a major immigrant destination while New Zealand's population was and has remained mainly Maori or Polynesian in origin, attitudes, towards English, towards Polynesian languages and certainly towards other languages such as German, are not necessarily the same. The 'battle' between English and Spanish in the USA is meaningless in Australia. Attitudes towards the differences between 'Catholic' and 'Protestant' English in Northern Ireland are quite different in England, where such language differences may not be recognised, do not correlate with religion, and the interreligious differences are in any case not felt in the same way. Attitudes towards the elite in Australia and Britain are quite different, and thus attitudes towards elite language and towards socially inferior varieties may be quite different. Similarly, even in one geographical area the subdivisions of society hold different language attitudes. Hence attitudes towards standard English or towards dialects differ according to social background, educational level and many other social factors within one society, and also as between different societies. The (language and other) attitudes of the wealthy and well-educated are definably different from those of the poor and badly-educated; attitudes of rural speakers are different from those in towns; those of tenth-generation descendants of immigrants differ from those of first-generation immigrants.

Another main difficulty is the difference between L1 and L2

language users in English-speaking communities, whether English is learnt early or late in life. L1 users need English for most, if not all, their communicative situations. For others, English is an instrumental necessity without which it may be difficult to eat, work or be entertained, but may not be their only means of communication with family and friends. For others who come to English late in life there is a positive attraction in learning to use the language of Shakespeare or Julia Roberts, but again this subdivides the language community. And yet another cause of subdivision is that between English-using communities where the history of language contact is different: between Malaysia and Belgium. Yet another depends on the amount and type of English required for international commerce or work as an airline pilot or telephone operator.

Even the British Isles thus contain many language communities, both within English (users of the standard, of rural and of social dialects) and outside it (users of indigenous and of non-indigenous languages). Unsurprisingly, language attitudes, whether towards English or another language, or towards the users of language, are not the same everywhere, as we shall see in the next chapter. In this chapter we concentrate on four different types of language community in Britain: users of standard English as their L1; users of regional or social dialects as their L1; users of territorial languages, although here the L1 is often and indeed usually English; and users of non-territorial languages, although here again the L1 may not be the non-territorial language.

There are of course many social and political characteristics and attitudes which differentiate Great Britain from other countries and which are common across all four nations and in all types of language community. One of these is that of the main political parties, with the Conservative Party being traditionally the party of big business and right-wing attitudes; the Labour Party that of the working class and the political Left; and a Liberal Democratic party usually between the two extremes. There are other, mainly single-issue parties, such as the nationalist parties in Scotland, Wales and Northern Ireland. Across these three classes and two main parties the annual *British Social Attitudes* survey plots three attitudinal scales: left-right, welfarism and libertarian-authoritarian. The left-right scale, for example, notes attitudes towards income redistribution, big business, the law ('one law for the rich and one for the poor'); while the libertarian-authoritarianism scale measures attitudes towards 'respect for traditional British values', equal opportunities for blacks and Asians, and the censorship of films and magazines. The welfarism scale asked questions about attitudes towards the level of government spending on benefits, the fairness or otherwise of social security. On these bases, the parties did not, in 1999, altogether repeat the class divisions, nor are the views of the social classes on welfare or liberty immediately predictable. But views on income redistribution and on some moral issues show the Labour party's attitudes still lay more to the left than those of the Conservatives.

Table 1.1 Left-right, libertarian-authoritarian, welfare and the Euro: views by class and vote, 1999

	Conservative	Labour	Gap
Salariat			
Redistribution	26	48	22
Welfare benefits	33	47	14
Censorship	26	33	7
The Euro	41	70	29
Self-employed			
Redistribution	16	41	25
Welfare benefits	34	44	10
Censorship	23	33	10
The Euro	22	71	49
Working class			
Redistribution	23	46	23
Welfare benefits	25	46	19
Censorship	39	33	6
The Euro	17	25	8

Notes: Figures are percentages of the sample with 'left-wing' views.
Source: Selected and adapted from Jowell *et al*. 2002: 63-4

In 1999, the single concern which most divided the parties had little to do with these major issues: it was the Euro, the common coinage of most countries in the European Union. In 1987, the main issue which divided the parties had been the debate over nuclear arms. Otherwise, it could be said that general attitudes did not show sharp divisions between the parties or the classes over important issues such as income redistribution and censorship.

Despite the existence of such characteristics common to the whole of the British Isles we concentrate below, less on 'British' identity, more on those of the separate language communities. Inevitably however there remains some confusion between 'British' and 'English'.

The Standard English Community

The total population of the United Kingdom, as recorded by the 1991 Census, was 54,888,844 people. Of these, 51,114,048 were born in the United Kingdom; those born in England itself 42,897,179. Does this provide us with a count of the users of standard British English? Hardly. The traditional definition of the community using British spoken standard English combines a geographical defining factor (south-east England) and two socially important factors: use by the educated, and use by the elite. 'The idiomatic use (of shall and will) comes by nature to southern Englishmen' (Fowler 1926:142); 'the grammar and core vocabulary of educated usage in English' (Strevens, 1985:5); 'Received Standard' is 'the best, that form which has the widest currency and is heard with practically no variation among speakers of the better class all over the country. This type might be called Public School English' (Partridge 1947: 306).

Most definitions used today stress one or the other of these social elements; the regional one is rarely included, and indeed is usually specifically excluded since standard English is (said to be) spoken across the country. Thus Trudgill (in Bex & Watts, 1999: 117-28), considers that standard English is a 'purely social dialect'. It is 'spoken as their native variety by about 12-15% of the British population, and this small percentage does not constitute a random cross-section of the population. They are very much concentrated at the top of the social scale'. This would give a figure for standard English speakers of some six to nine million, distributed through the country.

Definitions based on education usually start with the usage of Public Schools and Oxbridge, as with Partridge above. This would imply about seven or eight per cent of the population at most, since this has been the maximum proportion in independent education for most of the twentieth century: under five million people. Even if the definition is broadened to include all those who have completed secondary education (Greenbaum (1990:18): 'the language of the educated all over Great Britain') this would still imply a maximum of some fifty percent of the population. The terms used in National Curriculum documents in the year 2000 also stress the idea of 'educated' users: 'standard English, spoken and written, is the predominant language in which knowledge and skills are taught and learned'.

Sometimes, standard English is defined as a written form. Thus standard English is 'essentially the same form of English used in books and newspapers all over the world' (Honey, 1997: 1-3). This definition would imply a common international form for standard English and mean that there remained little connection between the standard and the UK. Whether in speech or writing, most commentators nonetheless still tend to identify at least two geographically distinct forms: American English and British English. Others would accord standard status to the English of each of the major English-speaking political entities, so that there would be a British, an American, an Australian, an Indian, a Canadian, a Singaporean and a New Zealand standard.

Other definitions use concepts such as that of a neutral, unmarked form, against which all others are 'deviant' or 'idiosyncratic'; of one against which notions of correctness can be tested; of a canonical form against which dialects can be defined; and of idealisation, so that standard English is never actually realised anywhere but is intuitively known by all users. This implies that standard English could be part of the linguistic repertoire of the total UK population, some fifty-eight million people or more in 2002, particularly so since the UK is essentially monolingual and only marginally bilingual, a majority have learnt English as their first language, and the English taught in schools has for long been the standard form (even more so since the introduction of the National Curriculum in the early 1990s),

The British Isles are, as we know, home to four nations: England, Scotland, Ireland and Wales. The facts, the history, the myths and the taboos which together create the self-identity and attitudes of citizens of the United Kingdom, its 'imagined community', are a mixture of those which derive from the individual nation, from the social status and personal history of the individual and those which rulers of England, Britain, Great Britain or the United Kingdom have from time to time manufactured to support their view of history or their agenda for government. The enduring nature of such myths means that identity concepts are often fuzzy, particularly as between the labels 'England' and 'Britain'. Thus the arrival of James I of England in 1603, uniting the crowns of England and Scotland, where he had been King since 1567, meant the need to rename the kingdom and create a myth of Britain, and to subdue the separate cultural identities of the four nations. Later, and after the civil wars of the 1640s, the Restoration of 1660 and the settlement of 1688, the Whig interpretation of history was to found an enduring set of attitudes which persist today as probably the most widely accepted background to civic and political life, and which can be found in all British political parties even though rarely stated. The main features of this background myth are the following (see e.g. Larsen, H. 1997: 38-9):

The Anglo-Saxons were the first true Englishmen.

Their liberties were withdrawn after the Norman Conquest.

The civil war merely replaced one tyranny with another.

The settlement of 1688, the 'Glorious Revolution', inaugurated a new age of English liberty.

The Constitution balances the powers of the monarch (the crown), the titled aristocracy (the lords), and the landed gentry (the commons).

Parliament is the forum for balancing and harmonising interests.

The legitimacy of Parliament is paramount and its independence is unquestioned.

Britain is committed to a non-interventionist state, an open market and a free international economy.

The English/British political system is superior to continental political systems.

Political/institutional pragmatism is preferable to grandiose, abstract, continental schemes.

Rights are to be justified as the traditional liberties once enjoyed by Englishmen (and to be enjoyed again) rather than asserted as the natural and inherent rights of man.

Parliamentary sovereignty is bound up with defiance of the European continent.

Figure 1.1 The Whig interpretation of history

This political and attitudinal background surfaces again and again today in widespread contemporary political attitudes. Parts of it are changing; parts of it remain very obvious, particularly in discussions of the European Union and the Euro; it is apparent in media attitudes towards universality and towards any grandiose and abstract schemes or centralised policies. English/British identity has continued to be a topic of debate, sharpened particularly as devolution was brought about in 1998. At that point, two speeches may be said to characterise the positions of the main contemporary political parties on the issue of national identity: that by the then leader of the Conservative Party, William Hague, on 24th January 1999, and that by Tony Blair, leader of the Labour Party, on 28th March 2000. Robin Cook, then Foreign Secretary, clarified this latter position further on 19th April, 2001, in what has become known as his 'tikka masala' speech. For Hague, 'there is one UK: 'we sink or swim together'. 'The English have always had a strong inherent sense of their own identity, but have never felt the need to express it'. There are four principal features of the British character: 'our individualism and spirit of enterprise; our social mobility and our loyalty to local institutions, which are both reflected in, and, in turn, are shaped by the political institutions of Great Britain'. Hague was careful to specify that 'local' did not mean 'regional': 'we are not a regional nation'. English nationalism is ' a backlash' and a 'sleeping dragon', provoked by Scottish and Welsh nationalism, which will lead to the disintegration of Great Britain.

For Tony Blair, also, 'we are stronger together than apart', although 'true Britishness lies in our values, not in unchanging institutions'. These values were tolerance, adaptability, work, strong communities and families, fair play (rights and responsibilities), and an outward looking approach to the world. Britain's mixed population showed, according to Blair, that outdated 19th century conceptions of blood and territory were inappropriate, and should be modernised and replaced by a devolved plural state.

Robin Cook responded directly to the three threats to British identity (multiculturalism, devolution, and Europe) which Hague had outlined. 'Pluralism is ... an immense asset that contributes to the cultural and economic vitality of our nation. ... Chicken Tikka Massala is now a true British national dish.' Britain is a European country 'in the more profound sense of sharing European assumptions about how society should be organised. ... we reject insular nationalism and the politics of fear.' Devolution has 'been a success for Scotland and for Wales, but has also been a success for Britain.' 'Centuries of living together and working together have created enduring bonds between each of the constituent nations that make up Britain. ... our common identity as British.' It is the diversity of modern Britain that is 'consistent with the historical experience of our islands' and which is a 'unique asset.'

No political leader had anything good to say about nationalism; all were talking of British, not English, national identity; Hague indeed was concerned that English nationalism might be a negative force.

Some small British political parties support 'Britishness' or 'Englishness'. The British National Party has a long history as a semi-Fascist group opposing immigration. In recent years a UK Independence Party has proposed independence from the European Union. Neither has mainstream support. Again, the confusion between British and English identity remains.

More scientific attempts at defining attitudes towards nationalism and ethnicity have been made in surveys of public opinion, particularly at the time of devolution in 1998. Thus the MORI surveying organisation conducted a poll for *The Economist* in September 1999 on the identity issue. One question posed to a representative sample across Great Britain (hence not in Northern Ireland) showed that overall only 40% of the population named Britain as a country with which they identified, even though respondents could name two or three 'communities'. 45% of respondents named the individual country, England, Scotland or Wales. In both Scotland and Wales percentages of over 70% identified with their country. In England, by contrast, the percentage identifying with England (41%) was by a long way the smallest of any in the three countries, slightly less than that including Britain among their responses. The numbers identifying with the Commonwealth, or regarding themselves as world citizens, were under ten percent in each case, with Wales seeming the least interested in such communities (3% with the Commonwealth, 2% with the global community). Europe, as a community with which to identify, scored slightly higher: 16% across Great Britain, with approximately the same percentages in each country.

Table 1.2 Communities with which the UK population identifies

Question: Which two or three of these, if any, would you say you most identify with?

	GB	Eng	Scot	Wales
This local community	41	42	39	32
This region	50	49	62	50
England/Scotland/Wales	45	41	72	81
Britain	40	43	18	27

Adapted. Original report available from from www.mori.com

Similarly, the National Centre for Social Research found that English people were changing their feelings about their own identity, even as between 1997 and 1999. Such changes could be related to devolution as well. In this survey the Moreno scale of nationalism was used, asking the questions 'Which, of the following, best describes how you see yourself?': English, not British; More English than British; Equally English and British; More British than English; and British, not English. This scale, first devised for examining the situation in Catalonia, has the advantage that it narrows the focus to the choice between two nationalisms, each or both of which might apply. The result is that there seems to be an increase in English nationalism, sparked by devolution. Nonetheless, in England at any rate, dual nationalism is still the most frequently chosen category: most people feel themselves to be equally English and British.

Table 1.3 British identity, 1997 and 1999

	1997	1999
English, not British	7	17
More English than British	17	15
Equally English and British	45	37
More British than English	14	11
British, not English	9	14
Other/none/don't know	7	7

Figures are percentages. Sample size: 3000
Source: NCSR, reported in *The Guardian*, 28.11.2000

Another way of measuring nationalism is to investigate feelings of pride. Here, while 69% of those who regarded themselves as unambiguously English were proud of the fact, 39% of the same group were still proud of being British. Among those who declared themselves as unambiguously British, 52% were proud of being British and only 20% of being English also. One conclusion could be that the name England/English provokes stronger feelings than does the name Britain/British. Put another way, for some, nationalism is not a sentiment with which they agree; they are happier with a less emotive, more consensual name like Britain than with a more specific, possibly more jingoistic one like England. Such feelings may be caused by any of a number of factors ranging from concern over the history of English political   domination in Britain and abroad to worry over football hooliganism.

The journalist Jeremy Paxman (1998: 12 - 21) also maintains that English nationalism has massively increased among the population since 1995. Paxman notes another significant point about English nationalism: a general and traditional view that 'almost any display of national pride is not merely unsophisticated but somehow morally reprehensible'. He quotes George Orwell's view that 'in left-wing circles it is always felt that there is something slightly disgraceful in being an Englishman'. That this should have been so derives, firstly, from self-confidence: 'the English have not spent a lot of time defining themselves because they haven't needed to.' Secondly, from dissolving English identity into British identity; only now are the English discovering the difference. Thirdly, the English, as opposed to the

Scottish or Welsh, have had no immediately identifiable 'enemy' against whom to sharpen their sense of nationalism. The nearest equivalent is the French, the traditional enemy, and indeed Paxman did discover that identity issues in England are sharpened by the contrasts the public feel between themselves and France. He found, admittedly on adhoc and anecdotal grounds, that many people agreed that while the English and British floundered with the name of their nation, 'the French know who they are'. But the contrast and the enmity are not particularly strong.

Communities using Rural and Social Dialects of English

Like standard English, the rural and social dialects of the language have both geographical and social settings. Because urbanisation and population movements have greatly affected language use for a considerable time, the social diversity of rural dialects has been generally ignored in dialect studies, many of which have been aimed rather at preserving fast disappearing regional dialects. Dialectologists have thus usually concentrated on identifying the lexical components and phonology of the language use of rural dwellers who have stayed in their local area all their lives. Such a requirement necessarily excludes the better educated, the richer, and those who travel to find work. 'Rural dialects', as studied in the bulk of dialect studies, are in effect the language of agricultural workers who are tied to the land - an increasingly restricted group. The language attitudes of such a restricted group may or may not be shared by the wider social mix of those living in dialect areas, who have often retained little more than the accent. Nonetheless, it is likely that some language attitudes will be common in dialect areas, shared even by those who do not necessarily speak dialect or whose accent is not normally regionally marked. Similarly, it is difficult to be absolutely sure about users of social dialects, except through specific sociolinguistic studies of variation where the class membership formed part of the investigation.

The English regions

The regional distribution of dialects of English in England during the twentieth century was extensively studied over the period between 1950 and 1961 and published as the *Survey of English Dialects* (see Trudgill, 1990; Orton *et al.*, 1978; Fennell, 2001). In general, and in England, at least four major traditional dialect areas are recognised:

North, East and West Midlands, and South. Ultimately, these dialect differences derive from those between the Germanic dialects of the Angles (East Anglia, Midlands and North), the Saxons (Essex and Wessex) and the Jutes (Kent); and from differential effects of the Scandinavian invasions (North and East); while the influence of French has not followed regional lines. Modern dialect areas can also be identified and do not exactly mirror the traditional ones. Modern dialects show differences between areas such as the Northeast; Northern (Yorkshire and Lancashire); the East, the West and the Central Midlands; East Anglia; the Home Counties; and the Southwest. In addition, Trudgill notes that the large urban areas such as London, Birmingham, Liverpool and Manchester have developed characteristic dialect forms of their own. Areas can be distinguished on the basis of pronunciation and some differential word and grammatical usage. Thus for example the pronunciation of _but_ divides southern from northern dialects; the final _g_ in _long_ is noticed in Liverpool, Manchester and Birmingham; and the vocalisation of _l_ in _milk_ is indicative of Estuary English (originally parts of East Anglia and the Home Counties, but now rapidly spreading). Word equivalents like _sneck/latch_ differentiate North from South, and _while/until_ differentiate Yorkshire from both North and South, although these usages are declining. Gross divisions like these can be further subdivided, and pronunciation and accent differences between even small areas can be recognised by many.

Dialect forms of English outside England itself include Scots and Ulster Scots, (see Chapter 8). Barbour (2000) considers these to be more dialectally marked than a third form, the 'standard language in Scotland' or Scottish English. There are recognisable, different pronunciations and accents of English associated with Scotland, but also with Wales and with Northern Ireland, although none of these is normally considered to have attained the status of a dialect. In terms of the relative sizes of the English regions, and the comparison of these with the populations of the other three countries of the United Kingdom, Table 1.4 shows comparative estimates of the population aged over 16 as in 2001.

We noted in Table 1.2 above that across Britain half the population associated with the region, slightly more than associated with the name 'England' or 'Britain'. Political regionalism and claims for regional autonomy have however not been a strong feature of England over the past two hundred years, except in some specific areas such as Northumberland, Yorkshire, Cornwall, perhaps Essex, where a tradition of cultural independence has been maintained. This is probably due to a number of factors. Historically, the Anglo-Saxon regional kingdoms disappeared after 1066; there have been no regional conflicts within England (the fifteenth-century Wars of the Roses were dynastic rather than regional). The Enclosure Acts, particularly between 1750 and 1830, changed the open field system and hence removed peasants from direct contact with 'their' land. Education, particularly the education of the elite in Public Schools, has been national since the early 1800s and destroyed local links. Parliament, also, has rarely split on regional lines. Parliamentary constituencies have been reformed constantly since 1832: in 1885, in 1948 and most recently in 1997. Local government was redesigned in 1835, 1894, 1974 and again in the mid-1990s, and regional loyalties have either disappeared or been weakened as a consequence. There are both unitary and two-tier authorities; small counties such as Rutland 'disappeared' in the 1960s and were recreated in the 1990s.

Table 1.4 Working population by region and country (2001)

Region	Population over 16
North East	2,033,000
North West	5,370,000
Yorkshire and the Humber	3,974,000
East Midlands	3,338,000
West Midlands	4,185,000
East	4,313,000
London	5,747,000
South East	6,408,000
South West	3,947,000
TOTALS	
England	39,315,000
Scotland	4,045,000
Wales	2,320,000
Northern Ireland	1,275,000
United Kingdom	46,953,000

Note: Population aged over 16 only.
Source: Labour Market Survey (September to November 2001).

The New Labour proposals of 1997 to develop stronger regional governance at the top level have resulted in the creation of Regional Development Agencies whose main function is the economic development of their region. The 'political' partner of these agencies, the Regional Assemblies or Chambers, which were proposed as elected 'governments' having a range of functions similar to those of the Welsh and Scottish parliaments, have not been received with open arms: a poll found only 45% in favour in 1999 (_Economist_, 26.3.1999), with greatest support in London, the North-East and the South-West. Policy as laid out in the White Paper of May 2002 (_Your Region, Your Choice_) was to conduct a referendum region by region on whether an elected Assembly would be established there. Possibly, nine such regional governments may then appear in England. Each would have a population at least comparable to that of Scotland, the largest of the devolved countries. As can be seen from the list of Table 1.4, only one has a regional name other than a simple geographical indication. Even this one, Yorkshire and the Humber, is divided by a major river, the Humber, and although it apparently combines two areas (the East Riding of Yorkshire and North Lincolnshire) these have traditionally felt little fellow-feeling. All in all, regionalism is not a strong factor in feelings of nationalism or ethnicity in England.

London already has an elected Assembly and an elected Mayor, while the other Chambers or Assemblies so far have appointed, not elected, members. None of the proposals for England show much interest in language matters, and the dialect boundaries do not necessarily coincide with the regions, or indeed, with the former counties.

The English social classes

Technically, class membership is usually derived from occupation. Thus the Office for National Statistics (previously the Registrar-General) allocates the population according to current or last occupation in a scheme established in 1911. This classification produces six social classes: I (professional occupations), II (managerial and technical), III (skilled non-manual), III (skilled manual), IV (partly skilled) and V (unskilled occupations). It is highly unlikely that such a scheme would enable us to pinpoint social dialects for each such 'class' in England. One of the factors making this even more unlikely is social mobility, mentioned by William Hague as a defining characteristic of (modern) Britain (see page 22). Analysing social mobility in Britain, Heath and Payne (in Halsey & Webb, 2000: 260) used seven classes: the higher salariat (professionals, managers and administrators in large enterprises); the lower salariat (semi-professionals, managers and administrators in small enterprises); routine white-collar workers; petty bourgeoisie (farmers, small employers and self-employed workers); higher working class and lower working class. Table 1.5 shows the percentage membership of these among men in Britain aged over 55, and over 35, in 1995, together with an indication of how stable class memberships have been. This latter figure shows how class structures have changed: there has been a large increase in the salariat, and a decrease in the working class. Table 1.6 gives summary indexes of social mobility for men in the same two birth cohorts, showing again that upward mobility, out of working class employments, means it is unlikely that social classes are stable enough to retain clearly differentiated social class dialects. The conclusion must be that social class solidarity is not a strong feature of modern Britain, and that class loyalties are unlikely to be strong enough to foster the retention of class dialects at this large scale.

Table 1.5 Social class structure and mobility in Great Britain

Class	Cohort born in 1930-39	Cohort born in 1950-59
I	17.1 (47)	23.2 (68)
II	15.0 (38)	19.1 (40)
III	5.8 (6)	4.5 (1)
IV	13.3 (31)	15.3 (31)
V/VI	25.6 (34)	22.0 (35)
VII	23.2 (35)	15.8 (33)

First figure is percentage of the total in each cohort; figure in brackets is the percentage of each cohort in the same class as their father.
Tables 1.5 and 1.6 calculated from Halsey & Webb, 2000: 260-5

Table 1.6 Summary indexes of social class mobility

Class	Cohort born in 1930-39	Cohort born in 1950-59
Percentage stable	34	35
Upwardly mobile	38	42
Downwardly mobile	18	13
Horizontal movements	10	10

Class membership, class-based attitudes and class loyalty, however, are often claimed to be a strong and continuing feature of British and particularly of English social attitudes. An anthology of 'Englishness' (Milsted, 2001) devotes thirty pages (118-148) to humorous quotations, mainly from literary sources, demonstrating strong awareness of class distinctions. These range from a 1577 description of the 'foure sorts of Englishmen, as gentlemen, citizens or burgesses, yeomen, and artificers or labourers' to John Stuart Mill's 'the very idea of equality is strange and offensive to them. They do not dislike to have many people above them as long as they have some below them' (1860); to Hilaire Belloc's

> The Rich arrived in pairs
> And also in Rolls-Royces ...
> The Poor arrived in Fords
> Whose features they resembled ...
> The People in Between
> Looked underdone and harassed (1932)

and to the Frost Report's television sketch of 1967:

> Cleese: I get a feeling of superiority over them.
> Barker: I get a feeling of inferiority from him, but a feeling of superiority over him.
> Corbett: I get a pain in the back of my neck.

Class awareness usually relies on a simple division of this type into two or three groups: middle class, working class and an intermediate group ('petty bourgeoisie') made up of the self-employed, farmers and owners of small businesses. Indeed, the simplest division usually made in sociolinguistic work is into Working Class, Middle Class and Upper Class (cf. Trudgill, 1974). Class membership and attitudes seem to differ according to which of the two main sociological and political traditions is followed, consciously or not: the Marxian and the Weberian. The Marxian model is essentially a two-class structure in which ownership of the means of production is significant and there is opposition between the working class and the ruling class or bourgeoisie. Thus Hoggart (1957: 62) identified the British working class's attitude towards 'them':

> 'They' are the 'people at the top', the 'higher-ups', ... 'get yer in the end', 'talk posh', 'are all twisters really', 'never tell yer owt', ... 'treat yer like muck'.

Hilaire Belloc acidly made his Justice of the Peace clarify right and wrong:

> Distinguish carefully between these two,
> This thing is yours, that other thing is mine.

You have a shirt, a brimless hat, a shoe
And half a coat. I am the Lord benign
Of fifty hundred acres of fat land
To which I have a right. You understand? ...
I do not envy you your hat, your shoe,
Why should you envy me my small estate? ...
Moreover, I have got the upper hand,
And mean to keep it. Do you understand? (quoted in Milsted,
2001: 139-40)

The Weberian multi-dimensional model uses a number of defining characteristics such as income, occupation, or education, each or all of which may define class membership; there is less opposition between the classes and movement between them seems to be recognised. British attitudes, however, remain fairly fixed. Thus, humorously and more seriously (Milsted, 2001: 138 and 146):

Bow, bow, ye lower middle classes!
Bow ye tradesmen, bow ye masses! ...
We are peers of the highest station ...
Pillars of the British nation! (W. S. Gilbert in *Iolanthe*, 1882)
Dear Michael,
I am always hearing about the Middle Classes. What is it they really want? Can you put it down on a sheet of note paper and I will see whether we can give it to them. (Prime Minister Harold Macmillan, memo to the Head of the Conservative Party Research Department, October 1957).

Heath and Payne (in Halsey & Webb, 2000: 260) give the following chart of changes in the size of the classes during the twentieth century.

Table 1.7 Class profiles of men aged 35 and over at the time of the survey: pre-1900 to 1959

	Pre-1900	1900-09	1920-9	1940-49	1950-9
I	7	10	16	21	23
II	11	9	13	16	19
III	8	8	7	4	5
IV	12	10	9	15	15
V/VI	32	31	32	23	22
VII	30	32	23	20	16

Percentages. Classes as in Table 1.5

Allum (1995: 69) considers a class structure, based on prestige and attitude, of five or six percent 'ruling class', 45-55 percent 'middle class' and 40-50 percent 'working class' to be characteristic of Britain between 1965 and 1980. , and it is probable that the trends then noticed, involving a general decline in the numbers of the traditional working class and an increase in those of the middle class, have continued.

The Territorial Communities

By this term is meant Scotland, Wales and Northern Ireland, which achieved recognition of their status, different for each, through devolution in 1998. In these countries, the languages involved are Scottish Gaelic, Welsh and Irish. There are or were other territorial languages within the geographical area of the British Isles, including Norn (last speakers disappeared in the eighteenth century from the Orkneys and Shetlands), Manx (last native speaker died in the 1970s), Cornish (the last native speakers died about 1800), and Channel Islands French (particularly Jersiais; some elderly native speakers of Channel Islands French remain). The Isle of Man and the Channel Islands are of course politically independent administrations as far as languages and most other internal matters are concerned, and retain some official role for their languages. Cornwall does have a political party, Mebyon Kernow, aiming at political autonomy, and a self-defined 'Stannary Parliament', recreated, from a 13th-century administration which regulated the tin trade, by the tin industry in the 1970s. Activists have defaced English Heritage signs, and a survey in 2000 by Plymouth University claimed to find 30% of children 'feeling Cornish, not English'. Although Cornish was not recognised at the time of ratification of the European Charter for Regional and Minority Languages, local activists expected an official recognition to occur in late 2002.

Scotland, Wales and Northern Ireland have retained awareness of their cultural differences from England despite their conquest and despite subsequent integration of their economies and political life over centuries. Awareness of language, particularly of the territorial language and its position in relation to English, and its role as a symbol of difference, has differed between the countries. Thus while the Welsh Language Society has actively campaigned in favour of Welsh the parallel organisations in Scotland have been limited in their outspokenness. In Northern Ireland language has become an integral part of the ideology and beliefs of those opposing British control, on a par with such symbols as different flags.

The Scottish Executive estimates the 2001 population as 5,100,000. This had decreased somewhat since a peak of some 5,200,000 in the 1980s, after falling to 4.7 million just after 1945. The 1991 Census showed 65,978 speakers of Gaelic in Scotland, 1.35% of the population at that time. This had decreased from 79,307 in 1981 (1.6%) and from 210,677 (5.2%) in 1901.

According to the Welsh Assembly, the precise population of Wales in 2001 was 2,949,000. The statistics for those able to speak Welsh, and perhaps more significantly those who speak Welsh only, show a consistent decline since 1921. 37.1% of the population spoke Welsh in 1921, with a monolingual population of some 6.3%. In 1991, the figures were 17.9% (508,000 people) who could speak Welsh, and a negligible monolingual population.

According to the Northern Ireland Executive, the population in 2001 was 1,577,816. This was divided in the following way between the religious communities:

Table 1.8 Religious affinities in Northern Ireland

Roman Catholic	605,639
Presbyterian	336,871
Church of Ireland	279,280
Methodist	59,517
Other	122,448
None	59,234
Not stated	114,827

Speakers of Irish were 45,338 in 1991 (3%). Other languages were not recorded at the time (but see page 168).

The three countries now enjoy devolution, having control of matters relating to education, health, transport, environment, home affairs and local government, leaving taxation, defence and foreign affairs to Westminster. They are the responsible authorities for the UK government's actions in relation to the European Charter for Regional and Minority Languages. Officially, each devolved country hence has full control of its own language policy. In practical terms all three countries use English as their normal means of communication and show little signs of changing this in the future. Their populations are essentially monolingual in English or contain a minority bilingual in English and the territorial language.

Nationalism, including political nationalism, is nonetheless significant in all three countries. In Wales and Northern Ireland, it is closely associated with language issues, so both political and language issues are treated together in Chapter 2. By contrast, the Scottish languages, Gaelic and Scots, have not acted as major symbols of nationalism. Scottish Gaelic has indeed played a role in the movement, since Gaelic is clearly different from English and symbolises the Celtic tradition. Scots, a dialect form of English, could be associated with English domination, although revived interest in Scots has accompanied its acceptance as a regional language in the European Charter. Political nationalism is strong in Scotland, widely symbolised by the flag, the Gaelic language, Highland cultural manifestations (haggis, bagpipes, the kilt), and such assertions of national economic independence as the discovery of oil and the priorities of the Scottish Parliament in social spending since 1998. Table 1.2 shows 72% of the Scottish population identifying with Scotland, and the Moreno scale of nationalism shows 32% feeling Scottish, not British (both England and Wales had 17%); 35% feeling more Scottish than British; 22% equally British and Scottish (against 37% in England and 36% in Wales); 4% feeling British, not Scottish.

The Non-territorial Communities

Britain has few monolingual communities not using English, except among recent immigrants and, in that case, principally among women. Even these monolingual communities are rare, although for example 40% of Edinburgh's ethnic minority groups say they do not use local shops because of English language difficulties. More usually, non-territorial communities are bilingual, using English and at least one other language in their everyday life. These communities have greatly increased in number and size since the 1950s.

An estimate of the possible size of the different ethnic communities was made by Parekh (2000), and is also periodically made by the Office for National Statistics (see Appendix). There were no official statistics before 1962, and indeed the accuracy of current ones is dubious. One of the main difficulties involved is the matter of definitions. The UK Census first collected information on ethnic groups in 1991. The results showed that 5.5% of the population, 3,015,050 people, classified themselves as such at that time. However, official ethnic group labels as used in the Census in Britain seem an almost hilariously unscientific mix of self-reported nationality, skin colour and geography, even though the origin of the labels derives from an assessment of the views expressed by the groups involved at that time.

The categories used in 1991 did not include those born in Ireland

(North and South), counted as 837,464 individuals. Although their housing pattern and employment groups   show a slightly more working-class pattern than the majority of the population, there has been little segregation, much intermarriage and little socioeconomic differentiation from the host population. Census results did include the nine categories of Table 1.8.

Table 1.9 1991 Census by ethnic group

White	51,873,794
Black-Caribbean	499,964
Black-African	212,362
Black-other *please describe*	178,401
Indian	840,255
Pakistani	476,555
Bangladeshi	162,835
Chinese	156,938
Other groups: Asian	197,534
Any other ethnic group *please describe*	290,206
TOTAL	54,888,844

The predetermined categories were accepted by about three quarters, but only three quarters, of 'ethnic' respondees. 7.1% of the minority group population described themselves as 'Black-other', while a further 16.9% placed themselves in 'Any other ethnic group'. The categories chosen to describe Britain's ethnic minority population have been criticised as an attempt to 'enforce the external boundaries given by the dominant group ... done in the name of combating discrimination and prejudice' (Isajiw, 1993), so skin colour or 'visibility', rather than ethnic group or nationality, is clearly the main discriminator applied. Indeed, the 1991 categories were unsatisfactory in a number of other ways (Aspinall, 2000). The first of these is 'hybridity'. Many mixed marriages have taken place and the resultant offspring prefer to regard themselves as 'Mixed' - some 230,000 in 1991 although the lack of an appropriate category means that this number is likely to have been underreported. Terms like 'Black Caribbean' had less relevance for second generation migrants, born in the UK, and indeed some 60,000 persons described themselves as 'Black British' in 1991, rejecting both the Caribbean and the African categories. One of the major problems was the use of 'outsider terms that defy difference' (Aspinall, 2000: 113) such as 'Asian' or even 'Indian', where cultural differences, particularly of religion, disappeared. Similarly, the 'myth of homogeneity' of the White population concealed the existence of those who regarded themselves as Irish, and presented problems for the significant numbers of both first and second-generation people with Turkish, Cypriot or other Mediterranean or Middle Eastern origins. Thus 26,597 people were born in Turkey, of whom 24,088 reported themselves as 'White'; 78,031 in Cyprus (75,516 'White'); 101,719 (55,023 'White') in the Middle East (Iran, Iraq, Israel, Jordan, Lebanon, Syria and 'other'). Even the other British nations (Welsh, Scottish, English) disappeared from view. New categories were developed for the 2001 Census, even though they vary between the four countries (England, Wales, Scotland, Northern Ireland). These included 'Mixed', 'Black British' and a question on religion. The idea of 'ethnic group' has been modified by that of 'cultural background'. In questions for the Scottish census, the term 'British' has been largely replaced by 'Scottish'. In terms of feelings of identity, ethnicity and 'belonging', there has been a notable development towards such labels as 'Black British' and 'British Asian' among young people born in Britain, which these categories are likely to clarify further.

Almost half of all ethnic group members in the country live in London, and make up 33.9% of the population of inner London and 23.8% of that of outer London. Other urban centres include Leicester (28.5%), West Midlands (18.3%) and West Yorkshire (10.4%). By contrast, Wales, Scotland and Northern Ireland each have less than 2% ethnic minority inhabitants. Rural areas throughout the British Isles have low concentrations of ethnic community members. This concentration, urbanisation and 'ghettoisation' was roundly condemned in a series of reports on disturbances which took place in Oldham, Burnley and Bradford in the summer of 2001, and was considered by some to be at the root of insular, closed attitudes towards other British citizens by some individuals and communities. Another factor tending in the same direction, also pointed out by these reports, was that of renewal from source countries. Thus it was a common practice for long return visits to be made to 'home'. Marital practices, too, in some communities led to young men seeking a bride from 'home' to maintain traditional practices concerning the status of women. Such brides entered Britain, often without English and without any understanding of British society. British immigration and refugee bureaucracy was speeded up and often waived for some categories of immigrant, particularly for religious leaders, and some arrived without any training, any English or any understanding of the British community or of British social norms. While such practices kept alive the contacts, languages, religions and traditions of the 'source' country within the 'host' country, together they also held the danger of keeping the community in Britain apart from the remainder of British society, and preventing the development of the immigrant community through the stages recognised elsewhere, where original first generation migrants became second and third generation descendants, more attuned to the norms of the host than of the sending communities.

Immigration to Britain is officially controlled through specific legislation including citizenship/nationality requirements. The British Citizenship Act of 1948 gave residence rights to about 25% of the world's population. In 1962, the Commonwealth Immigrants Act massively reduced this; the 1971 Immigration Act restricted entry even more, although it had to be temporarily modified as Idi Amin expelled Asians from Uganda in 1972. In 2002, control was effected by the Home Office Immigration and Nationality Directorate through the 1981 British Nationality Act and the 1999 Immigration and Asylum Act, pending a new Act in late 2002.

Peach et al. in Halsey and Webb's *British Social Trends* (2000: 128-75) reviewed the development and characteristics of the main immigrant groups, using the 1991 Census for estimates of size. The Black Caribbean population of 499,964 members was probably underreported for a number of reasons, although the figure of about half a million has remained stable since the primary immigration of the period 1948-1973, with a peak in 1961. Family structure remains characteristic, with households headed by a single female, often with dependent children. Unemployment is approximately double that for white groups, while the occupational structure is skewed towards blue-collar employment. On the other hand, there was also evidence of increasing integration: there is high participation in the labour force, a major increase in home ownership and a high level of mixed marriages, as well as dispersion from inner-city ghettoes. In terms of languages, English Creoles have a special position within the non-territorial languages. Since there was a large influx of migration from the West Indies between 1950 and 1965, Jamaican Creole, often called British Black English (BBE) in imitation of American terminology, has been extensively studied (Sutcliffe, 1982). Such studies date mainly from the 1970s and 1980s, although 'It is not the case that British Black English has disappeared' (Fennell, 2001: 206). As generations follow, BBE may remain in isolated features rather than in the full system. Accent certainly remains a strong feature, and the identity implications of accent and language remain strong among the Black community. Immigrants in the 1950s were often recruited for, and entered, specific types of employment in transport and the National Health Service. This characteristic has not continued with subsequent generations.

Black Africans have come mainly from Nigeria and Ghana. Immigration started with student populations being trained for the end of colonialism, while the economic collapse of much of Africa has prevented their return. Characteristic family practices include fostering, and both religion and national origin seem to facilitate the emergence of a distinct cultural and social life, supported by many regional, ethnic and national associations themselves maintaining well-developed social networks. As with Black Caribbeans, unemployment and underemployment is high, with much part-time or casual work. Since the population is young, mostly under 45 in 1991, and first-generation, languages tend to be maintained as part of these networks.

The Chinese group is the smallest, and split between those of Hong Kong origin (48%), mainly poorly educated, and those from the Chinese Republic (17%) and Southeast Asia, professional and highly educated.The proportion of Chinese with first degrees is double that of the white population. Unemployment is low; 41% work in the catering trade; households are often multi-family, indicative of extended family structures. Overall, the Chinese are regarded as the most successful ethnic group among immigrants to Britain since the 1950s. In terms of languages, the population is diverse, with many different Chinese languages in use among the mainly young population.

Nearly half the three million ethnic minority population of the UK in 1991 came from South Asia: Pakistan, India and Bangladesh. These national labels conceal major differences in religion, place of origin, employment characteristics, socioeconomic profile and language. Indians are mainly Hindu or Sikh; Pakistanis and Bangladeshis mainly Muslim. Indians of rural origin originate from the wealthier areas of the Punjab while Pakistanis came from the poorer rural parts; Indians also came from a higher socioeconomic base, or from East Africa where they formed the middle classes. All three national origins in fact relate to small, specified areas of the sending country. A sample of Indians declared language abilities as Punjabi (62%), Hindi (33%), Gujarati (20%) Urdu (20%) and Bengali (2%); most of the sample, responding in 1994, were multilingual. All groups share support of traditional family structures: marriage within the group, households with more than one family. Indians have made rapid economic progress while Bangladeshis and Pakistanis are more represented in blue-collar occupations and have higher unemployment. Pakistanis and Bangladeshis have a large household size, with significant overcrowding particularly among Bangladeshis. The Bangladeshi population is heavily concentrated: many lived in inner London, 25% of the British population in one borough, Tower Hamlets, and Bangladeshis have remained more segregated than other groups. Pakistani groups are strongly present in the Northern textile towns of West Yorkshire and Lancashire, while Indians are present in the South and Midlands. Although all three groups are present in London, it is mainly the Indians who have located in the suburbs.

The official categories have no connection to language use. Neither do the published tables of country of origin. Estimates given in 2000 varied between 450,000 and one and a half million people 'with little command of the English language' (Grover, 2000). The lack of any form of language question except for the 2001 Census in Wales, Scotland and Northern Ireland, where the questions ask only for knowledge of the territorial language, means that there will still be no adequate information on speaker numbers or type of knowledge (spoken, reading, writing) for non-indigenous languages. Even in education, statistics to identify need are hard to come by, often lack clarity, and definitions vary. A 1999 survey of languages used in London schools (see Appendix) found considerably more Yoruba speakers than either French or Spanish ones, and separately identified such languages as the English and French Creoles.

One language-related group, the Romani, present since the Middle Ages, have generally avoided involvement with the political life of Britain. Their sense of identity is closely identified with the tradition of nomadism and travel, and with the international spread of the group. Wherever Gypsies have travelled, they have absorbed religions, languages and customs of those among whom they have lived, while maintaining a sense of identity and difference which today enables international contact.

Similarly, the Jews, present since the Norman Conquest, have maintained the sense of a different identity while at the same time accepting the norms and behaviours of those among whom they live. The population is estimated at around 290,000, having declined from about 430,000 in the 1950s; it is mainly urban, and five London boroughs contain half the British Jewish population. There is a dense network of organisations; a third of Jewish children attend Jewish schools.

Nonetheless, the use of Yiddish has declined among 'European' Jews; synagogues are closing and British Jews have joined political parties, demonstrate a range of attitudes and share the identity attitudes of the territorial communities where they live. Both these two long-established communities, the Romani and the Jews, have maintained distinctive cultural identities while at the same time absorbing political and national identities.

Communities, Individuals and Linguistic Repertoires

We have discussed communities to this point as though they were distinct entities, with hard edges and impermeable boundaries. But facts like the social mobility of individuals entering or leaving the elite, of young people changing their linguistic habits as they grow older, of migrants moving between countries or from country to town mean that regional, social and ethnic communities are not hermetically sealed, impervious to the movement of individuals. A widespread misunderstanding of correlational sociolinguistics implied that lower class and upper class 'codes' belonged to their respective classes, and that the purpose of education was to force lower class users of a 'restricted' code to adopt upper class 'elaborated' code along with upper class social and family practices. By contrast to this, the notion of 'linguistic repertoire' is that individuals are not tied to a particular form of language, but may use different codes or varieties in different circumstances. Every individual thus moves between different social and regional dialects, vocabularies and indeed accents as circumstances and settings change. The example of using a regional accent at home or in the pub, while communicating in a less marked variety at work or when teaching, is familiar to many. Individuals may thus belong to more than one language community at one and the same time, as they belong to a diversity of religious, ethnic, social and political communities. In both the strong and the weaker versions of the Sapir-Whorf hypothesis, attitudes towards language(s) and language varieties are regarded as being closely associated with, if not determined by, other links that unite communities, and with the boundary features such as territory, skin colour, wealth, political ideology, that distinguish them. It is likely however that attitudes to language, to language varieties and to languages will vary according to the amount of travelling the individual has done, the degree of mobility they have experienced or the number of groups in which he or she moves - home, work, family, church, sports club, political party - and the extent to which their linguistic repertoire indicates sensitivity to communication. It may well thus be that any one individual, as he or she moves between languages, may adopt different language attitudes at different times or in different circumstances.

Nonetheless the identity issues we have examined in this chapter enable us to locate the different communities within Britain in relation to the identity sequence outlined in the Introduction. There is, clearly, a degree of fuzziness about the identity of Britain and that of the four territorial countries, England, Scotland, Wales and Northern Ireland. The latter three countries continue to regard identity and national issues as important, despite their conquest by England and centuries of subsequent administration in which they have played major roles. Each can point to a range of symbols and characteristics, from folk dance to flags and food. Each of them has strengthened its national feeling through contrast, and even conflict, with England. Each of them can identify its national symbols, its national myth of origin and its unique customs. Each, importantly, has an 'enemy' against which to construct and defend its identity: England. Despite the efforts of James 1st and his successors, England still has an identity problem. England's traditional 'enemy' is France, and Lord Nelson is famous for his views: 'I hate the French most damnably' (quoted in Paxman, 1998: 37). But despite recurring irritation with our nearest neighbours this conflict is not a major defining feature of contemporary England. England has a lack of symbols: Hague's set is the Houses of Parliament, Big Ben and Buckingham Palace, none of which is specifically English, while all of them are major symbols of Britain (or even of London). The Whig interpretation of history, even though it retains strength for some, was designed for British, not English, identity.

The self-awareness of ethnic communities varies according to such factors as size, recency of immigration, and location. From time to time specific events (Gulf war, Bradford riots) sharpen or reduce this sense of identity. Many interest and pressure groups exist and are keen to convey their views (see, e.g. p. 100).

The following chart outlines and summarises the identity situation, as it could be described for the communities we have discussed in this chapter and as at the year 2002. This picture may well be modified as we consider further the language-related attitudes held by such communities.

Identity: *the creation of personal identity*
Identity: *the creation of social identity*
>England may be at this early stage in the identity sequence. The changes caused by devolution, membership of the European Union and increased immigration are causing a closer examination and reexamination of identity issues than for a considerable period.

Ideology: *the development of a 'myth' underpinning identity*
>Underlying ideologies of nationalism have been strong in Scotland, Wales, and Ireland. In England, ideological support for identity issues has generally been lacking. If anything, there is an ideology of shame for a colonial and oppressive past mixed with pride, rural romanticism and anti-Europeanism. The Whig interpretation of history is a powerful myth for England, and basic political ideologies remain rooted in left-right opposition.

Image: *developing or protecting the image of the identity*
Insecurity: *fears for the identity*
Maintain identity
>Both the maintenance and the defence of identity have been noticeable in relation to Scotland, Wales and Ireland. Devolution has acted as the spur to reconsiderations of regional identities, while multiculturalism has acted as the spur for reconsideration of the identity of Britain.

>Some ethnic communities are sensitive to 'attacks' on cultural practices (halal butchery, consumption of bush meat, marriage practices, 'genital mutilation').

Defend identity
Maintain inequality *among social groups*
>Social distinctiveness, particularly as between the elite and the rest, has been notable: class is a significant feature of British make-up.

Correct inequality *among social groups: pluralism*
>The correction of inequality has been a traditional component of the policies of the political Left, and it could be felt that policies on such issues as devolution as well as multiculturalism are motivated by such an impulse.

Integrate *with a social group in order to understand it*
Improve use of instrument *in order to strengthen economic support for the identity*
Despair *at the potential loss of the identity*

Figure 1.2 Identity sequence for United Kingdom communities

Chapter 2

Language Attitudes

Attitudes towards a dominant language, which is not in particular danger and whose speakers may be supremely unaware even of the existence of other languages, are likely to reveal that speakers consider it outstanding, important for every domain of activity, and very attractive. Action is not called for. English speakers might therefore be expected to show this picture for English as L1 in England:

Attitudinal structure

Excellence		Vitality		Attractiveness		Action	
L1	L2	L1	L2	L1	L2	L1	L2
3	1	3	1	3	1	1	1

where L1 is English and L2 is any other language. Strong attitudes (3) are shown by the existence of formal texts such as books, articles or speeches; weak or negative (1) by their absence (see p. 9 above).

By contrast, a language in danger of disappearance like Welsh or more particularly Scottish Gaelic would be felt to lack vitality, even though speakers of it might feel the language to be both excellent and attractive in itself. Activists would feel it essential to call for action in order to save it as an L1. Insofar as the other language is concerned, English in these cases, activists might doubt its 'excellence' but ruefully agree on its high level of vitality or use in many domains, and on its undoubted attractiveness for economic if for no other purposes:

Attitudinal structure

Excellence		Vitality		Attractiveness		Action	
L1	L2	L1	L2	L1	L2	L1	L2
3	1	1	3	3	3	3	1

where L1 is the relevant territorial language and L2 is English. Note that these are the likely attitudes of activists, not necessarily those of language planners.

Attitudes Towards English

Barbour (2000: 29-30) agrees that the English-speaking indigenous population of England lacks generally accepted symbols of its national identity, as we have seen in the previous chapter. The language does not constitute 'an effective symbol of Englishness', nor does it play much part in issues of ethnic or national identity. Contemporary attitudes towards English do include pride, however, as the following summary indicates (based on Bailey, 1991: 267-87; see also Cameron, 1995. Note that terms in quote marks themselves reflect some of these attitudes; terms in italics are examples):

- some minor doubts about the spelling system, 'irregular' grammar and 'unrestrained' vocabulary but also about 'inbuilt racism, gender bias and a history of linguistic oppression' both within the British Isles and abroad;
- greater prestige for middle class ('standard') forms ('U' - _napkin_) than for lower class vocabulary and syntax ('non-standard') ('non-U' - _serviette, ain't, I don't want none_);
- greater prestige for Received Pronunciation (RP) and for southern English accents than for northern ones;
- while some regional dialects and accents please (Somerset, Scottish), others don't (Cockney, Birmingham);
- a belief that 'standard English' is 'correct', 'neutral' and 'unmarked', is substantially uniform and is used by 'educated people' everywhere in Great Britain;
- a feeling that Anglo-Saxon terms are 'real' English while Romance/Latinate vocabulary is a 'difficult', superimposed layer;
- pride in cultural and literary history, with a particular belief that Shakespeare is the greatest literary figure of all times and countries;
- pride in a simple grammar, a large lexicon and the ability to borrow words easily from foreign languages;
- pride in the ease with which English can be learnt, an associated pride in the world-wide role of the language, and tolerance towards non-British forms including 'foreigner talk';
- pride in the 'modernity' of the language, enabling it to be used in all domains, particularly prestigious ones like science and technology.

Standard English and language ideologies

Randolph Quirk (1990) quotes the definition of standard English given in the American *Webster's International Dictionary*:

(1)   the English that is taught in school;

(2)   English that is current, reputable and national;

(3)   the English that with respect to spelling, grammar, pronunciation and vocabulary is substantially uniform though not devoid of regional differences, that is well-established by usage in the formal and informal speech and writing of the educated, and that is widely recognised as acceptable wherever English is spoken and understood;

(4)   all words entered in a general English language dictionary that are not restricted by a label (as slang, dial., obs., biol., Scot.).

He continues 'there is nothing esoteric, obscure, or special about (standard English): whoever or wherever we are in the English-speaking world, we have been familiar with it all our lives'. This common-sense, if circular, approach poses a number of problems about the attitudes it implies. Thus sociolinguists are by no means in agreement about the attitude that specialists should adopt towards standard English or even about its definition (see pp. 19-20 above and Coupland, 2000; Davies, 1999). Davies (pp. 173-4) pointed to the attacks on 'common-sense' definitions of the standard like Quirk's from:

- post-modernists ('standard English as one kind of universal metanarrative seems to have met its fate');
- Marxists ('language standardisation is first a matter of hegemony');
- feminists ('what a small group of unprincipled people speak');
- those who identify an inner, middle and outer circle of influential language users ('the exclusive prerogative of those in power');
- proponents of linguistic equality ('all normative statements refer only to the high code, thus leaving the masses to an undervalued vernacular status').

The term was first used in 1836 (according to the *Oxford English Dictionary*) or 1775 (according to McArthur 1999), although the sense dates from 'the middle of the sixteenth century' (Honey, 1997). McArthur distinguishes three senses, which we could label 'correctness', 'legitimacy' and 'prestige', or 'social primacy':

- a standard and a range of dialects, with inevitable overlap;
- only standard English is English, and any leakage of dialect into it is reprehensible;
- "standard dialect" is first among equals, the other dialects being good in themselves. (McArthur, 1999: 165)

Trudgill (in Bex & Watts, 1999: 123) makes the same distinction between the correct and the social aspects: 'standard English is simply one variety of English among many. It is a sub-variety of English', although 'it is ... by far the most important dialect in the English-speaking world from a social, intellectual and cultural point of view'. Others prefer to select one or other of the meanings: 'standard English is not merely one dialect among many, but instead is a specially important and valuable variety which derives its value from a set of qualities which are not shared by other, non-standard dialects' (Honey, 1997: 5); 'the minority of pupils who are already speakers of standard English are unfairly advantaged' (Carter, 1999: 163).

James Milroy investigated language attitudes in relation to standardisation (e.g. Milroy & Milroy, 1991 and Milroy, 2001). He also identified three attitudes supporting preference for a particular language or variety to act as standard: it is prestigious; it is legitimate; it is correct. Milroy then examined 'ideologies' which might lie behind such attitudes towards a particular language or variety in a 'standard language culture'. The following discussion interprets Milroy's approach, adds to it and attempts to systematise the 'ideologies' involved in these three attitudes towards standard English in Britain.

Thus, an early 'ideology' was that English was a divine gift. In the early seventeenth century, words were deemed to have been originally monosyllables, created by Adam on naming-day in Eden (Genesis 2:19) as he named every living creature (see Bailey, 1991: 39-57). Some believed that the 'Teutonic' monosyllables were 'close to the primitive, prelapsarian lexicon ordained by divine providence'. 'Real' words were thus those that came closest to a Teutonic origin, and later borrowings into English, particularly polysyllabic ones, must necessarily lack the divine legitimacy of the Anglo-Saxon stock.

Non-religious language ideologies are usually divided into language-internal and language-external types. The first language-internal ones rely on beliefs about the nature of contemporary British English as a language system: firstly that legitimacy derives from the known, historical evolution of the language; secondly, that correct English is a self-defining system with its own internal structure. In the nineteenth century, with the growth of Darwinism, philology defined correctness as based on scientific observation, and resulting from the process of evolution. Thus James Murray, together with the Oxford University Press, was eventually approached by the Philological Society to produce a *New English Dictionary* 'on historical principles', which would define the original meaning of words and trace their history. The proper sense of a word, the Society felt, is its original sense, and the 'real' meaning of a polysyllabic form can be deduced from the history of its development. The historical approach, not limited to lexis, aimed at discovering and deducing language origins and development, but also at confirming that English 'had a continuous unbroken history, a respectable and legitimate ancestry and and a long pedigree' (Milroy, 2001: 549). Milroy quotes Skeat (1873: xii), declaring that contemporary English 'is absolutely one ... with the language that was spoken in the days when the English first invaded the island'. The ideology is circular: the history of English is that of standard English, so standard English is both correct and legitimate, because it has a history. The second language-internal ideology is the belief that the correct form of language has its own internal structure, recognised because it is chosen by most speakers. This, more modern, ideology, not mentioned by Milroy, currently lies behind the use of large corpora of spoken language and written texts to support dictionaries and grammars of usage. Thus the COBUILD programme, based at Birmingham University, uses enormous corpora of written and spoken texts (450 million words in January 2002) to provide The Bank of English, used by Harper Collins dictionary department in Glasgow to search for evidence to support dictionaries and other reference works. In this way the frequency of usage of *different from* or *different to* can be checked and related to language style and context.

The second set of language ideologies is language-external: legitimacy, correctness and particularly prestige derive from social judgements about language use. All these imply that some form of socially accepted authority is involved. The first authority, indicated by Milroy, is that the canonical form of the language is recorded in grammar books, in rules and norms, and is known to experts, 'high priests', and those who have devoted care and attention to it. This form is precious, has to be protected and cared for, and not left to the careless and ignorant. The presupposition is that language is a cultural artefact, like religion or the legal system, and like them is protected by a specially educated and selected group of citizens, although these are not necessarily language specialists. This is the ideology behind the creation of a language academy as originally set up by a group of interested individuals. English has no academy, no single group of recognised intellectuals who could be said to wield authority: intellectuals, indeed, are commonly derided as 'too clever by half' or as 'eggheads'.

The second language-external authority is that which relies on the expertise of language specialists. The battle between 'professional linguists' and 'the Conservative government and the popular press' (Bex & Watts, 1999: 1; see also Chapter 8) turned on the claims from one side to expertise; from the other to 'common sense'. This battle was bruising for professional linguists and educationalists, who had assumed that their expertise gave them a basis for judgement in language matters. The professional opinion states that all languages/varieties are equally correct, in that there is no scientific basis for regarding one as more developed or legitimate than another. All languages and varieties are equally adapted to the present needs of their speakers. Only some professional linguists (e. g. Trudgill as noted above) are prepared to accept a greater social value for standard English than others, and even then not on linguistic grounds. A third authority is those who have some official appointment in relation to language: here, an example is the state-appointed committees, usually made up of members of the policy network, who moderate the work of consultants charged with devising the details for the National Curriculum. Part of the hatred directed by many in Britain against the French Academy relies on the belief that it is a state-appointed bureaucracy, rather than what it actually is, a rather haphazard collection of forty 'immortals'. Bryson (1990: 131) talks approvingly of the British 'lack of a stultifying authority', quoting the 'depressive effect on change' allegedly exerted by academies. He then promptly cites numerous British authorities whose prescriptions and proscriptions seem just as fierce, including 'British Conservative politician Jock Bruce-Gardyne' for the split infinitive. Having shown that English is no stranger to powerful prescription and proscription he then maintains that 'English is a fluid and democratic language in which meanings shift and change in response to pressure of common usage rather than the dictates of committees.' A moment's research would have shown that meanings are as shifty and democratic in French, apparently heavily controlled by an official academy, as they are in English, in that the Academy itself is as controlled by social pressure as are British authorities such as Conservative politicians. The example Bryson quotes, of the power of the Academy - the Academy's rejection of the spelling reform of 1988 - was in fact the result of a political campaign by *France-Soir*, *Le Figaro* and the Right (Ager, 1996: 119-25), since the Academy had at first accepted the reform. So much for official control of language!

Another authority for correct and legitimate English is literary English: that recorded in the works of good authors. The canon of literary works involved is sometimes specified, as in the National Curriculum, but often undefined. A much more widespread belief, and probably that which forms the commonest ideology of language in Britain, is that the usage of the social elite represents the correct and legitimate, high-prestige form. Thus Bex, in Bex & Watts (1999: 89-109), maintains that three authorities (Fowler, Gowers and Partridge) 'have been of immense significance in shaping lay people's perceptions of what counts as "good" English'. The authority that these writers possessed was derived, in Bex' view, from the symbolic capital of their representations of the language of public schools and Oxbridge. They hence derived authority from the elitism of British society. Bex' purpose is not necessarily to praise the three authors: in fact he characterises them, negatively, as 'influential in constructing a model of the language ... male, class-based, largely drawn from the written mode, and (which) appealed to a particular view of history that privileged the English'.

These have not been the only authorities to be cited in the search for a social justification for standard English. The authors of the *Guardian Style Guide* (Marsh & Marshall, 2000) claim to base their judgments on the 'values of society'. This approach has considerable difficulties: social values are notoriously difficult to define and differ considerably from one group to another; words and terms that are acceptable to some are not so to others, as the editors of dictionaries find when they include derogatory terms because they are part of the language. Direct reference to political, rather than social, values is rare, although for example a political preference for social stability and cohesiveness on the one hand (which implies a single correct English), or to celebration of social diversity on the other (which implies a variety of correct forms) come to mind.

English, with its ability to borrow words from other languages and to constantly change, was frequently condemned in the eighteenth century as a fleeting and inconsistent means of expression. Latin, with its 'lasting marble', provided a source of certainty. Dryden's notion that Latin 'guides our language' proved so popular that the teaching of English grammar relied on Latin grammatical distinctions, such as the six cases, gender distinctions for pronouns and notions of agreement, for centuries. The model of Latin is less often used today, but is still cited as an authority for English usage.

Dr Johnson based his dictionary decisions on three criteria: the usage of 'good' authors, etymology and reason. Such intellectual values as expressive clarity, clear thinking behind the formulation of expression, and simplicity are sometimes cited to define what is correct in English. 'Logical' reasoning in particular is cited as determinative of correctness, despite the evident lack of reason or logic in many uses in language. Finally, following Chomsky's approach to linguistics, a new definition of the acceptability of grammatical structures and their relationship with words has been based on the native-speaker's intuition, arising from an innate universal grammar. Intuition as a source of authority in language implies a psychological rather than a social justification for usage. In sum, Figure 2.1 lists the ideologies that seem to lie behind the three attitudes towards the standard language: legitimacy, prestige and correctness.

A further issue is to discover how widespread such attitudes and supporting ideologies are. McArthur (1999: 167-8) identifies three groups: strong or mild traditionalists, and liberal/progressives. The strong traditionalists, a diminishing group, define standard English as the speech and writing of educated people belonging to the upper and middle classes of south-eastern England. Strong traditionalists are those who consider that standard English includes a particular accent, that baptised Received Pronunciation. Mild traditionalists define standard English as 'the usage of educated people ... (used by) print and newscasters'; also, usually, mild traditionalists accept RP as standard 'because it is the only non- or supra-regional accent ... the best-described and longest-established model.' Liberal-progressives, a growing group, define the standard as the language of those who have 'completed secondary-school education, may have gone to college, and manage the language competently ... (they) dissociate "standard" from "accent"'. For these, standard English can thus be spoken in any accent. Most people however remain uncertain and 'move around on a continuum of viewpoints'.

It is hardly surprising that standard English should sometimes be regarded positively, as a sensible means of communication or as a useful resource for all, as with Honey, 1997; or negatively, as the symbol of an oppressive, authoritarian and class-based minority as with Bex in Bex & Watts, 1999. It is this debate that was at the heart of the 'battle' over the curriculum in the 1980s, examined in Chapter 8, and which has continued since.

Language-internal
- Known historical evolution produces a pure, legitimate language.
- Internal structure (e.g. of collocations as actually used) demonstrates legitimacy and correctness.

Language-external
- Canonical form is legitimate because it is recorded in dictionaries etc. and is to be protected by careful, educated (if self-appointed) guardians such as an academy (prescriptivism).
- By contrast, linguists consider that all varieties are equally correct and hence legitimate (descriptivism).
- State-appointed committees (e.g. for the National Curriculum) define legitimacy and correctness.
- The literary canon of good authors defines correctness and legitimacy.
- The high prestige usage of the elite is the legitimate form.
- Social values define legitimacy and correctness.
- Political ideologies define legitimacy and correctness.
- Model of Latin defines correctness.
- Reason (and other intellectual values such as clarity, clear thinking and simplicity) define legitimacy and correctness.
- Native-speaker intuition defines legitimacy and correctness.

Fig 2.1 Ideologies of the standard language

Purism

Thomas (1991: 75-81) defined main categories of linguistic purism as archaic ('reverence for the past'), elitist ('negative, proscriptive attitude to substandard and regional usage'), xenophobic ('eradication or replacement of foreign elements'), ethnographic ('rural dialects are purer than city speech or the standard') or reformist ('conscious efforts to reform, regenerate, renew or resuscitate a language') (see Chapter 4).

Purism, of whatever sort, is a strong, 'visceral' language attitude. Public reactions to the 1996 Reith lecture series by Professor Aitchison demonstrated the strength of British concerns about correctness and about 'corruption', seeming to mix archaic and elitist purism, as Lesley Milroy (1999: 180) notes. Lesley Milroy's belief is that 'underlying British concern with class' means that this attitude is 'more saliently divisive' than, for example, race (see pp. 29-31 above). Elitist purism would thus seem to be the strongest British language attitude. This type of purism is not new. As George Bernard Shaw noted in the Preface to *Pygmalion* (1916): 'It is impossible for an Englishman to open his mouth without making some other Englishman despise him'. The popularity of the Ross/Mitford 'discovery' of U and non-U English in 1956 (see p. 80 below) came from the recognition of an underlying attitudinal reality: 'One single pronunciation, word, or phrase will suffice to brand an apparent U-speaker as originally non-U' (quoted in Milsted, 2001: 121). Attitudes towards the class-based nature of Received Pronunciation echo this view; 'in all occupations for which an educated person is required, it is an advantage to speak RP, and it may be a disadvantage not to' (Abercrombie, 1951, quoted in L. Milroy, 1999: 187).

Other types of purism remain important. Ethnographic purism has a long history, as Wordsworth showed in his Preface to *Lyrical Ballads* of 1800:

> The language of these men (i.e. of humble and rustic dwellers) has been adopted ... because, from their rank in society and the sameness and narrow circle of their intercourse ... they convey their feelings and notions in simple and unelaborated expressions.

Lesley Milroy (1999: 180-189) considers the stigmatised urban dialects as 'the lowest layer of all' in Britain, quoting Keith Waterhouse's declaration that 'most regional accents ... are attractive enough (although I'm afraid I can see no case for Brummagem)'. She notes particularly strong reactions to Estuary English, the 'cockneyfied accent of the South-East'. Waterhouse condemned this urban dialect of Milton Keynes, also recognised as 'classless' since the Princess of Wales spoke it, as a 'slack-mouthed patois'.

> Many separate investigations have confirmed that the most stigmatised varieties are those of Glasgow, Birmingham, Liverpool (Scouse) and London (Cockney). The rural dialects of Northumberland, Cornwall, Devon or Wiltshire, however, are generally thought to be attractive. Both urban and rural Yorkshire accents are usually positively rated.

Xenophobia, too, is an important attitude. Baugh & Cable (2002: 393-5) note that in nineteenth-century Britain 'any impurity in the language was more likely than not to be described as an Americanism'. The attitude remains: ' "Get to" do something is an otiose Americanism. "You will get to go to the Moon"' (Philip Howard in *The Times*, 24.01.2002).

Complaints and guidance

The British public's language attitudes have indeed long shown a widespread desire for authoritative linguistic control of some sort, through a tradition of complaint about language usage which Milroy & Milroy (1985: 37) classified as of Type 1 ('implicitly legalistic and concerned with correctness ... *them houses'*) or Type 2 ('moralistic, and attack abuses of language which might mislead and confuse the public ... *the distance between centralised bureaucratic language and the "real" usage of ordinary people'*).

Many, if not most, of the complaints newspapers receive from their readers are concerned with the use of English. Thus the *Guardian* Readers Editor considered (15.12.2001) 'the *Guardian's* (mis)use of the English language' to be readers' 'favourite subject ... some of this correspondence is so strongly evocative of the past and the faintly chalky atmosphere of the classroom that it might make your eyes water'. One of the examples he then considered was the use of 'whom', quoting extensive examples of cases where readers were right or wrong to complain. Another was the split infinitive. He ended his column with a seasonal comment on yet another, the apostrophe, mentioning its absence in the *Guardian's* own Christmas Card ('Seasons Greetings').

Moralistic complaints, particularly about bureaucratic language, obfuscation, and political spin, are similarly frequent. The Plain English Campaign (Chapter 6) was founded as a direct consequence of complaints about the unnecessary difficulty of official forms. In complaints of this type the main concern is that the public should not be misled, as the Milroys point out. But moral, religious and ideological views also lie behind a number of complaints about language use in advertising and in the media. This is shown in research into public attitudes towards swearing commissioned in 1998 by the Broadcasting Standards Commission and in 2000 jointly by the Advertising Standards Authority, the British Broadcasting Corporation, the Broadcasting Standards Commission and the Independent Television Commission (Millwood-Hargrave, 2000). The survey, of 1,033 adults aged 18 and over, was as representative as possible of the adult population of Great Britain, and was supported by qualitative analysis of group discussions and depth interviews. It looked first at attitudes towards swearing and offensive language 'in life', and then more specifically in the media. Participants in the research 'say they have noticed an increase in the use of swearing and offensive language in daily life. It was generally disliked, but ... their acceptance of 'strong' language did not signal an approval of it'. A list of words tested for reaction showed little change between the two years, except in the case of terms of abuse, particularly racial abuse, which was generally condemned as 'very severe'. The 'topography of bad language' found by researchers indicated an increase in the severity of reaction to different types of swearword, ranging from baby talk to racial abuse:

Least severe

baby talk	poo, wee, bum
rhyming slang	berk
double entendre	salad tosser
puns	peace off

More severe

blasphemy	Jesus Christ, God
Abbreviations	b******s, f.c.u.k.

Severe

expletives	shit, fucking hell
sexual references	shag, dick, pussy
adjectival	fucking, pissing

Very severe

directive abuse	wanker, slag
abuse of minorities	spastic, poof
racial abuse	nigger, Paki

(Millwood-Hargrave, 2000:8)

The general public

There is little large-scale statistical evidence for the language attitudes of the general British public. Small-scale research evidence (e.g. Giles & Powesland 1975 on evaluations of speech styles) tends to support the views expressed above, particularly concerning the continuing importance of RP, of class and regional differences, and of purism generally. Bex (see p. 49 above) took it that the continuing high sales of his three authorities (Fowler, Gowers and Partridge) indicated that their attitudes remained widespread. The occasional newspaper article or opinion poll on language matters reflects a largely purist approach among the public. Thus Matthew Engel in *The Guardian* (27.02.02): 'L'academie anglaise, founded in this space last month to try to prevent the British version of the English language being overrun by superior transatlantic firepower, has been overwhelmed by support.' Most reported attitudes are therefore those of influential individuals comparatively expert in the field, and an accurate statement of the views of the general population is lacking. In sum, as Bailey (1991: 237) notes, the many evaluations of English swing widely between extremes of celebration and deprecation.

> Those who celebrate its perfection usually find some aspect in need of improvement; those who deride its imperfections often conclude that it is not much worse than other human languages, or, with modest amendments, the best language ever spoken. (Bailey, 1991: 237)

From the evidence that is available, the attitudes of English speakers towards standard English in the UK would seem to fall into the following pattern (compare with p. 43 above).

Attitudinal structure of the English-speaking community in Britain

Excellence		Vitality		Attractiveness		Action	
L1	L2	L1	L2	L1	L2	L1	L2
3	1	3	1	3	1	2	2

where L1 = standard English and L2 = any other language. The desire for action on the standard language reached 3 in the 1980s but has traditionally been at a low level, while desire for action on languages other than English has probably now risen above the lowest level (see Chapter 8).

Attitudes Towards the Territorial Languages

While sharing the general attitudes of the English-speaking population towards English, language attitudes towards the territorial languages in the three countries seem clearer. Statistics on these are easier to come by than on English. Much material is however published with a campaigning purpose, usually for, occasionally against increased use of the territorial language. In Wales, for example, 'political pressure (i.e. in favour of Welsh) is high in profile, if not vast in terms of numbers' (Thomas, 1997: 341). One key attitude in the territorial communities has often been that of opposition towards the dominant role of the English language and particularly towards standard English:

> For English is a killer ... It is English that has killed off Cumbric, Cornish, Norn, and Manx. It is English that has now totally replaced Irish as a first language in Northern Ireland. And it is English that constitutes such a major threat to Welsh and to Scottish Gaelic, and to French in the Channel Islands, that their long-term future must be considered to be very greatly at risk. (Price, 1984: 170)

Attitudes towards Irish, Welsh and Scottish Gaelic in the relevant countries are not however all the same. None of the countries is ethnically homogeneous and population movements both in and out affect a large number of people. Language plays different roles in each country, and the extent to which devolution has been popular also differs.

Northern Ireland

In Ireland itself, language attitudes have mirrored political ones. The Gaelic League, founded in 1893 with Douglas Hyde as president, claimed an Ireland not only free, but Gaelic-speaking as well. Gaelic revivalism played a major part in the Irish Free State, whose first President was the same Douglas Hyde. Irish continued its role in the identity politics of Ireland in the Constitutions of 1937 and 1948. Attitudes towards the language remain one dividing point between the nationalist and unionist communities in Northern Ireland. Since devolution and the creation of the North-South Ministerial Council, language support, for Irish and for Ulster Scots has become a requirement, underlining the political importance of language. In these circumstances, it is hardly surprising that attitudinal surveys simply reflect political attitudes, with support for Irish strong in the nationalist community and weak among Protestant groups, and vice-versa for Ulster Scots.

The Northern Irish linguistic scene involves three languages: Irish, Ulster Scots and English. In general Ulster Scots is spoken, if at all, by Protestants; Irish, if at all, by Catholics; and English by both main 'ethnic' groups. The word 'ethnic' is used here to label the two main differing groups in Northern Ireland following the practice of McCafferty (2001: 68-9), relying on six defining features for an ethnic community: a collective name, a myth of descent, a shared history, a distinctive shared culture, an association with a specified territory, and a sense of intra-group solidarity. The reality of the divisions between the two communities is clear from page 3 of that study: 'the active - though at times unreflecting, maybe even unconscious - sectarian thinking and practices that reflect life in Northern Ireland entails focusing on the ethnic boundary between Catholic and Protestant'. McCafferty concludes in his study of (London)Derry (p. 211) that 'people are aware of the ethnic distribution of the population in general, and the ethnic make-up of their segregated neighbourhoods. ... The reality of the boundary is obvious, it is difficult to cross, and is unlikely to be broken down in the near future' . Furthermore the divide is not affected by class: indeed, 'sociolinguistically speaking, the middle class is more divided than the working class'. More broadly, and in their use of English, individual politicians across Northern Ireland tend to use Ulster-Scots dialect features if they are Protestant (Democratic Unionist Party) and Southern Irish English features if they are Catholic (Sinn Fein). It is hence not just in the maintenance of Irish and Ulster-Scots that the sociolinguistic situation in Northern Ireland reflects the 'ethnic' differentiation, but also in the use of (different varieties of) English.

The correlation of Irish with the Catholic population is not altogether simple, however. A small number of Protestants and Unionists in Northern Ireland see Irish as part of their cultural heritage, and as divorced from political connotations. 'However, for the majority of Protestants, Irish represents unification with the Republic of Ireland, and acts as an "irritant".' (Northover and Donnelly, 1996: 34).

Language attitudes across Northern Ireland could probably be summarised as follows, with a number of provisos as we have pointed out.

Attitudinal structure of communities in Northern Ireland

Excellence			Vitality			Attractiveness			Action		
L1	L2	L3	L1	L2	L3	L1	L2	L3	L1	L2	L3
3	3	1	2	3	1	3	3	1	3	1	1

where L1 = either Irish or Ulster Scots for the relevant community; L2 = English and L3 = the other of Irish or Ulster Scots.

Wales

In Wales, attitudes towards the maintenance and revitalisation of Welsh have similarly formed a main strand in Welsh nationalism. Welsh nationalism itself is a complex set of beliefs, with at least three main components (C. H. Williams, 1994). The cultural strand is important, stressing the history, the myths and traditions, and the cultural artefacts of the indigenous culture. Language is of course a central component in this tradition, whose main drawback for a less dependent Wales is its stress on history and on ethnicity as the fundamental defining characteristic. At the extreme, cultural nationalism is rooted in the past and in language matters rejects language borrowings, developments in the slang of the young, and indeed any language change. The Welsh language, for cultural nationalists, bears the risk of being regarded as an untouchable, holy museum-piece. The second strand of attitudes is formed from the core-periphery approach to inclusive states, seeing Wales as an example of internal colonialism. England, and particularly London, is seen as primarily an economic enemy, interested only in asset-stripping and exploitation. Wales is merely the mass labour force for enterprises based in England, and produces solely for export, with the resulting resources going to Head Office in London. Both the industrialisation of the nineteenth century and the deindustrialisation of the later twentieth are seen as forms of marginality, provoking either the ghettoisation of Welsh workers in valley communities or their reduction to social inequality and economic deprivation. Even rural communities are peopled only by small-scale tenant farmers, separated from their landlords by religion, language and social class. The Welsh language, for core-periphery analysts, is the shameful badge of the colonised. The third strand of attitudes described by C. H. Williams is based on conflictual approaches, defining the Welsh as being of one social class in permanent opposition to the elite. Ethnicity is of little importance per se; 'the ethnic group is seen as a social rather than a cultural group' (G. Williams, 1980: 367). Language, here, is the battle flag for the fight against injustice.

In terms of formal political parties, Plaid Cymru is the main nationalist party. We should be careful in dealing with Welsh nationalism, particularly in view of two contradictory survey results which show that not all those living in Wales are necessarily nationalists. While Table 1.2 shows that 81% of respondees identified with Wales, 27% with Britain, in 1999, in the same year the Moreno scale of nationalism showed 17% of the sample feeling Welsh, not British; 19% more Welsh than British; 36% equally Welsh and British; 7% more British than Welsh; and 14% British, not Welsh. As with England, Britishness is not necessarily felt to be opposed to Welshness. Welsh nationalism is, however, opposed to England and the English, and protests about 'Wales swamped by tide of English settlers' (*Guardian*, 01.03.2002) recur frequently. Meibion Glyndyr, an activist group, firebombed 300 'English-owned' homes between 1979 and 1994; an activist was jailed in 1993 for sending letter bombs to Conservative politicians. New pressure groups arise, like Cymuned, challenging the established protest organisation, the Welsh Language Society and aiming to keep local houses for local people, appealing to UNESCO that oppression of the Welsh 'native people' continues.

Baker (1992) attempted to measure language attitudes among a group of nearly 800 young people in 1990, proposing twenty statements with which respondees could agree or not. The raw results of (a small part of) his research showed agreement with the following twelve of these statements, which we have rearranged to fit our pattern of excellence, vitality, attractiveness and action:

Excellence
I like speaking Welsh
Welsh is not a difficult language to learn
Welsh is a language worth learning
Vitality
It's hard to study science in Welsh
I do not prefer to watch TV in Welsh
Attractiveness
Welsh has a place in the modern world
I'm likely to use Welsh as an adult
If I have children, I would like them to be Welsh speaking
You are not considered a lower class person if you speak Welsh
Action
We need to preserve the Welsh language
Welsh should be taught to all pupils in Wales
It is not a waste of time to keep the Welsh language alive.

The Welsh Language Board, necessarily sensitive to the Welsh public's attitude towards its work, needs to be constantly aware of attitudinal change. It has commissioned two general language surveys, in 1995 and 2000, which broadly support these views. The 2000 survey (Table 2.1) was intended to inform the Board's marketing strategy, involved interviews with 1,192 adults of whom Welsh speakers were 43% (as compared with the 17.9% of the 1991 Census figures). 74% of the sample were born in Wales; 76% claimed Welsh identity, while 51% claimed 'British', 20% 'European' and 19% 'English' (multiple responses were accepted).

In practical terms Welsh is declining, and this practical proof of language attitudes would seem to indicate a decreasing interest in the language. Both before and after devolution, with educational policy and the requirements for bilinguality in public service employment of the 1993 Welsh Language Act, attitudes which indicated general support for the use of Welsh showed marked resistance when monolingual English-speaking individuals were faced with the need to learn a language they did not know. In such cases issues of human rights are regularly raised, and minority-language activists are sometimes accused of becoming even more oppressive than the dominant group.

Table 2.1 Attitudes towards Welsh

Support the language: strongly 67%; opposed 5%; indifferent 23%.
Percentages feeling that Welsh will continue as a living language for the foreseeable future: definitely 40%; probably 35%; possibly 12%; don't know 7%; no 6%.
Net % score (proportion disagreeing deducted from proportion agreeing):

Welsh is important for Welsh culture	84
Welsh is something everybody can be proud of	78
It is important that children speak Welsh	74
Speakers should ask for a Welsh language service	49
Welsh is relevant to modern life in Wales	49

Source: adapted from Report on the State of the Welsh Language, March 2000.

Language attitudes for a sample such as that in the Welsh Language Board's second survey (i.e. with 43% Welsh speakers) could probably be summarised as

Attitudinal structure of Welsh speakers in Wales

Excellence		Vitality		Attractiveness		Action	
L1	L2	L1	L2	L1	L2	L1	L2
3	2	2	3	3	3	3	1

where L1 = Welsh and L2 = English

Scotland

In Scotland language attitudes have not played so great a role as in either Wales or Ireland. 1.35% of the population of Scotland, 65,978 people over the age of 3, spoke Gaelic in 1991, a figure that has decreased from 210,677 (5.2%) in 1901 and 79,307 (1.6%) in 1981. As in Wales, such a decline gives practical proof of language shift, as a consequence of 'an overall ideology of linguistic assimilation and the stranglehold of a dominant language and powerful external forces', while 'Gaelic has been neither an official nor promoted language' (Macpherson, 2000). The attitudes of activists are perhaps predictable: 'Ultimately, the issue of Gaelic is not just a Scottish issue. It is an issue of human dignity, of belonging, and of justice'. Commentators identify fairly large changes in attitude over the twentieth century. Around 1900, as in Ireland, pro-Gaelic attitudes came to the fore with the 1891 creation of An Comunn Gàidhealach whose aim was 'to develop Gaelic nationally and locally as a living language'. By the 1990s it had some 3,000 members world-wide and concentrated through the century on providing education and on the Arts, relying on voluntary funding for most of its existence. From 1920 to 1965 attitudes were generally less supportive: 'Gaeldom in Scotland sang itself asleep' (McKee, 1997). It was not until 1965 that attitudes changed, developing into a 'Mini-Renaissance' that led, eventually and after a change of government in London, to devolution in 1998. A survey of parental attitudes in the Western Isles in 1989 showed 86% of parents wishing their children to be bilingual, with 71% supporting Gaelic-medium education (Scottish Office, 1994: 8). Gaelic is now recognised as a national asset, and has been used in debates in the Scottish Parliament.

Scots, also called Lallans (Lowland language), may be considered either as a a group of northern English dialects or as a separate language, since it was probably standardised and codified in separate ways from English in England. Despite the existence of a major poet (Robert Burns) writing in the language, Scots has not acted as a major symbol of Scottish identity. Indeed, neither Lallans nor Gaelic has become a central symbol of Scottish independence for the main nationalist political party, the Scottish National Party.

Attitudinal structure of the majority of the population in Scotland

Excellence		Vitality		Attractiveness		Action	
L1	L2	L1	L2	L1	L2	L1	L2
3	3	1	3	2	3	3	1

where L1 = Gaelic and L2 = English

Attitudes Towards Non-territorial Languages

Among non-territorial communities, language attitudes have generally prioritised language maintenance in religious practices (Hebrew, Classical Arabic) and education, although foreign languages can be widely seen across the country on shop fronts and school signs, in advertising and newspapers, and there is a number of foreign-language TV and radio channels aimed at dwellers in Britain, particularly serving Hindi, Urdu and Bengali speakers.

Activists are strong in support of the teaching of community languages in the schools, and have exercised pressure in favour of such languages, for example at the time of the revision of policy towards the teaching of modern foreign languages in 1991 (see Ager, 1996: 148-9). There exists a number of such pressure and interest groups, which are generally concerned with cultural matters as well as language. The Centre for Information on Language Teaching and Research (CILT) runs a website where many practising teachers exchange information and are informed of teaching resources and of official schemes such as that for achieving Qualified Teacher Status, and publishes a regular bulletin concerned with community languages.

Attitudinally, many individuals and communities, representing probably the majority view, appear to prize their own language and wish to ensure its preservation among their own community, particularly in education and among the young, while recognising the fact that it will not provide for more than a part of their linguistic needs, and hence recognising also their own need to acquire English. But two other attitudes are also present. A 'separatist' group wishes to isolate the community from what they see as Western decadence, supporting frequent contact with 'home' and maintaining the language. In some cases, new non-English-speaking members of the community are actively sought and welcomed. Children are encouraged to study the 'home' language (see Appendix to check the GCSE and A-level entries for Urdu). A different attitude actively pursues a policy of integration, and encourages the community to adopt the host country's language, sometimes even denigrating its own. This may happen particularly where the language concerned is a non-prestige variety.

Many factors affect language attitudes for immigrant communities. In some cases, language practices are intimately connected to religious practices. Language may be used, sometimes deliberately, as a symbol of difference from the host community. This is probably true also of speakers of British Black English, where some culturally-related language practices such as verbal duelling, the (Caribbean) accent and other isolated features 'can be used for effect, for example in expressing ethnic or group solidarity' (Fennell, 2001: 206).

In these circumstances it is difficult to present a coherent picture of attitudes. Every community, every language, and every part of the country is different. If one had to summarise across the total picture, most communities regard English as itself excellent but their own language, in some cases, as less so; English as vital but their own as clearly not sufficient for communication in all domains; both their own and English as attractive; and, if there is any need for action, it is to acquire English and, in some circumstances and for some communities, to maintain their own.

Attitudinal structure of members of non-territorial communities

Excellence		Vitality		Attractiveness		Action	
L1	L2	L1	L2	L1	L2	L1	L2
1-3	3	1	3	3	3	1-3	3

where L1 = community language and L2 = English.

Chapter 3

Planning and Policy: from 880 to the 1950s

What Actors Attempted to Influence Language for what Ends?

Anglo-Saxon, French and Latin

British official language planning for English can be said to start with King Alfred's decision in 880AD to translate the materials of education into Anglo-Saxon, with the consequence that the Wessex form became a written standard for the clergy, in effect the only literate group. This chapter's brief account of the succeeding eleven centuries is deliberately limited to pointing out the actors and the aims involved in LPP, since the history is well known (see, for example, Baugh & Cable, 2002; Fennell, 2001). Alfred's political aim was to create an identity, to ensure that his kingdom could recognise itself and could be coherent enough to lead.

The 1066 Conquest of England by Duke William of Normandy had no such overt or obvious linguistic aim. As would continue to be the norm for centuries, the spoken language usage of the mass of the population was of little concern to the aristocracy. For official written purposes, Latin was the normal language of record, mixed with English as in the Domesday Book and, mainly later, Norman French. The ruling elite used its own spoken language, Norman French, and employed English only insofar as it was necessary to provide instructions for the Anglo-Saxons. This diglossia, itself a convenient oversimplification of a complex situation, was not without its problems, however. The conquered Anglo-Saxons were by no means uneducated, did not lack a developed economy in the terms of the time, nor were they without cultural life. The Bayeux Tapestry commemorating the Norman victory was probably made in Kent, by Europe's foremost artistic producers of the time, and certainly represents a major achievement. Anglo-Saxon organisation was, by European standards, sophisticated and advanced: the Domesday Book would have been impossible without Anglo-Saxon administrative genius. Indeed, William's officials used English themselves, certainly in the early years and until the dispossession of Anglo-Saxon clerks had taken place.

The dispossession of the Anglo-Saxon aristocracy and its replacement by the Norman did indeed replace the language by French throughout England in political life, but ecclesiastical matters, education and most serious writing was in Latin, as indeed it had been under the kings from Denmark and those of Anglo-Saxon origins. English itself started to be used again at the political level within a century, a process that was continued and confirmed as the knights were forced to choose where their lands were to lie after Philip II of France conquered Normandy in 1204, and where their social allegiances would be in 1244. In 1215 the Magna Carta was in Latin; in 1258 the Provisions of Oxford were in English. The fact that these were recorded in English was a specific, unusual action, deliberately chosen by King Henry to mollify the (now English) barons and to stress what, it was beginning to be clear, would be a specifically English political entity as he expelled his French supporters and renounced his claims to territory in France. French had by this time taken over the dominant roles and domains in society, but, in 1333, Parliament had to instruct 'all lords, barons, knights, and honest men' to teach French to their children, while universities prescribed that students should converse in Latin or French, not English. Such actions were by this time rearguard ones; by 1362 the Statute of Pleading admitted that English should be used in the courts 'because the laws, customs and statutes of this realm be not commonly known in the said realm for that they be pleaded, shewed, and judged in the French tongue, which is much unknown in the said realm'. Both courts and Parliament moved to English in 1362; the grammar schools construed in English from 1385. Parliamentary statutes, in Latin until about 1300, were in French until 1489 and in English thereafter.

The English that emerged in the fourteenth and fifteenth centuries from diglossia had been fundamentally modified from the Anglo-Saxon of the eleventh century. The three actors usually identified as the language planners of the following age were Chancery, the state bureaucracy; the Church, with its roles as principal educator as well as preserver of documents and everpresent task of listening to the populace as well as talking to it; and Chaucer, perhaps the foremost of the literary figures including Langland and Wycliff, although Caxton's role in codification and systematisation of spelling and other aspects of language should not be forgotten. As before, official LPP affected only the written language of the elite; the politically unimportant mass of the peasantry was left to its own linguistic devices. But all three main actors had to communicate on a daily basis with the populace, and were as much affected by the language that was used to them as by the language they, in their controlling and directing roles, used to it. Among the major choices that were made at this time was that of the dialect to be chosen to form the standard written English of the future. Here, the main actor was Chancery and the law courts, and the selection depended as much on official needs for consistent administration as on the growing social requirements for literature and education.

There was little official interference, but much social pressure, in the three LPP decisions that were needed for English between 1500 and 1700: status to allow English to replace Latin in all the important public domains, including scholarship; the codification of spelling; and elaboration of the vocabulary to cope with the increasing demands of the Renaissance in new technology, social change and a wider European, and later international, political role after Elizabeth. This was the time when literature defended English against Latin; when patriots recognised the role of English as the national speech; and when the Renaissance encouraged learning, and the new learning demanded dissemination, in English. The flood of translations increased the English vocabulary, despite grumbles at 'inkhorn terms'; more significantly, the elitism of the Romance and Latinate layer of vocabulary pushed English native terms even more into the subordinate role, while confirming the openness of the latter language to borrowing. Once strengthened by these additions, English could nonetheless start to hold its own, particularly when standardised and codified. The headmaster of St. Paul's School, Richard Mulcaster, in his _Elementarie_ of 1582 showed the growing influence of educators, rather than politicians, in establishing and codifying it, a process eventually more or less achieved for spelling about 1650. Dissemination and confirmation of the new standards relied on technological developments like printing, but also on the role of literary figures like Shakespeare. Probably the single most important element in standardising the language might have been the King James Bible, the Authorised Version, in use until at least 1960. This confirmed and symbolised the 'Britishness' of the religious battles.

Codification

Two 'them and us' oppositions which still affect language planning today are side effects of the LPP which had taken place to this point in the history of English. Diglossia between an 'official' higher (H) and an 'everyday' lower (L) language had long been present. The H language, that used in public, official domains, had been in turn Latin, then Norman French, then Parisian French, then the dialect of the East Midlands and London. In the seventeenth and eighteenth centuries the opposition, very similar in its effects, was between 'refined' and 'vulgar' speech. Even in contemporary Britain the social division continues, between standard English and non-standard forms, but also between accents, both regional and social. It was not until the 1950s that Received Pronunciation started to lose its role as the ideal. The second opposition is that between the Romance and the Anglo-Saxon strata, particularly in vocabulary. It is revealed in the contrasts between an essentially Germanic grammar and a lexical stock which does not altogether match; between concrete and abstract vocabulary; but also in use of the Franco-Latinate layer as the preferred vehicle of advanced scholarship and learning. The impression is that long words from Latin roots are the difficult ones which require the support of a strong and systematic educational system. The more advanced the education, the more Latinate vocabulary is acquired and needed, so the greater control a speaker has of this vocabulary, the better proof of (a longer) education, and hence of elitist standing. It is hardly surprising that education in the Public Schools, until the late nineteenth century, required that members of the elite, the only ones for whom secondary education was possible, should confirm their membership of this select social group by mastering its language, Latin.

By 1700 the need was for codification, for rules and for certainty. Samuel Johnson in his _Dictionary of the English Language_ of 1755, Bishop Lowth in his _A Short Introduction to English Grammar_ of 1762, acted knowingly or not, on behalf of the social and political structure of their time in their task of codification. These and other language actors influenced language, not immediately in pursuance of political aims, but for wider social purposes. In 1714 however Britain had very nearly created its own language Academy to formally consecrate this as a state process, as France and Italy had before it. English was said to face three problems: to reduce the language to rule and set up a standard of correct usage; to refine it - that is, to remove supposed defects and introduce certain improvements; and to fix it permanently in the desired form. The Royal Society resolved in 1644 that it should establish a 'committee for improving the English language', with a detailed programme of language planning outlined by the important public servant John Evelyn. Major literary figures (Dryden in 1660 and Defoe in 1697) supported the idea of an official organisation, which was taken up again by Jonathan Swift in 1712 in a letter to the Lord Treasurer of England. The opposition to the idea, like the idea itself, was political: the Whigs, populist and pro-Parliament, saw an Academy as one more manifestation of the monarchy's authority and took the opportunity of Queen Anne's death to reject the plan.

The eighteenth century efforts at LPP seem, on the face of it, to be the results of public-spirited work by disinterested individual benefactors, in the same way the Royal Society in effect founded scientific exploration and discovery by a similar process, led by gifted amateurs. Both widely read 'Dictators' of language, Lowth and Johnson, relied on etymology, the model of Latin; the notion of the usage of the best authors, sometimes described as 'refinement'; and, in cases of last resort, on 'reason'. The extent to which such guides were disinterested can be judged by the (then) meaning of terms like reason and refinement. Reason was interpreted to mean consistency, analogy, and occasionally the logic of universal grammar. 'Universal', however, itself usually meant Latin, the language accessible only to those who could afford secondary education. Similarly, refinement was defined by contrast to vulgarity, the customs of the mass. Parliamentary usage of the term in the eighteenth century shows how the pleas from the growing middle class against the burden of taxation without the right to be represented in the House of Commons, were simply excluded from consideration, since they were not couched in 'refined' language. 'To speak the vulgar language demonstrated that one was morally and intellectually unfit to participate in the culture ... Ideas about language justified class division and even contributed to its formation' (Smith, 1984: 2-3). Even when the usage of the 'best authorities' was cited, as in Priestley's _Rudiments of English Grammar_ (1761) and Campbell's _Philosophy of Rhetoric_ (1776), the 'diction' of the 'laborious and mercantile part of the people' was rejected as 'mere native English' (Priestley) or as casual and mutable, 'fugitive cant' (Samuel Johnson). The codification of English was hence a social process, constructed by representatives of a social dictatorship as effective in erecting barriers to social mobility as the aristocratic, centralising French Academy. But it was also motivated by 'morals', by the pervading sense that to use correct language was a duty, and that only persons lacking a moral sense could use incorrect or inappropriate language. Rejection of a British (language) Academy did not mean the rejection of the idea of controlling language: Samuel Johnson was delighted to be called a language Dictator by Chesterfield, despite his hope that 'the spirit of English liberty will hinder and destroy' Swift's Academy.

In the nineteenth century, the aims and purposes of the language planners remained in the social sphere rather than returning to the political ones of the fourteenth or earlier centuries. The Public Schools, defining acceptable language use across the country, acted on behalf of the elite as gatekeepers to social advancement, using knowledge of the classical languages as the key and hence ensuring the reproduction of the controlling social category and its maintenance in power. The Eldon judgment is a significant pointer to how this was done. Using Samuel Johnson's definition of a grammar school as a school for teaching grammar (i.e. Latin), Eldon supported the desire of the Public Schools to be released from their charitable aims of providing free education. The resulting insertion of fees into what had been the only form of secondary education in the country ensured that only those with money could be educated beyond the primary level, transforming the leading schools into what they have remained: non-local, fee-paying closed agents of social uniformity, aiming as much at ensuring entry to the professions and the elite as at reproducing the elite by educating its offspring. Thomas Arnold of Rugby School was perhaps one of the foremost thinkers involved, enunciating a convincing moral code as the schools selected pupils on the basis of their background. The schools created a remarkably uniform social category, a remarkably uniform common language and set of values, even a uniform pronunciation and vocabulary. Until the beginning of the twentieth century, these language planners followed a social aim which had clear political consequences, inspired by a strong sense of duty and morality.

The British Isles

Outside England, language planning as a consequence of political conquest had already imposed English as the language of Wales, Scotland and Ireland. LPP aims in the Celtic periphery were, and have remained, essentially political. In the three conquered countries, dissension was never far away. Formal texts imposing English in Ireland started with the 1366 Statutes of Kilkenny, threatening landowners with forfeiture of their lands if they did not teach English to their young, while a sixteenth century Act required that 'every person ... inhabiting this land of Ireland ... shall use and speak commonly the English tongue and language'. Legal provisions there may have been, but Henry VIII's control of the Church meant that Catholics who wished to remain so used Irish, and English was less and less used until James I's settlements in the North started the colonisation that eventually brought English to the fore. The 1536 Act of Union between England and Wales made English formally official in Wales, provoking a massive attitudinal shift by the Welsh gentry who flocked to learn English. Henry VIII's Act of 1536 ensured that access to the law was only possible through English, a condition that continued until 1942, and that 'any manner office or fees within this realm of England, Wales, or other the King's dominion' could only be maintained by those using the English speech or language (cf. Grillo, 1989: 95). The Scottish and English crowns were united in 1604 as James the Sixth of Scotland became James the First of Great Britain, setting about a massive propaganda battle to use 'Britain' and not 'England' as the name of his realm. Scottish Acts of 1616 required that the children of clan chiefs be 'trained in virtue, learning and the English tongue'. The 1707 Act of Union of the two parliaments formally imposed English as the one language of the state.

The political aims of LPP in the periphery were associated with moral and religious purposes, too. Protestant beliefs in the need to read the Bible for oneself meant that, on some occasions, local languages like Welsh were encouraged. Indeed, although Parliament denied Cornish prayer books in 1549, it allowed translations of the Bible and Divine Service into Welsh in 1563. The consequence, paradoxically, was that the peasantry, without access to 'office or fees', became cut off from its own elite, increasingly English-speaking, and was in effect isolated in a linguistic ghetto. Well-intentioned civil servants in the nineteenth century saw how far this ghetto was disadvantaging people in Wales, and, for different but equally 'moral' reasons, tried to help: 'the Welsh language is a vast drawback to Wales, and a manifold barrier to the moral progress and commercial prosperity of the people' (Kay-Shuttleworth 1847, quoted in Grillo 1989: 47). The Irish famine of 1846-7 convinced many of the Irish peasantry that survival lay in learning English, but only in order to enable emigration to America where they retained their Catholicism. On the other hand, the increasing anglicisation of Ireland and Wales led to the rebirth of nationalism, another ideological cause, and to awareness of the central role of cultural identity through core values such as language. It is thus that the Gaelic League was born in 1893, and the aim of an Ireland 'not only free, but Gaelic-speaking as well' led eventually to the Easter Rising of

1916, the Irish Free State of 1922 and the Irish Republic of 1948 with its Constitutional role for the language. In Scotland it took the clearances of the 1840s and 50s to ensure the near disappearance of the Gaelic-speaking linguistic reservoir and its dispersal, mainly to America but also to New Zealand. Scottish Gaelic survived only in the islands to the north-west of the mainland.

Empire and after

The political solution of insisting on a central role for English was continued in the spread of the language abroad to colonies, Empire and Dominions. Motives were equally mixed, seeing no problem in covering economic gain by religious and moral fervour. In the seventeenth century John Smith was encouraging 'people of small means', 'if hee have any grain of faith or zeale in Religion, what can he doe lesse hurtful to any, or more agreable to God, than to seeke to convert those poor Salvages to know Christ and humanity, whose labours with discretion will triple requite thy charge and paine' (quoted in Bailey, 1991: 68). An 1838 address to Australian Aboriginals was crystal clear, demanding that the Black Men build huts, wear clothes, worked and made themselves useful. Above all they had to love God.

Jakob Grimm, speaking to the Royal Academy of Berlin in 1851, praised English to the skies, considering that it 'combines extreme simplicity with all the qualities demanded of a language expressing the thought of the most advanced civilization'. There was of course widespread satisfaction among the English at the prospect of an English-speaking world, backing up the military, commercial and ideological facts of conquest and control. The creation of Empire was also a linguistic action, and Britain 'civilised' its conquests by encouraging the 'natives' to adopt Christianity, Victorian values, clothes and English, if necessary by the use of force. Britain's success with English abroad was due to its military and naval might, its commercial activity and its encouragement to local elites to imitate and adopt both language and attitudes. (Some) Indian rulers were thus encouraged to take up education in English, retaining their leading roles, rather than all being simply crushed as in Algeria or Indochina. The eventual founding of the British Council in 1934, and its support by the Foreign Office in order to disseminate British culture including the language, one of the consequences of this type of encouragement, has only been regarded as itself an imperialist, political, action in very recent times (Phillipson, 1992). Throughout the nineteenth and early twentieth centuries the same ideas about English accompanied its spread. English was the language of the arts and sciences, of trade and commerce. It was inevitable that it, and it alone, should be the language of civilisation and of religious liberty. Almost exactly the same terms were used by French colonisers of the time, only, of course, about French.

As the nineteenth century advanced, as the Empire was developed, Britain's power was indeed based more and more on her economic weight. While in 1851 half the population lived by agriculture, by 1901 the proportion was a quarter. The shift towards industry and away from an agrarian society meant drastic changes. The productiveness of British industry, the impetus given to economic development by the abolition of the Corn Laws and the development of Free Trade, and the growth of technology meant that language use had to be planned to ensure that the workforce could be more productive. While rural peasants could please themselves how they spoke, when industrial workers massed in towns and left the Welsh countryside they had to learn a common language. An obvious consequence of this type of LPP was the destruction of dialects and local languages. A second was that, during the nineteenth century, as the Public Schools educated the elite and attempted to restrict it, economic development increasingly enabled uneducated people to rise in society. The delocalisation of the elite and the transformation of Public Schools into social gate-keepers provoked a flood of advice on negotiating the social divides, from Mrs Beeton's _Household Management_ to _Vulgarities of Speech Corrected_ (1826) and _Society Small Talk or What to Say and When to Say it_ (1879). The period saw the rise of the amateur as language planner. It saw, also, the rise of formal education for the mass, so that the mass could play its economic role. Sunday Schools gave some training in reading, as did the Anglican National Schools and the Nonconformist British Schools, between them educating just over a million boys by the 1850s. The Elementary Education Act of 1870 offered a place for children to age 10 with a curriculum of the three Rs, fee-paying until 1891. The school-leaving age rose to 14 in 1918, to 15 in 1944 and to 16 in 1973. Girls, of course, were trained for domestic service or marriage until the typewriter and the telephone provided them with suitable economic opportunities. Religious foundations played a main part in education, if an ad-hoc one, until the Education Act of 1944 systematised their relationship with the state. Even this Act was very clear that the compulsory secondary education it introduced should have three purposes: the grammar schools were for education; the technical schools were for training for the world of work; the modern schools were for the mass, ensuring basic levels in the three Rs and providing such specialisms as the poorer resource levels available to these schools than to the other two could provide. Even so, the social aims of Butler's Education Act of 1944 were clear: to bring about a cohesive society where education could be offered to each according to (a view of) his or her need.

The aftermath of the World Wars saw an increase in a new type of language policy. Language was to be learnt not just as an aid for economic life but for its own sake. The increasing wealth of society meant that leisure time was becoming available. Easier and wider access to grammar schools meant that even children from the working classes could gain access to scholarship as well as to economically oriented training. The entertainment industry blossomed. Qualification and certification did start to replace the traditional ways of defining the elite, by birth or wealth. In all these changes, LPP lost both its economic aims of the nineteenth century and its social aims of the eighteenth. Political differences were no longer so clearly defined by issues of class, and LPP actors could no longer be so clearly identified with social background, economic roles or with ideologies of domination.

Political actors were concerned with the educational and examination system. There were numerous reports on the state of English teaching, many of which revealed views on language which were to suffer many changes as the century drew on. Newbolt's Report of 1921 confirmed the central role of English in education: 'every teacher is a teacher of English'. Sampson's *English for the English* of the same year clarified some of the thinking involved: standard English was to be recommended, and the purpose of education was to destroy the 'evil habits of speech' and the 'degradations' of dialects.

Social, Political and Economic Aims

If language planning and policies had mainly political motives, even in corpus planning, to 1800, aims of social engineering rose in importance through the nineteenth century and the early twentieth as language became one of the key elements in structuring society, and particularly in maintaining class divisions (Smith, 1984). As social structures changed with the Industrial and the Agricultural Revolutions, recognition of social differences through language became more difficult. Dialects mixed and education spread the standard language at the same time as rural workers moved to the town and landowning was no longer the only proof of wealth and status.

Logically, greater use of the standard language, becoming known as the 'Queen's English', should have acted as a social leveller. In fact, the opposite happened, and for this education in the Public Schools, the only secondary education available, is probably responsible. The Public School version of English, and Received Pronunciation, maintained the class divisions through ensuring the association of money and symbolic linguistic capital. In this way, the educational gatekeepers ensured the definition and reproduction of the ruling elite.

By 1900, economic motives for language planning became more important, since this type of 'planning' blocked advancement and produced a static society. The technical advances of manufacturing, and the requirements of industry meant that language planning increasingly targeted the working class through acquisition policy as the new century arrived, as new Education Acts were passed, and as demand increased for a workforce able to read, able to understand the standard language and ready to accept the social norms it encapsulated. Marxists see such planning as a negative reinforcement of elitist domination (Holborow, 1999); others will regard it as a necessary and unavoidable move towards modernisation.

Language planning by social and economic pressure is in essence a way of managing society without involving the state. In both cases, management may involve ensuring that things happen or continue to happen, that outcomes and outputs occur. In order to do this, successful political control may be just as effective when it leaves things alone as when it changes them. If it ain't bust, don't fix it: evolution is just as good, and often better, than revolution. Much British language planning at government level before the 1950s seems to have followed this approach, aiming at social management and the efficient use of human resources by muddling through rather than by the grand symbolic gesture. The other side of this course is that society can be 'managed' to be cohesive mainly by keeping people in their place, by oppression and restriction if need be to ensure that revolutions and rejections of the established order do not occur. Either way, there is little doubt that governments took little interest in the precise nature of the curriculum until nearly a century after the creation of large-scale public education in the 1880s.

By contrast with social and economic motives, political aims are generally concerned with instituting change in society, usually in pursuance of a particular ideology, world view or agenda. In most cases, politicians are in a hurry for revolution and change. If it stands still, abolish it: politics is the art of the possible, of doing things. Not all

British LPP has been as static and cohesive as it might at first appear. The ideological aim had been present in many centuries and in many specific examples, even though the word 'moral' is the preferred cover term. Thus the aim of forcing the Welsh to learn English had the 'moral' aim of ensuring their material advancement; the 'civilisation' of Africa was conducted for the moral benefit of the natives. The moral impetus behind education was stated many times. Indeed, even the planning of the nineteenth century, driven by economic pressures, was presented as a moral imperative, and the development of public education in Great Britain reflected an almost religious aversion to the Dickensian squalor and poverty in which the urban poor lived. Certainly enough was done to avoid the worst excesses of uprisings and revolutions.

It has not been until the last half of the twentieth century that overt, organised, and ideological attempts to influence language use, often indeed through legislation, have started to affect all three main LPP areas of corpus, status and acquisition.

Planners: the State, Social Categories and Individuals

If the aims and purposes of LPP in British history have often been clearly linked to social and economic origins and intended outcomes, with only occasional and strictly identifiable political intentions, the actors who brought about significant changes seem to have come as much from civil society as from the official state.

There have of course been cases of official, state language policy. King Alfred's actions were official; William the Conqueror's, even though incidental to his main purpose, were those of a government; the Education Acts of the 1870s were political actions. But many times, in Britain, language policy has been carried out without flamboyancy, without a Parliamentary Act or even a major debate. Leading politicians, like Gladstone or Balfour, may occasionally make comments about the glories of English, although they did not often do much for it or about it. It is often the quiet actions of the state's bureaucrats, rather than the noisy declarations of rulers, which have inspired specific, and productive, LPP actions. The institution of education among the Welsh peasantry in the nineteenth century, as the financial support for the British Council in the twentieth, were behind-the-scenes actions of civil servants, carried out by stealth and often with the best of motives.

The elite, a social category defined differently at different periods of history, were significant actors. The first major break in domination by French occurred as the Angevin Empire collapsed about 1200, when a deliberate choice had to be made for England and English rather than French by the elite who had to decide, at the insistence of the French King, whether they wished to retain their lands in France or opt to give these up so that their possessions were entirely in England. Language behaviour was the consequence of language choices by the land-owning elite, symbolising their own political, but also social and economic interests. Later, too, although the formal power was in the hands of Royalty or officials, the elite were by no means powerless. Whig philosophy in the eighteenth century aimed at restricting the Royal power, and its strength was shown in the issue of the failed Academy.

In late medieval times the actors represented three social forces that have come to share, fairly equally and even today, the role of instigator of LPP: Chancery or officialdom; Church or the moral urge; and Chaucer or the cultural and literary world. Individual planners can often be traced to one of these three backgrounds. Cable's list of the ten people responsible for creating standard English showed how (quoted in Honey, 1997: 84).

Thus from officialdom one could identify Henry V, king of England from 1413 to 1422, promoting the use of English in government and probably the founder of English nationalism at Agincourt; Thomas Elyot, sixteenth century Clerk to Henry VIII's Council and educator, author of _The Governor_ in 1531 which advocated a humanist education, in English; and Richard Mulcaster, headmaster of St Paul's school and author of the _Elementarie_ in 1582, advocating and codifying spelling.

From the Church and its concerns with philosophy as well as with the basis for an English state religion, came John Wyclif, fourteenth century founder of the Lollards who used English rather than Latin in his writings and paved the way for the Reformation; and William Tyndale, translator of the Bible in the sixteenth century.

From literature Geoffrey Chaucer, fourteenth century poet and writer, author of the Canterbury Tales and one of the main reasons why the Midlands dialect became standard; William Caxton, fifteenth century merchant whose use of the printing press moved the language towards standardisation; and above all William Shakespeare, sixteenth and early seventeenth century dramatist whose plays did more than anybody else to shape English as a language capable of expressing every aspect of life and emotion.

The two eighteenth century planners named by Cable, Samuel Johnson and Bishop Lowth, are perhaps less easy to pigeonhole.

Although Lowth was a bishop, his systematisation and codification of grammar in 1762 reflected little of the Church's LPP motivations. Samuel Johnson, author of the *Dictionary* in 1755 was a working journalist before receiving a pension from Lord Bute. Johnson's particular facility was to be part of society, to reflect the pressures and opinions of the elite as well as to create them, since the list of his friends is the list of the major cultural figures of the eighteenth century, usually members of the Literary Club.

The same three sources have produced planners in modern times: officialdom and the management of the state (Sir Ernest Gowers); the moral impetus of changing ideologies, including those of social categories as well as those of a specifically religious belief systems (Thomas Arnold); and LPP actors with a more cultural intent, and sometimes a less coherent motivation (George Orwell). The role of officialdom has not been preponderant, although it has been significant: in James I's attempts to recast British identity and to use the English language as the means for doing so; in Parliament's eighteenth-century attempts to repudiate increasing democracy and resist reform by insisting on a particular form of language; in the official control of education from the late nineteenth century on; in the awards of knighthoods in 1908 and 1928 to two of the editors of the *Oxford English Dictionary*; and in continuing control of both the periphery in the British Isles and of the Empire and later Commonwealth. Literary figures, too, have been significant actors: Shakespeare's language has always been held up as the ideal, and the acceptance of poetry with its essential refusal of obedience to strict rules of grammar in pursuance of expression is a recurring motif in LPP statements.

But it is the moral impetus that was significant in much British LPP up to the twentieth century. In cases where the Welsh had to be taught English for their own good, or the African savage had to wear clothes and read the Bible, as in cases where society's decadence had to be protected by insisting on the use of standard English, on 'correct' spelling, and on 'decent' language in the media, there has been no lack of public figures prepared to liken these preferences to the word of God or to derive them from an ideological basis founded in the goodness of man. The significant figures of the eighteenth century, Johnson, Lowth and Swift among them, are at one in their desire to codify and fix the language in pursuance of social cohesion and harmony, a moral aim if there was ever one.

Chapter 4

Non-political Language Planning

Individuals, private societies and the media have played major roles in influencing or trying to influence language usage. Indeed, it is these public-spirited and generally non-political groups and individuals who are traditionally regarded in Britain as the most significant, if not the only, language planners. Most of these efforts by non-political people and organisations have been driven by purist motivations of various sorts. Among these, those which seem to have the strongest attraction for the British are elitist, archaic and reformist purism. These have resulted in campaigns to protect, defend or conserve the characteristics of the past, of the 'best' speakers, of the canon of 'major' writers, and to oppose the 'sloppiness' of the uneducated, the socially deprived and the young, as well as the simply modern. Reformist purists have produced innumerable campaigns to regularise spelling, to simplify grammar or to improve style. All these motivations, although they are outwardly non-political, may actually reflect political ideologies, particularly when the aim of 'defending' English against the attacks of modernity, the uneducated or the socially deprived are associated, as they frequently are, with condemnations of those who would 'modernise' society, 'reform' education or give rights to the 'inferior' social categories.

In this chapter we shall examine avowedly non-political language planners who have been active during the late twentieth century. Although this cannot be an exhaustive survey, we shall be interested to see whether the moral or ideological motive is in fact as important as it seems to have been for many before the twentieth century. We shall also limit most of the discussion to LPP for English, partly because the territorial languages are dealt with separately in Chapter 8, and partly because the motives for exercising influence are so different for each of the languages.

Individuals and Purism

During the twentieth century a number of prominent individuals, from George Bernard Shaw to Keith Waterhouse, have found language of interest. Many of these have used their writings on language to make political, social or other points. Even when they say they are dealing with language, their real interest is elsewhere, and they comment, not so much on matters of linguistic or sociolinguistic interest as on politics, culture or society. Raymond Williams, in *Keywords* (1976) is an example. Williams' interest was to clarify the interpretation of terms commonly used in a particular semantic field. He noted that *Keywords* had been called an exercise in 'cultural history, in historical semantics, the history of ideas, social criticism, literary history and in sociology'. His *Vocabulary of Culture and Society* is not an LPP document but an attempt both to track changing interpretations and to map the field of culture in such a way as to allow him a critique of the field. Martin Amis' *War Against Cliché* (2000) is a selection of literary reviews and essays published between 1971 and 2000, and is little concerned with clichés in language. Kingsley Amis, in The *King's English*, which first appeared in 1985, was rather more concerned with language issues. Occasionally, Amis condemns or approves a term, although the majority of the book is aimed at definitions and distinctions, and at 'correctness' in language use. Bill Bryson's *Penguin Dictionary of Troublesome Words* (1983; 3rd ed 2001) was also intended to help rather than pontificate, while his *Mother Tongue* (1990) deals with various aspects of the English language, again without much expectation that his views will influence the corpus, status or learning of English. Indeed, the popular tone of *Mother Tongue* is reflected well in reviewers' comments such as 'A delightful, amusing and provoking survey, a joyful celebration of our wonderful language, which is packed with curiosities and enlightenment on every page'.

Despite these examples of mixed motives, most of those trying to influence language, including indefatigable members of the public writing to newspapers and magazines, have followed the purist tradition (McArthur, 1998: 98-117; see also p. 37 above). McArthur quotes many such who have written to him as Editor of *English Today*, bemoaning 'the decline of our language' and seeing the language as 'a vehicle of high culture, a protection against Outer Darkness.' Thus Jack Conrad (aged 73) was 'very concerned about the way the English language has been rapidly deteriorating during the past few years ... the process of deterioration has become a landslide.' One common factor has been the desire for a language authority: someone or some body who is authorised to rule on matters of language; to be the 'arbiter of standard English if not crusaders for the standardisation of all deviant forms'.

Xenophobes

Xenophobic rejections of the language of foreigners have long been directed at Greek and Latin, French and Italian. In the twentieth century, the main target has been Americanisms.

The tone of almost religious fervour occasionally heard in British anti-American xenophobia is by no means new: the word 'Americanism' was first used in 1781, and 'In the beginning English comment was uniformly adverse' (Baugh and Cable, 2002: 390). The tone is now sometimes regretful: 'Sadly, this battle has now been lost and *hopefully* is now widely used to mean it is to be hoped; mercifully, this is not the end of the world although it seems to upset the pedantic.' (Marsh & Marshall, 2000). Sometimes, still, comment is negative: Prince Charles is reported to have said Americanisms were 'corrupting and should be avoided at all costs' (*Guardian*, 6.4.1995). Americanisms change, as does their acceptance or rejection in Britain. Bryson (1990: 169) notes that *billion, airplane, gimmick* and *phoney* are accepted in Britain without question, and wonders why in America the Post Office delivers the mail while in Britain the Royal Mail delivers the post. Burchfield (1985: 163-66) noted, on the other hand, how some Americanisms 'remain firmly unborrowed'. He quoted *scam* and *schlepp*, both of which however had become frequent in British newspapers by 2000. Fennell (2001:221) also points out how American spellings, formerly rejected, have entered standard English: *judgment, medieval*; while others have not: *tire, plow*. Purist attitudes in many cases reflect political or social ones: dislike of American films accompanies dislike of the violence, the swearing and the sex, as well as the language, while dislike of US politics accompanies dislike of terms like *globalization*.

Archaism

We have noted how preferences for the language of the past may find their origin in such ideologies as the Whig view of history (Chapter 1), which regarded the Norman Conquest as an unmitigated disaster for the language. A recurring view is that the Germanic, Anglo-Saxon stratum is preferable to Romance and Latinate terms.

Preference for a previous form of the language, regarded as correct even though idealised, often seems to date this ideal to the time of the writer's youth. Thus Keith Waterhouse (1991) allocates blame for present-day poor English to the disappearance of grammar teaching in the 1950s and teachers' insistence in the 1960s that 'what the pupil had to say was more important than the way in which it was said'.

Elitists

Elitist preferences for southern, educated standard English over other regional and social dialects are frequently encountered. Elitism is by no means confined to this particular aspect of the linguistic ecology. Although generally Kingsley Amis avoids overly elitist comments, some, like the following, smack of the social snob.

> Servants and other inferior persons have from time immemorial been promising they will follow an order by saying or shouting from near by, something that means 'at once' and then dawdling or delaying indefinitely. Following their progress, or lack of it, expressions that formerly meant 'at once' have come to mean 'in a little while'. The most familiar of these is 'presently'. (Amis, K. 1997:110)

The most obvious example of elitist purism in twentieth century Britain is the discovery of U and non-U speech, academically by Professor Ross and publicly by Nancy Mitford, whose 1955 *Encounter* article sparked much debate and discussion, with notable contributions from Evelyn Waugh and John Betjeman (Mitford, 1956). Ross noted upper-class terms like sick, writing-paper, pudding and napkin and their lower-class equivalents such as ill, note-paper, sweet and serviette. The debate struck an immediate chord with the wider public, and the phrase *U and non-U* has become part of the language even if the examples have changed.

Elitism is also evident in two other types of purist: the reverse elitists who utterly condemn aristocratic outpourings and are convinced that the 'lower orders' hold the key to the purest English; and the anti-urban brigade ('ethnographic' purists) who similarly approve solely of rural speech.

Reformers

It is particularly on ideas for a pure new language, freed from the misunderstandings of traditional English, that reformist purists have spread their wings. Fifty-three proposals for new languages were made between 1880 and 1907, although of these only Esperanto has achieved wide recognition. Reformist motives have generated many proposals for English, too, most frequently for spelling reform.

Suggestions have been made for using a reduced form of English in specified circumstances. C. K. Ogden invented Basic English in 1929. British American Scientific International Commercial English, as the name indicates, was intended to make learning English easier for an international audience and to simplify communication. Basic English, using a vocabulary of 850 words, was not actually as simple as that: the 850 words have something over 18,000 senses as listed in the *Oxford English Dictionary*. Basic English remained in use until the American General Service List of 2,000 words replaced it to provide a learners' essential vocabulary, itself remaining valid until the 1970s. A similar, and similarly scientific, approach to defining which words are needed for particular purposes lies behind the specification of prescribed subsets of English for different subject areas. Such a subset of words and phrases, often internationally agreed as significant, is more efficient for communication, easier to learn and prevents misunderstandings. Thus Essential English for Maritime Use, commonly known as Seaspeak, was invented during the 1980s, replacing the possible variety of phrases for use at sea like 'I didn't hear you' or 'Please repeat that' by one standardised phrase 'Say again'.

International agreement on such reforms is not easy to obtain. Canada continued, and continues in Montreal, to use French rather than English in aviation. Although the International Civil Aviation Organization recommends English, certain phrases and words (e.g. *Roger, Wilco,* and the use of the phonetic alphabet (*Alpha, Bravo*)) not all pilots obey. Probably the worst result of linguistic misunderstanding occurred at Tenerife in 1977, when a KLM pilot misunderstood the Spanish controller's use of 'at take-off' and set off down the runway as another plane was landing in fog (Crystal, 1997: 100).

Following Sir Isaac Pitman's invention of shorthand and proposal for a new alphabet in the 1840s, and keeping things in the family, Sir James Pitman's Initial Teaching Alphabet, commonly represented by lower-case letters as ita, and published in 1959, had considerable success in the 1960s and 1970s and was widely used by teachers in the UK. It aimed, not at developing a new alphabet, but at representing phonemes more accurately and at aiding the transition to ordinary spelling for young children. Although many teachers liked it and promoted it, finding it easy to manage the transition to ordinary spelling, the alphabet gradually fell into disuse and was no longer recommended after the 1970s.   Spelling reform is still urged on National Curriculum authorities.

George Bernard Shaw bequeathed his royalties, for a period of twenty-one years after his death in 1950, to devise a new alphabet (Carney, 1992: 484). The motive was principally economic: Shaw claimed in 1944 that 'Shakespeare might have written two or three more plays in the time it took him to write his name with eleven letters instead of seven'. His will was successfully challenged by the British Museum and other legatees, but some provision was still made for the design.   The 40-character alphabet   that appeared was designed for writer not reader, was difficult to learn and to print. It consisted of completely new letters, making no use of the existing Roman alphabet. No psychological tests were made to ensure readability, and some of the symbols can be easily confused. But one of his plays was published in the new alphabet to show that it could be done, and although Shaw was convinced that the simple demonstration would suffice to convince readers of the excellence of his proposal, it was quietly dropped thereafter.

Mont Follick, a vigorous and enterprising reformer who died in 1958, managed, as an MP, to introduce a Private Member's Bill in 1949 and 1953 aimed at introducing an alternative alphabet. This proposal, for New Spelling, was sponsored by the Simplified Spelling Society, and would have had the effect of changing the appearance of over 90 percent of words on a page. The second Bill, although approved at first reading by 65 to 53, was withdrawn after official assurances that the Ministry of Education would investigate the proposal. Spelling was not Follick's only concern: he proposed a number of radical simplifications to grammar in a book written in 1914 but not published until 1934. Some of the suggestions included doing away with plurals, articles, cases and genders of pronouns, the imperfect and the future tense. His principal aim was to help foreign learners of English, an aim that was the stronger since he managed a successful language school. His original motivation does not seem to have been commercial, however; if anything he was driven by a desire to end wars by proposing an international language to help understanding.

One recurring theme among purists is the belief that thought is modified by language. If language is clear and pure, then so will be the thoughts conveyed. Likewise, if the message itself is clear and clearly understood by the writer, the style, diction and expression will automatically themselves be perfect. George Orwell was particularly concerned about clarity in writing. His six rules for 'an instrument for expressing' were:

(1)   Never use a metaphor, simile or other figure of speech which you are used to seeing in print.
(2)   Never use a long word when a short one will do.
(3)   If it is possible to cut a word out, do so.
(4)   Never use the passive where you can use the active.
(5)   Never use a foreign phrase, a scientific word or a jargon word where you can think of an ordinary English equivalent.
(6)   Break any of these rules sooner than say anything outright barbarous. (quoted in Crystal, 1987: 2)

In a particularly well-known and influential article (Orwell, 1946), he advocated a 'plain and transparent' style aimed at 'letting the meaning choose the word'. Orwell invented Newspeak, exemplified in his novel *Nineteen Eighty-Four* (1949), as a lesson in how language could be subverted by totalitarian regimes. The novel was itself a set book for generations of British schoolchildren, and, thus tacitly supported by the state, was for decades a principal weapon in the ideological struggle against what was later called the 'evil empire' of Communism.

Shaw died in 1950 and Mont Follick in 1958. After the flurry of interest over U and non-U language in the late 1950s, public concern with language declined somewhat in Britain until the 1980s brought renewed interest. Possibly the most significant individual to have written recently on the subject of the English language has been John Marenbon, a relatively obscure Conservative thinker and pamphlet writer who happened to pen a pamphlet on *English, our English* (1987) for the Centre for Policy Studies, the think-tank whose opinions lay behind much of the mood of Margaret Thatcher and her radical Conservative government. It may be this pamphlet that was the trigger for the more aggressive and more politically inspired language policy approach that was adopted by that and subsequent governments. Keith Waterhouse, novelist and film director, wrote a column in the *Daily Mirror* and then *Daily Mail*, following this by *Waterhouse on Newspaper Style* in 1989 and *English, our English* in 1991. As a 'constant campaigner for improved standards of English in our schools' Waterhouse allocated blame in the latter volume for the poor standard of English to the education system: 'the rot set in back in the late Fifties when clause analysis ... was abolished from O-level

English ... the switch was more ideological than educational ... lowered the general level of literacy.' 'Bad English ... is part of the general corrosion of the quality of life, like vandalism, litter and graffiti.' The analysis almost exactly follows that of the Thatcherite educational reforms of the late 1980s (Chapter 8). His contribution to correcting the situation, like that of Kingsley Amis and indeed Bill Bryson, was to discuss specific examples of improvements people should make to their own writing. His list (Waterhouse, 1991: 143-7) is similar to Orwell's, and indeed to Gowers' (Chapter 6), although he does add 'Connect your unattached participles' to the recommendations.

Societies and Associations

Organised groups and societies aiming to influence language and language behaviour are not numerous in Britain. Their aims and methods are various; their resources and membership generally small; and their support comes from a variety of sources including occasional government grants or Lottery funds. Many of them are concerned as much with supporting Englishness or Britishness, or the world-wide influence of the English-speaking peoples, as with the language itself. Others are more directly concerned with the language, which indeed they sometimes regard as divorced from its users. The following brief list does not consider some important associations, particularly those whose main aims are not linguistic or which are semi-humorous (The Apostrophe Protection Society). It excludes academic societies and research organisations, including in particular the European Language Council, 'a permanent and independent European association, the main aim of which is the quantitative and qualitative improvement of knowledge of the languages and cultures of the European Union and beyond'. It excludes societies aimed at publicising artificial languages such as Esperanto, and developing and promoting communication systems such as Sign Language. It excludes dialect societies, of which there are many, and, with some exceptions, those defending or promoting the territorial and the non-territorial languages. It also excludes groups with specific interests such as the National Association of Teachers of English, the English Place-Names Society, 'Clarity', an organisation of lawyers 'supporting the simplification of legal language' and similar groups.

The Simplified Spelling Society was founded in 1908. Its members included both scholars such as Gilbert Murray and Daniel Jones and public figures such as George Bernard Shaw, H. G. Wells and

Archbishop William Temple. It found a major supporter and publicist in Mont Follick. Its major success was probably the submission of a Bill to Parliament in 1949, which failed only by 87 votes to 84, and a second Bill in 1953, accepted at first reading and which was withdrawn only after strong opposition by the Ministry of Education. The 1949 Bill proposed a ten-year programme after which only new spelling would be taught, which would be compulsory for the award of copyright in all new publications. Lobbying by the Society continues strongly in the 2000s, particularly for the National Curriculum, and the case is made that 'English spelling makes it very difficult for young children to acquire "phonic knowledge" and "to make phonetically plausible attempts at more complex words" (both aims of the curriculum) because large numbers of even the simplest essential high frequency words have phonetically implausible spellings.' The Society discusses a number of ways of simplifying spelling, including for example 'Cut Spelling', essentially a simplification of existing rules such as double consonants and a rationalisation of variant spellings of the same sound.

The Society for Pure English was founded by the Poet Laureate Lord Bridges in 1913. It attracted many significant members, among them Balfour, Prime Minister from 1902 to 1909. Its Tracts appeared from 1919 to 1945, while its Manifesto of 1925 revealed the moral earnestness of its origin and the belief that language was declining rapidly, partly due to 'communities of other-speaking races who ... learn enough of our language to mutilate it'. The theme of its work was basically xenophobic and anti-American, although without extremism, and ethnographic purism also enjoyed a high profile: 'we would prefer vivid popular terms to the artificial creations of scientists'. The Society was by no means unopposed: Robert Graves called it 'literary Fascism', and the general opinion in the 1930s was that its lack of success simply proved that language change is a process of 'impersonal drift'. The Society closed in 1945, although it had already lost much of its popular appeal after Bridges' death in 1930.

The English-Speaking Union was founded in 1918 by the journalist Evelyn Wrench and sixteen friends, with the aim of promoting closer ties with English-speaking peoples. The first public meeting was addressed by the then former Prime Minister A. J. Balfour, while its headquarters then and since, Dartmouth House, was opened by Prime Minister Stanley Baldwin in 1927. The Union prides itself on the support and guidance it has received since from many public figures. Its declared aims in 2001 are 'to promote international understanding and human achievement through the English language'. It organises programmes of scholarships, awards and a variety of educational schemes, all aiming to encourage 'sharing thoughts and feelings, to transmit information, to explain, discuss, argue and persuade', so that the young people who participate 'emerge better equipped to contribute to their society and with a better understanding of the world they live in'. ESU 'embraces 47 countries in all five continents, with thousands of members in the UK'. Although the ESU is not, strictly speaking, a language association and its activities are similar to those fostered by the Commonwealth, it insists on the use of English although it provides a forum for all countries whether or not they formed part of previous British spheres of influence.

The Queen's English Society is a campaigning organisation. It 'aims to promote and uphold the use of good English, and to encourage the enjoyment of our language. The Society aims to defend the precision, subtlety and marvellous richness of our language against debasement, ambiguity and other forms of misuse'. Its objects are

> to promote and uphold the use of good English in schools ...
> Children must be brought up to recognise that there is a formal
> structure to the language, and that the literature of the past is a
> worthy and useful source of writing style. Although it accepts
> that there is always a natural development of any language, the
> Society deplores those changes which are the result of ignorance,
> and which become established because of indifference (website
> queens-english-society.co.uk)

In the British Isles there are active language support groups for the territorial languages, as well as the state-funded organisations such as the Welsh Language Board, Comunn na Gaidhlig and the North-South Language Body in Ireland (North and South). The Welsh Language Society has thus long campaigned for Welsh. It specialises in active protests, holding rallies, calling for action in favour of Welsh at the BBC and at public sites such as, in 2001, a shop for Orange mobile phones. It is in favour of a new Welsh Language Act, aimed at ensuring effective bilingualism throughout Wales. In Scotland, a number of Gaelic organisations promote language and culture. These received government grants totalling £608,100 in 2000-1. One of these, An Comunn Gaidhealach, organises the annual Royal National Mod and other cultural festivals and was founded in 1891; it had over 3,000 members in 40 branches in 1994. In Scotland also, the Scots Language Society was founded in 1972 'to further Scots in literature, drama, the media, education and in everyday usage'.

The Publishing Industry

The role of printing and publishing in the standardisation and codification of a language has been well known since Caxton. In the twentieth century, still, the importance of the printed word in enforcing uniformity of language usage is key. As Deborah Cameron has pointed out (1995: 33-77) 'vested interests', particularly those of 'craft professionals' such as copy editors, have greatly, perhaps excessively, influenced publishing and journalism by 'hyper-standardization: the mania for imposing a rule on any conceivable point of usage, in a way that goes beyond any ordinary understanding of what is needed to ensure efficient communication'.

Most publishers give guidance, not usually so extreme, on how they expect authors to present their work. Such guidance typically covers a large range of language-related items, from punctuation to the use of American or English spelling or the use of -ise as opposed to -ize. It is at the stage of copy-editing, when the completed manuscript is checked by the editor, that Cameron's 'hyper-standardization' may come into effect, and the author's use of gender-related pronouns, repetition and a number of stylistic choices may well be questioned. In recent times, of course, copy-editors are used less frequently as authors type-set their own works for publication, and the use of electronic spell-, grammar- and style-checkers has become more frequent. These also have their own preferences, some of which derive from their origin in one country or another. Few of these automatic copy-editors are as pernickety, as capricious, or as quirky, as copy-editors sometimes were; their advantage is their consistency and the fact that they give choices to authors rather than imposing a style of their own.

The Media

The influence of the Press, particularly the written Press, on language is well-known. It is particularly in creating and spreading neologisms that newspapers and broadcasting have a unique role. Since it is their duty to report things as they happen they are often in need of new terms to describe new happenings, ideas and events. Baugh & Cable (2002: 308) give a number of examples: to *back* a horse, to *comb* the woods for a criminal, to *spike* a rumour; a *probe*, a *deal*, a *go-between*. Verbal novelties abound: *zillion-dollar*, *nobelity* for winners of a Nobel prize. Some newspaper headlines, apart from being occasionally witty, introduce new terms or influence the use of existing ones. *Up yours, Delors*! is a classic *Sun* headline, as is *Gotcha*!

The written press, too, offers general guidance to journalists wishing to write in its house style. Newspapers' policy recommendations on language can be effective, as has been shown for example by Fasold (1987) for America, where the use of titles (Mrs, Miss, Mr, Ms) changed drastically in the *Washington Post* after the publication of its 1978 guide. The *Guardian Style Guide* (Marsh and Marshall, 2000) covers a range of language topics. The guidance seeks to maintain house style as well as simply to correct mistakes, and in this it 'bases its advice on the Guardian's values', although it does advise 'short trips' to Gowers, Partridge, Fowler, Amis (*The King's English*) and Orwell.

> House style is the means by which a newspaper seeks to ensure that where there are permissible variants in spellings, the use of acronyms and so forth, a unified approach to these matters is adopted in disseminating a sense of rationality and authority in the use of language. (Introduction, Marsh & Marshall, 2000)

For Mrs, Miss or Ms? the advice is to 'use whichever the woman in question prefers ... (otherwise) use Ms'. Entries for *e* include among others

Earls Court	no apostrophe
earring	no hyphen
east end	inner east London north of the river (the equivalent district south of the Thames is south-east London); but West End
Easter Day	not Easter Sunday
effectively	not a synonym for in effect. 'The Blair campaign was effectively launched in 1992' means the intended affect was achieved; 'The Blair campaign was in effect launched in 1992' means this was not the official launch, but the event described did have the effect of launching it, whether intended or not
England	take care not to offend by saying England or English when you mean Britain or British.

The *Economist Style Guide* (1991 edition) is rather more direct about its aims: it proposes to 'give some general advice on writing, point out some common errors, and set some arbitrary rules. The arbitrary choices are those of the paper's editors over many years'. It requires its contributors above all to be understandable, and repeats Orwell's six 'elementary rules', giving no other authority for its pronouncements.

Examples of its entries under *e* include

-ee:	employees, evacuees, detainees, referees, refugees but, please, no attendees (those attending), draftees (conscripts), escapees (escapers) or retirees (the retired).
effectively	means with effect; if you mean in effect, say it. The matter was effectively dealt with on Friday means it was done well on Friday. The matter was, in effect, dealt with on Friday means that it was more or less attended to on Friday. Effectively leaderless would do as a description of the demonstrators in East Germany in 1989 but not those in Tiananmen Square.
enormity	means a crime, sin or monstrous wickedness. The enormity of his crime is tautologous.
ethnic groups	Avoid giving offence. This should be your first concern. But also avoid mealy-mouthed euphemisms and terms that have not generally caught on despite promotion by pressure-groups. If and when it becomes plain that American blacks no longer wish to be called black, as some years ago it became plain that they no longer wished to be called coloured, then call them African-American (or whatever). Till then they are blacks.
	Africans may be black or white. If you mean blacks, write blacks. People of mixed race in South Africa are coloureds.
	Anglo-Saxon is not a synonym for English-speaking.

For spoken language, the BBC found it necessary to create an Advisory Committee on Spoken English almost from its beginning in 1921. It recommended Received Pronunciation as that 'least likely to cause offence'. Todays Pronunciation Unit advises on the correct pronunciation of foreign terms, names and place names. Since the 1990s, and even more so after devolution, regional accents are widely heard, as they have been from the start of the commercial ITV, and, interestingly, in sports coverage.

Dictionaries, Grammars and Style Manuals

Standard written British English is now described in widely distributed works. The most authoritative dictionary for British English is probably the _Oxford English Dictionary_ and more recently the increasingly corpus-based dictionaries like _Collins_ and _Penguin_. Quirk _et al._'s _Grammar of the English Language_, published in 1985, is probably the fullest statement, although its sales do not approach those of the Oxford dictionaries. Oxford University Press (OUP) had six different reference works with 'grammar' in the title available in 2002, by four different authors (Chalker, Cobbet, Greenbaum, Seely). For style, grammar and points of usage, three works are regularly republished and can be easily found in most high street bookshops. H. W. Fowler's _Dictionary of Modern English Usage_ was first published in 1926. New revised editions have appeared regularly since, srevised by such major figures as Gowers or R. W. Burchfield, formerly editor of the _Oxford English Dictionary_. Gowers' _Complete Plain Words_ was first published in 1954 as a guide to clarity in the civil service (see Chapter 6), and again has been constantly revised and republished. Eric Partridge's _Usage and Abusage; a Guide to Good English_ was first published in 1947, and has also reappeared in new editions.

Publishers which consistently produce dictionaries, grammars, style manuals, advice on 'good' English and other language reference works include Oxford University Press (OUP), Cambridge University Press (CUP), Collins, Penguin, Cassell, and many others. OUP alone had 78 works of 'language reference' available in 2002, including dictionaries of literary terms, of idioms, of modern slang and of euphemisms; advice on spelling, on better wordpower, and on style. Most high street bookshops have a number of such guides to good or better English available, and sales are high. The English Language Teaching (ELT) market is a multi-billion-pound industry, in the UK and abroad.

The publishers of dictionaries and other language reference books themselves necessarily act as their own authorities on the nature of language. They usually work by committee and many associate academic and other experts with their productions. Professor David Crystal has long been thus associated with Longman and with Cambridge University Press; Professors Randolph Quirk, David Abercrombie, John Sinclair and Peter Strevens have had significant effect on many language reference works over the period from 1975 to 2000. Tom McArthur has long been associated with the language publishing industry.

Chapter 5

Language Rights

From this point we shall concentrate the discussion on the period since 1975. This chapter will explore the question of rights to use language, and will concentrate on the rights of what are often regarded as aggrieved minorities. Chapters 6 and 7 discuss LPP for language as a resource, while Chapter 8 examines issues that have become problematic. To a certain extent, all 'rights' issues are also social 'problems', in that declaring and exercising a right almost always involves an obligation on other members of society to concede rights that had not previously been recognised. Hence the inclusion of some examples here and others in Chapter 8 is arbitrary, and this is particularly true for the territorial languages in Wales, Scotland and Northern Ireland.

We start with a consideration of the rights outlined in the Human Rights Act itself. We then consider other examples of LPP. The first of these is sexism; we then deal with racism and discrimination more generally in language, and examine how Britain has tackled such questions. The next issue is that of the rights of non-English-speakers, mainly those who have entered the country since 1945, to maintain their own language and culture. This example is closely connected with more general issues of multiculturalism, dealt with separately in Chapter 8 as a language problem. The issue of rights for non-English speakers living in the UK is also connected with acquisition policy for foreign languages, including English as a foreign, second or additional language. These are dealt with, for English in the schools, in Chapter 8, since it was this topic that was at the centre of a major problem during the 1980s. English and literacy for adults is considered in Chapter 6. For policy regarding the teaching of foreign languages, the issues are discussed in Chapter 7. These divisions, as we have said, are for convenience of treatment: rights, problems and resources cannot always be easily separated from each other.

Human Rights Act, 1998

It was one of the main tenets of the Labour Party, newly elected to power in 1997, that human rights had been neglected during the years of Conservative party power from 1979, and indeed previously in British history. That this should be so may go back to the Whig interpretation of history (see Chapter 1), which set its face resolutely against any acceptance of rights, preferring instead the concept of (English and British) liberties and freedoms. It particularly opposed the idea of universal rights, and took exception to the formulation of the Rights of Man as expressed in the French Revolution and the incorporation of rights in the United States Constitution. The Human Rights Act was thus a major break with British political (and legal) tradition, and its implications and workings are closely monitored by the Lord Chancellor's Department.

The Act enshrines the European Convention on Human Rights as British law. The rights guaranteed in Britain are described in Schedule 1 to the Act. The Schedule contains specific mention of language rights in Articles 5, 6, and 14:

Article 5
Right to liberty and security
2.   Everyone who is arrested shall be informed promptly, in a language which he understands, of the reasons for his arrest and of any charge against him.
Article 6
Right to a fair trial
3.   Everyone charged with a criminal offence has the following minimum rights:
(a) to be informed promptly, in a language which he understands and in detail, of the nature and cause of the accusation against him.
(e) to have the free assistance of an interpreter if he cannot understand or speak the language used in court.
Article 14
Prohibition of discrimination
The enjoyment of the rights and freedoms set forth in this Convention shall be secured without discrimination on any ground such as sex, race, colour, language, religion, political or other opinion, national or social origin, association with a national minority, property, birth or other status.

Articles 5 and 6 had been the practice in British courts for a number of years. Indeed, the problem had occurred in a very specific form in 1936, when Welsh activists used Welsh in court in Caernarvon and refused to testify in English at the retrial in the Old Bailey in London. In this case there is little doubt that the accused were fully competent in English, and the point of their protest was not that they did not understand English but that they preferred to have their case heard in Welsh. The problem continues today in that the courts, and, indeed, the police, have to be convinced that the defendant cannot understand English before an interpreter or translator is employed. A simple preference for one language over another is not guaranteed by the Human Rights Act.

Article 14 extends the grounds for discrimination beyond those already catered for in the Sex Discrimination Act of 1975 and the Race Relations Act of 1976. Many of the additional grounds of possible discrimination mentioned in Article 14, such as association with a national minority or birth, derive from the particular history of countries like France or Italy and hence from the Europe-wide antecedents of the Act, although recognition of them was tacit in the practice of the British courts. Some grounds for discrimination, like disability or age, are more general and represent changing views on the causes of, and remedies for, society's attitudes towards those who are in some way 'different' from the norm.

Article 14 also outlines a distinction to which we shall return later: that between the rights of the individual, which are the main concern of the Human Rights Act, and those of groups or categories. The rights of social categories such as race are not dealt with in the Human Rights Act.

There are other Articles in the Schedule which have relevance for language rights. Article 8, Respect for private and family life, requires the state to ensure the right to respect, not merely for private and family life, but also for correspondence. Article 9, Freedom of thought and religion, ensures that everyone has the right to 'manifest his religion in worship, teaching, practice and observance'. Many religions have scriptures or holy works in languages other than English, and in some cases these languages themselves are regarded as holy. Article 10, Freedom of expression, although it is heavily restricted by considerations of security, territorial integrity and public safety, gives the right to 'receive and impart information and ideas without interference by public authority'.

Since the passage of the Act in 1998 the Lord Chancellor's department has kept a close watch on how the issues have been dealt with in the Courts. The Human Rights Unit maintains statistics on cases, gives guidance and provides training opportunities for those involved in implementing the Act, and keeps track both of the Parliamentary history of the Act and of relevant policy statements. Between 2nd October 2000 and 13 December 2001, for example, of some 297 cases 233 had found no remedy to the complaint in the Act, 3 had led to administrative action and 23 had led to the quashing of the particular order or decision referred to. As far as the author is aware, no cases involving language rights alone had been submitted to the British courts by the end of December 2000.

Despite the nature of its judicial system and case law approach to justice, the British legal system was well aware of the rights approach of Roman codified law and subsequent modifications such as the Human Rights embodied in European Community law and in the United Nations Charter. Britain's acceptance of the Human Rights Act was by no means the first use of rights in British law, as we shall see below in the case of racial and sexual discrimination in employment. Issues of disability are a case in point. The Disabled Persons Employment Act of 1944 and an Act of the same title in 1958 had both legislated against discrimination in the employment of the 'physically handicapped'. A change in terminology, representing a change in approach, took place in 1995 from the terminology of the earlier Acts, 'persons registered as handicapped by disablement', to the 1995 term 'disabled persons'. Indeed, the Disability Discrimination Act of 1995 shows the change in attitudes over the thirty-year period, a change later strengthened as the New Labour government came to office in 1997, in other ways as well. Changes in approach even during the 1990s are revealed by changes in terminology. The 1995 Act set up a National Disability Council which was itself replaced in 1999 by the Disability Rights Commission. The move from a 'top-down' Council to a Commission was matched by the move from the concept of national disability to the rights of the disabled themselves. These significant changes of words are typical of changing approaches. Membership of the European Community and then Union has also had continuing effect on the rights issues, as greater awareness of codified law had come about through the operation of the European Court of Justice.

In December 2001, new governmental proposals to tackle discrimination at work were published, aiming to amend the Race Relations Act and the Disability Discrimination Acts, together with new legislation to outlaw discrimination at work on the grounds of sexual orientation, religion and age. These new proposals would be implemented over the period from 2003 to 2006. They represent a further indication of the extent to which British law is changing under the influence of European Union Directives, since the purpose of the changes is to bring British law into conformity with Directives on Employment and on race. At the same time, of course, it must be remembered that Britain, as an EU member, itself took an active part in negotiating and establishing such Directives.

Sexism in Language

As the oil crisis of 1975 ended the post-war illusion of economic stability and growth in a cohesive, balanced society, reformist approaches to language planning in opposing discriminatory language use increased across the world. In the area of gender and gender preferences language planning in Britain has reflected action and opinion elsewhere in the English-speaking world, and deliberate or ignorant sexist language use has become rare internationally. In Britain, the policy has some legal backing. Indeed, the most successful pressure group in campaigning for language rights has been the feminist movement (Cooper, 1989: 14-21; Cameron, 1998; Coates, 1993).

In Britain, the movement early noted the 1850 Act for shortening the language used in statutes, ruling that 'masculine gender should be taken to include females', a practice which continues even, remarkably, in the Human Rights Act: 'No one shall be deprived of his life...his liberty...in a language which he understands...his civil rights'. Significant individuals like Virginia Woolf and later Germaine Greer, together with academics like the American Robin Lakoff, started by pointing to sexist language ('generic *he* and *man* and titles that mark women's marital status') and sexist language use ('the ways in which women are denied the right or the opportunity to express themselves freely'), particularly in the media and publishing. The idea that women suffered from linguistic deficit (lack of assertiveness) soon gave way to the notion that male use of language represented both dominance and difference, bred into the sexes by early upbringing and social conventions, and which should be corrected by performing gender differently in the hope of changing not merely language but also recurrent unequal pay, sexual harassment, rape and domestic violence (see Cameron, 1998).

Official policy responses tackled the issue of discrimination in employment, with the Equal Pay Act of 1970 providing for an individual to be treated not less favourably than a person of the opposite sex who works for the same employer, as regards pay and other terms in the contract of employment. The antidiscrimination legislation was broadened by the Sex Discrimination Act of 1975, which outlawed discrimination on the grounds of sex or marriage. Discrimination could be maintained if the person involved was employed in a private household or in small business, although these provisions were abolished in 1987. Direct and indirect discrimination are outlawed, as is victimisation, so membership of trade unions, employers' organisations and clubs related to particular professions or employments are covered. Discriminatory advertisements are banned. Positive action in favour of one or other sex may be permitted in the case of training organisations and employers, but is not permissible in recruitment or promotion. While the main responsibility for implementing antidiscrimination procedures in firms is the employers', individual employees are also responsible for ensuring that equal opportunities prevail. The legislation also set up an Equal Opportunities Commission to monitor the situation. The Commission regularly issues guides and reports on the working of the legislation, aimed at individuals and at employers, such as the Code of Practice on Sex Discrimination or that on Equal Pay (both available from www.eoc.org).

The Sex Discrimination Code makes a number of points about language. Thus the use of words like *waiter, salesgirl* or *stewardess* in an advertisement 'is taken as an intention to commit an unlawful discriminatory act' unless the advertisement specifically states that the job is open to men and women. Advertisements must be worded to avoid presenting men and women in stereotyped roles. Recruitment solely by word of mouth should be avoided. Tests must be unbiased, in content as well as in scoring mechanisms. Detailed questions about marital status, children and domestic obligations 'could be construed as showing bias against women'. Both age and length of service may be discriminatory against women. It is unlawful to imply that applications from one sex only will be considered in recruitment, so only some 'genuine occupational qualifications' may disqualify one sex from applying or being employed: considerations of strength and stamina do not justify restricting a job to men, nor do considerations of decency and privacy mean that all sales assistants must be women in clothes shops.

The Commission regularly receives large numbers of complaints about the provision of goods, facilities and services, which must also be provided without discrimination. The issues were being considered for possible extension in the general review of discrimination legislation announced in late 2001.

Continuing popular awareness of the issues of gender difference and discrimination has been raised not merely by the Commission, but by widely read works such as the volumes by the American author Deborah Tannen (e.g. Tannen, 1990). 'In 1982, when I first considered writing a book about gender differences in language, the topic was perceived as being of interest only to a specialist minority ... the book has been reprinted many times since it was first published in 1986' (Coates, 1993: ii).

Other Discrimination in Language

The topic broadened to include official proscription of all types of discrimination, particularly racist language use, in Britain during the mid-1970s. Again, the movement has been world-wide, reflecting attitudes in most of the English-speaking world as much as in the UK. Pressure to ensure the use of 'appropriate' language in Britain has been widely exercised by individuals like Stuart Hall, and by associations and pressure groups working in areas from race to disability. A speech by a major Conservative politician, Enoch Powell, on 22nd April 1968, had prophesied 'rivers of blood' as 'in 15 or 20 years time, the black man will have the whip hand over the white man'. Powell was ejected from the Conservative party as a result of the speech.

Official British anti-racial-discrimination legislation started with the Race Relations Act of 1976. This Act also set up a monitoring organisation, the Commission for Racial Equality. In 1986 the Public Order Act Part III made it an offence 'to use threatening, insulting or abusive words or behaviour with the intention of stirring up racial hatred'. The MacPherson Report into the murder of Stephen Lawrence, published in 1999, and its acceptance of the notion of institutional racism, widened the concept of racial discrimination still further, and a number of high profile legal cases in the late 1990s and later have also served to keep the concept of racial discrimination in the forefront of public awareness.

There is little doubt that attitudes towards sexism, racism and disability have changed drastically during the twenty-five years since 1975, and continue to change today. For example, the survey conducted by the broadcasting and advertising regulators, of the general public's attitudes towards the use of bad language in the media (see pp. 53-4 above), noted changes in attitudes even between 1998 and 2000. 'One of the most striking differences, qualitatively, ... was an increased awareness and sensitivity towards other people. ... This was most notable in terms of racial abuse, but other groups were also mentioned: people with disabilities, those from different religious faiths, homosexual men and women, and also national minorities'. Anti-discrimination policy seems to have preceded, rather than simply followed, this attitudinal change. Nonetheless, official language policy in favour of antidiscrimination rights has accompanied a general social movement in this direction: by 2001 journalism, publishing and public speeches carefully avoid provocative language use. Prescriptions contained in guides or style manuals often make little difference between discrimination against women, against disability or against race:

> Avoid the word 'immigrant' which is very offensive to many black and Asian people
>
> Use positive language about disability, avoiding outdated terms that stereotype or stigmatise. Terms to avoid, with acceptable alternatives in brackets, include victim of, crippled by, suffering from, afflicted by (prefer person who has, person with); wheelchair bound, in a wheelchair (wheelchair user); invalid (disabled person); mental handicap, backward, retarded, slow (person with a   learning disability); the disabled, the handicapped, the blind, the deaf (disabled people, blind people, deaf people); deaf and dumb (a person who is deaf and speech-impaired, or a person who is hearing and speech-impaired)
>
> Our use of language should reflect not only changes in society but also the newspaper's values. Phrases such as career girl or career woman, for example, are outdated (more women have careers than men) and patronising (there is no male equivalent): never use them. (Marsh & Marshall 2000)
>
> Don't use phrases which refer to women through their husbands: e.g. architect's wife Elsie Smith, Philip Grey and his wife Jean. (*Watch your Language! Non-sexist language: a guide for NALGO Members* 1987)
>
> Replace victim of, crippled by, suffering from, afflicted by, by person who has, person with, person who has experienced. Replace mental handicap by people with learning difficulties. (*Disability Etiquette*, Employers' Forum)

Conservative governments in power in the UK between 1979 and 1997, while not repealing earlier antidiscrimination legislation and indeed occasionally promoting it as in the case of disability, generally treated such planning as a product of the 'loony Left'. Their attacks, usually rhetorical exercises, were supported in almost evangelical condemnations published by think-tanks such as the Centre for Policy Studies and by philosophers such as Roger Scruton. It may be such attacks that provoked a condemnation of some outdated attitudes said to be still present in the Conservative Party in 2001, in a letter to his constituents by John Bercow in 2002 (*The Times*, 17.01.2002). The letter said that Conservatives were perceived by some as 'racist, sexist, homophobic and anti-youth', accusations that were immediately repudiated by the leader of the party.

Antidiscrimination language planning, which has continued since the advent to power of the Labour Party in 1997, has not always been favourably received by the wider public. The report of the Commission on Multiethnic Britain, set up by the Home Secretary to advise the Labour Government, received a less than favourable public reception for its contention that 'the word "British" will never do on its own ... Britishness, as much as Englishness, has systematic, largely unspoken, racial connotations ... Britishness is racially coded' (Parekh, 2000: 38). This latter phrase was deliberately recast as ' "British" is a racist term' by some newspapers. The Home Secretary was very nearly obliged to reject the whole Report as he made clear that the Commission's proposals would not necessarily be adopted as they stood. September 11th 2001, the date of the terrorist attacks on the Twin Towers in New York, also had considerable effects on attitudes and on policy towards discrimination. The first reaction of the Prime Minister was to counsel against verbal and other attacks on Muslims, and the Anti-Terrorism Bill presented to Parliament in December 2001 attempted to formalise a crime of religious hatred on the same lines as the sexism and racism Acts. At the same time, there was considerable pressure to change the stress of multicultural policy towards integration if not assimilation, and there were repeated calls for greater and better awareness of English by groups and individuals (see Chapter 8).

From time to time impatience with 'political correctness' in language surfaces in the Press. Thus Mary Riddell, writing in *The Independent* (18.08.2002) considers that much legislation has gone beyond the reasonable and that some attitudes are e now excessive:

> The fuss over (the thoughtless use of 'nigger') was spurious nonsense. ... imagined legions of politically correct lentil-slurpers who forbid the use of spoon (Cockney rhyming slang for coon) ... Islington teachers singing 'Baa Baa Green Sheep'.

The Maintenance of Non-indigenous Languages

The recent history of official language policy towards non-indigenous languages, and the difficulties that have beset it, is marked with strong attitudes, the growth of official 'interference' with the school curriculum, and with some rather strange characteristics which seem to be peculiar to Britain (see also Chapter 1 for a description of UK ethnic communities, and Chapter 8 below for a discussion of multiculturalism). The first problem for any formal language policy is that basic language, and indeed ethnic group, statistics simply do not exist in the UK, as we have noted in Chapter 1 above. Official language policy hence responds to whatever pressure is placed upon it, so documents are sometimes produced in languages other than English. Which languages are chosen depends on the pressure received by the individual Department or branch of local government, and varies from case to case, as in the versions of the Small Claims leaflets, available through the Lord Chancellor's department only in Welsh and English up to 1998 and in these plus Arabic, Bengali, Chinese, Gujarati, Hindi, Punjabi and Urdu thereafter; the National Health Service Plan Summary of 2000 (Arabic, Bengali, Chinese, Greek, Gujarati, Hindi, Punjabi, Somali, Turkish, Vietnamese, Urdu); or the information leaflets and questions for the 2001 Census in England, available also in Albanian/Kosovan, Croatian, Farsi/Persian, French, Italian, Japanese, Polish, Portuguese, Russian, Serbian, Spanish, Swahili and thus in 24 languages.

Parliamentarians are well aware of the multicultural and indeed multilingual nature of modern British society. In introducing the Registration of Political Parties Bill in the House of Commons on 4th June 1998, for example, the Home Secretary Jack Straw noted:

> These days we are a multicultural, multiethnic society. Many of my constituents have a first language that is not English, but Gujarati, Urdu, or Punjabi. There are similar groups across the country. If they put forward a name, it is important there is a translation attached in English so that the returning officer can make a judgement on whether the name is consistent with the criteria in the Bill. (*Hansard Debates* for 4 June 1998 Column 517)

The discussion on this occasion went on to make the point that Welsh and English were the only statutory languages in the United Kingdom, and that Welsh therefore required no translation into English. On the other hand, other British languages such as Cornish did. The translation proviso was presented as an aid for returning officers, to ensure that 'prohibitions regarding obscenity, for example' were not contravened. The other prohibitions concerned such issues as ensuring that parties did not present themselves as national parties, royal parties or otherwise claim special status.

The second area of interest for British language policy in this field is the existence of a pressure and interest group network, and its relations with formal governmental policy-making (see, for example, Smith, 1993; Ager, 1996). In many cases, formal 'fora' have been set up to ensure that policy-makers try out policies and discuss positions, while formal consultation periods are the normal requirement for policy proposals. The Home Office Race Relations Forum acts as an official sounding board for matters affecting race relations in the UK, and its list of members indicates many with connections to a range of interest groups, including the African Youth Trust, the Bar's Race Relations Committee, the Asha Foundation, the Caribbean Advisory Group at the Foreign Office, the Blackburn and District Indian Workers' Association, the Muslim Council in Britain, the Jewish Council for Racial Equality, the Runneymede Trust's Islamophobia Commission, and the Martin Luther King Memorial Trust.

In terms of official requirements in educational policy, matters became significant after the issue of the European Economic Community's Directive 4861 of July 1977 (Thompson, Fleming & Byram, 1996). This required member states to 'promote the teaching of the mother tongue and culture (of the children of migrant workers) in accordance with normal education'. DES Circular 5/81 made it clear that although at that time the curriculum was not under central control, 'For the local education authorities in this country, (the EEC directive) implies that they should explore ways in which mother-tongue teaching might be provided, whether during or outside school hours, but not that they are required to give such tuition to all individuals as of right'. The Department for Education and Science also funded a major investigation of the 'other' languages of England in the Linguistic Minorities Project (Stubbs, 1985: see Chapter 8). This strongly advocated greater recognition and value for minority languages, for bilingualism and for low-status varieties of English. By 1984, only about two percent of primary school children from homes where languages other than English were spoken in fact received tuition in those languages. Her Majesty's Inspectorate of Schools, at that time the only body able to put curriculum recommendations to schools from the central government, made various suggestions including, in 1984, 'It is educationally desirable that bilingual children in primary schools should be given the chance to read and write their mother-tongues and to extend their skills in these languages'. But by 1985 the Conservative party had concluded that schools were not the place for teaching low-status English and languages other than English.

At about this time the National Association for Multicultural Education, a pressure group aiming to improve educational provision particularly for black children, and which had been founded in the 1960s, changed its name to the National Anti-racist Movement in Education. The change of name marked a number of developments in this and other pressure groups: the development of anti-racism as a stronger idea of 'struggle' than the 'cooperative' one of multiculturalism; an increased politicisation of such groups; and their adoption of the themes of anti-colonialism, anti-imperialism and anti-racism within British society. The intention was to combat racism across society; and educational provision was seen by some as a main area for the struggle. The political conditions of the time (see under multiculturalism in Chapter 8) strengthened ideas of opposition to central authority, and it may have been this strengthening that often concealed the 'rights' issue and transformed it into a 'problem' one. Certainly this was a time when discussions over the school curriculum became subject to direct action by parental groups exercising their right to bring matters to the attention of Local Education Authorities, school principals and individual teachers.

The Swann Report on _Education for All_ appeared in 1985. As noted above, one of its main conclusions was that 'Essential to equality of opportunity, to academic success, and broadly, to participation on equal terms as a full member of society, is a good command of English and that the first priority in language learning ... must therefore be given to the learning of English' (p. 426). It recommended that separate provision of English as a Second Language should cease, and that the needs of bilingual children should be met within mainstream education. To avoid this becoming a problem of discrimination, the suggestion was made that all children should have a form of language education as part of their studies. In this way, too, all children would receive some understanding of other cultures.

The Swann Report of 1985 thus suggested that communities, rather than central or local authorities, should be responsible for the maintenance of their own language(s). It was firm that mainstream schools should not seek to assume the role of community providers, whether for language maintenance or for bilingual forms of education. It did indeed recommend that bilingual support should be available for children making the transition from home language to English; and that, in secondary schools, community languages should be made available as foreign languages where there was sufficient demand. There was a further significant note that 'All pupils in those schools where community languages are in demand should be encouraged to consider studying them'.

This is the approach that has been officially followed since. In many respects however official support for non-indigenous languages is made available, locally if not centrally, and indirectly if not directly. Local Education Authorities, faced with large numbers of non-English-speaking children beginning school, have responded in various ways. The most common response has been the employment of bilingual assistants in schools, whose task is to act as interpreters and helpers for children who have no English, in order to help them to enter mainstream education as rapidly as possible. Their purpose is not therefore to maintain the non-indigenous language, but to help in the acquisition of English. Nonetheless, a secondary purpose is to ensure that the home language is not denigrated in the process, and to provide role models of native speakers of the language other than English.

CILT, the London-based Centre for Information on Language Teaching and Research funded by the Department for Education and Skills, acts as a resource centre for teachers of 'community languages', and publishes a bulletin from time to time on matters of interest. This bulletin, also available on the web, provides information on such issues as resources and training provision for community language teachers. Teachers themselves are employed directly by those Local Education Authorities which do provide classes in languages other than English, at whatever stage in education these are provided.

In 1988, with the introduction of the National Curriculum, central government was at last able to require that schools provide certain elements, certain subjects and allocate adequate time to them. The two reports which affected the design of the curriculum insofar as English was concerned (the Cox Report: Cox 1989) and for foreign languages (the Harris Report: Harris 1991) appeared in 1989 and 1991 respectively. Both included a chapter on bilingual children, but neither recommended a specific programme of support for non-indigenous languages in mainstream education.

Multicultural language policy, even after its profile was raised with a new government after 1997, has thus centred on the acquisition of English (see Chapter 8 below), while policy for foreign languages (Chapter 7) is mainly concerned with Britain's role in Europe (Ager,

1996: 89-101). Pragmatic help, in the form of translations of official documents and in interpreting in court or the National Health Service, is indeed made widely available by Local Authorities, the police or by central government, but on an ad-hoc basis. By the year 2002, and despite the issue being known and occasionally discussed in Parliament, policy for language maintenance seems to remain a simple washing of the hands, with no direct provision except for territorial/indigenous languages, and certainly no formal policy or formal legislation.

Motivation in Rights

Almost by definition, policy concerning the rights of groups or categories of people is motivated by concerns for the correction of inequality in society. The recognition of group rights by the political authorities confers a number of obligations on society at large. These apply particularly to sexism, to race and to disability, although recognition of the inadequacy of the present position means that the extension of the approach to other areas is under discussion in 2002. The policy, or lack of it, in the UK towards the issue of the maintenance of indigenous languages is somewhat more intriguing. Here, the motive is rather more oriented towards mainstream Britain in that politicians are more concerned with English and with maintaining the cohesiveness of society than with the minority language groups themselves. The immediate objective is not to support identity problems among migrant groups or the claims to implement the mosaic model of society, but to 'allow' individual communities to go their own way by, in effect, ignoring the issue. As we shall see later, the policy approach, including that followed by the Labour Party after 1997, is similar to that found in policy decisions on multiculturalism.

The Human Rights Act is concerned, not with group rights, but with those of the individual. It reflects the dominant policy form in Western democracies from the French to the American Revolution, and indeed from the Magna Carta on. The distinction between it and the other legislation in this Chapter is important, if only that the liberalism which gave rise to policies on individual rights logically leads to policies which should be blind to group characteristics. 'Race-conscious policies appear to subvert this tenet of liberal individualism, and, for some, raise the spectre of a return to the times when race was determinative of individuals' prospects' (Edwards, 1994: 55).

Another difference between the Human Rights Act and the other legislation is that the HRA applies to public authorities, whereas the other legislation applies also to private individuals or organisations.

We have not dealt in this Chapter with the correction of the inequalities involved, although the most usual form of correcting the wrong is by the payment of compensation, with the amount decided by the judge or jury involved.

Our motivational structure as outlined in the Introduction is dependent not merely on identification of a stage within the main identity creation sequences - personal and social identity construction, ideology, image, the maintenance and defence of the created identity, the correction or maintenance of social inequality, integration or instrumentality and despair - but also on an understanding of attitudes and the clarification of the social ideals and practical objectives planners have in mind. It seems fairly clear that in all the cases we have reviewed, English, the L1 of the majority of the population, is not necessarily regarded as in the top category of excellence. The reason for this is that the arguments of those condemning both sexism and racism feel that English as a language may be inherently sexist and racist. Centuries of such attitudes have resulted in inclusion of attitudes in the language itself, as much as in its use. The motive of reformers in this area is to a certain extent purist, in that they seek to reform the language as a symbol of the attitudes it embodies. The vitality of the language is accepted without a doubt, in that English is undoubtedly the appropriate language for all domains of use; its attractiveness is undeniable, too. In the case of sexist and discriminatory language there is a clear attitudinal penchant for action; only in the case of (lack of) support for non-indigenous language maintenance, however, is it demonstrable that action, whether in support of English or for other languages, is not thought to be necessary.

The political objectives behind policy, or the lack of it, seem to promote social cohesion in the case of sexist and discriminatory language. Here, it is clearly felt that a more precise objective through which to realise this ideal is corpus change. Indeed, it is in this area that much of the symbolic nature of 'rights' LPP becomes clear, as opposed to resource policy where the state provides or ensures the flow of support, and problem-resolution policy where the state is obliged to take resolute action. The purpose of LPP here is to change minds and influence beliefs through changing the language. For policy on non-indigenous languages, the objective is closer to that of maintaining social cohesion by, in effect, ignoring the issue.

Overall, the motivational picture for British LPP in policy on rights seems to follow the pattern of Figure 5.1. This represents motivation according to the display described on pages 8 to 11 of the

Introduction, placing the three cases of policy we have discussed into the two aspects of identity creation involved, the maintenance of identity and the correction of inequality. It shows the relevant attitudinal structure, as identified from the rhetoric, actions and discussions around the topic as we have reviewed it here; and summarises the ideals and objectives planners seem to have had, again according to the information as we have discussed it here.

Motivation for policy on language rights									
Identity sequence	Attitudinal structure								Ideal/objective
	Exc'nce		Vitality		Attract		Action		
	L1	L2	L1	L2	L1	L2	L1	L2	
Maintain Identity									
Non indigenous languages	3	1	3	1	3	1	1	1	cohesion / ignore issue
Correct Inequality									
Sexism	2		3		2		3		cohesion / change corpus
Other discrimination	2		3		2		3		cohesion / change corpus

For an explanation of the Figure, see pp. 8-11 in the Introduction.
Note that motivation as analysed here is that of the policy makers. Thus the L2 referred to above is, in this case, any non-indigenous language and it is presumed that such a language would not normally be used by the policy-makers in question. The L1 in each case is English.

Figure 5.1 Motivation for policy on language rights

Chapter 6

Language as a Resource for Citizens

The second group of LPP examples is those concerning language resources. A modern society needs an educated population, able to express itself, enjoy its environment and to use its skills in order to survive economically. Internally, the United Kingdom needs to help its citizens to have adequate capability in English and in literacy. Not merely for the purposes of government but for more elevated motives, too, it needs to ensure that its governmental machine can communicate clearly with the population. Managing and controlling these types of language use is an important duty, recognised as such by successive governments. But there are also issues of discourse, particularly the way language is deployed by politicians themselves, which are of importance to every citizen and which are planned and controlled as much as any other aspect of political life. Throughout this chapter and the next appears a tension between two motives for LPP: instrumentalism, the desire to ensure that language makes things happen and that the skills of language use are improved; and ideology, the desire to ensure that things happen, and that skills are used, for a particular reason or in pursuit of a particular agenda.

Adult Literacy

One recurring issue, affecting both corpus policy and acquisition policy, is the linguistic competence of citizens, and particularly the level of literacy. Literacy has been at the top of the international agenda of organisations such as UNESCO since the 1950s, its definition and its measurement going through phases of 'mass literacy', 'functional literacy' and later 'economic literacy'. European governments at first had to be persuaded that such issues should matter to them, since they were the first to introduce mass education at the beginning of the twentieth century and a hundred years of education had, they often thought, meant that their populations were now literate. France, for example, at first refused to accept that its population was anything other than 100% literate. In 1974 however, in response to a Europe-wide study of literacy which provoked action across the continent, the UK government founded an Adult Literacy and Basic Skills Unit (ALBSU). Provision was made for teaching English and improving literacy for adults, mainly through the further education system.

After 1979, with the election of the Conservative government which was to remain in power for 18 years, there began a series of radical policy initiatives in the field of education and training. Generally speaking, the aim of party policy was to involve industrialists and employers more in both education and training post-16, whether this took place in Further Education Colleges, in Universities or outside the state's formal institutions. One of the first moves was to clarify relationships. Those doing the education or training became 'providers' from whom education was 'bought' by the government and private employers. The students, who had organised themselves in Students' Unions, could not be trusted with any direct role. It was no longer the providers' job to decide what should be taught: their duty was to provide what the market (i.e. the employers) wanted. The involvement of employers in adult education came about through the creation of 'Training and Enterprise Councils', whose function was to 'buy' the 'products' of the 'providers'. By these and other means the government took control of all aspects of the educational agenda away from the educationalists. To ensure adult education and training a 'Further Education Funding Council' was created to channel government funds to Further Education colleges, while universities had their Higher Education Funding Council. Both Councils had a majority of employer members. In the case of higher education, the Council replaced the former University Grants Committee whose membership was principally Vice Chancellors, and which had had the formal duty of advising government on the needs of the universities. The change of title to Funding Council indicated that its purpose was to distribute the funds the government had decided were appropriate. Whatever the universities or colleges felt they needed was irrelevant. Such changes were not cosmetic: they signalled a degree of distrust of the education 'mafia' and its 'trendy, progressive' ideas developed through the 'permissive' 1960s; they made clear that the function of education was to provide what society wanted, not what it thought society needed;

and they made clear that the government, along with its Councils, would decide not merely the funding but also the curriculum, previously the preserve of the institutions themselves. To add to this ideological stance, funding per student was reduced in real terms in almost every year of the 18.

The government's basic ideological stance was that adults were, or should be, responsible for their own education, while training was, or should be, the responsibility of employers. A 'Family Literacy Campaign' was set up in 1993, aiming to bring together schools and adults. The Press Conference introducing it was notable for its concern, less with countering the lack of basic skills than with a political condemnation of 'the rot in education which had set in in the 1960s' discovered by John Patten, then Education Secretary. But the Family Literacy and Numeracy Project, managed by ALBSU, was introduced in 1994 and by 2000 was helping more than 50,000 parents a year to support childrens' needs where they themselves have poor skills, at a cost of £17M.

Nonetheless, UNESCO's International Adult Literacy Survey of 1996 showed continuing poor scores in Britain (cf Ager, 1996: 80-4). Research quoted in the White Paper 'Skills for Life' showed that by 1999 only a third of adults in literacy and numeracy education had improved their skills, half stayed at the same level, and 20% indeed got worse (DEE, 2000).

The New Labour government of 1997 was still faced by a functional illiteracy rate of 20% of adults, just as in 1974. While in opposition, it had developed a 'National Literacy Strategy' involving a compulsory daily hour of practice in primary schools, developed into a full-blown 'Framework for Teaching English' and incorporated into the National Curriculum for both primary and secondary schools. For adults, it inherited a complex maze of institutions, programmes, funding and qualifications. It set up a working party under Sir Claus Moser to examine the whole area of adult education and training, which recommended a 'Fresh Start':

- a clear framework of standards
- a national curriculum framework which identifies the skills to be learnt
- sound assessment
- high quality teaching
- a range of learning opportunities
- provision integrated with other programmes of learning and vocational training. (Moser, 1999)

Literacy was then tackled through the White Paper 'Skills for Life', published with the government's plans in December 2000. To a large extent, the plans, slowly implemented during 2001 and continued with the newly elected Labour government of June 2001, involved a major restructuring and reorganisational effort aimed at bringing together education and training: they were a good example of constituent or agency planning, restructuring the machinery of policy as well as changing the 'sharp end'. Still, however, when new potential learners contact the Department on the web, they are met with a formidable list of 19 possible agencies and organisations, listed as follows on the Department's 'Adult Learners Gateway':

Qualifications website
> Information for parents, teachers, pupils, lecturers, students, employers and anyone with an interest in qualifications.

Get On
> The aim of the Get On campaign is to help adults improve their reading, writing and maths. This website is to enable training providers and other partners to support the Get On campaign.

learndirect
> Learn what you want, where you want, when you want.

Further Education Student Support
> Website providing details of sources of financial support for adult students in further education in England.

Department for Education and Skills Student Support
> This website is for students living in England and Wales who want to know what financial help is available to them as Higher Education students.

NIACE
> The National Institute of Adult Continuing Education is the leading non-Governmental organisation for Adult Learning in England and Wales.

Lifelong Learning website
> The leading site for the encouragement, promotion and development of lifelong learning.

International Students website
> Guidance for international students wanting to study in the UK.

UK online Centres
> A new programme designed to help bridge the gap between those in society who have access to ICT and those who do not.

National Vocational Qualifications (NVQ)
> This website is designed to give you a background to NVQs - why they exist and how they can help individuals and key players in the employment, training and qualifications world.

The European Choice
> A guide to opportunities for higher education in Europe.

The Union Learning Fund (ULF)
> promotes activity by unions in support of the Government's objective of creating a learning society, by influencing the increase in take up of learning in the workplace and boosting unions' capacity as learning organisations.

New Deal
> New Deal has been created to help unemployed people into work by closing the gap between the skills employers want and the skills people can offer.

University for Industry (UfI)
> UfI is a new kind of public-private partnership which will boost the competitiveness of business and the employability of individuals.

National Grid for Learning
> A collection of resources brought together by the UK Government to help raise standards in education and to support lifelong learning.

The Basic Skills Agency
> Working with organisations to improve basic skills for all.

Adult Learners' Week 2001
> What would it be like to go back to learning? Adult Learners' Week offers a chance to find out.

Read Write Plus
> The homepage of the Adult Basic Skills Strategy Unit, which leads and co-ordinates all aspects of the national strategy to improve levels of adult literacy and numeracy in England.

Childcare and other Financial Help for HE students 2001/02
> This guide gives detailed information on the Childcare Grant and other financial help available to HE students in 2001/02.

Even this list makes no mention of the overarching body 'responsible for all post-16 education and training' in England: the Learning and Skills Council. Confusingly, this LSC is the national body; 47 other LSCs were created at the same time across England, although each of them is called The Learning and Skills Council! In brief, the Adult Basic Skills Strategy Unit devises the strategy; the Learning and Skills Council funds the provision; **learndirect** is a guide to where the courses are and provides some; the Basic Skills Agency manages (some) provision; 'Get On' is a campaign, aimed at inciting media interest through such information as that 5% of people write nothing in Christmas cards, 68% send minimal name and greeting, and that writing confidence is probably a factor in this.

The policy outlined in 'Skills for Life' described the challenges, specified priority groups for immediate action, and set out a plan. Some seven million people in England 'cannot read or write at the level we would expect of an 11-year-old.' Individuals lose out financially, have low confidence and suffer social exclusion. One in five employers noted a significant skills gap, and the cost to the country of poor literacy and numeracy skills was 'as high as £10 billion a year'. The priority groups were, firstly, those with which the government was in direct contact: those in receipt of state benefits (mainly the unemployed), prisoners, and public sector employees; secondly, low-skilled people in employment; and thirdly, groups at risk of social exclusion, such as the homeless, refugees and those living in disadvantaged communities. The policy's aim was 'to reduce the number of adults in England with literacy and numeracy difficulties to that of our main competitors' - from one in five to one in ten or better. The intention was to raise the standard of provision, by robust assessment, a national core curriculum, national tests and commissioning new materials; by new qualifications for teachers and a new inspection regime. The levels of achievement, for example, newly devised, equate 'Level 1' with the expected achievement of 11-year-olds (Level 4 of the National Curriculum); and 'Literacy Entry level 1' with the expected Level 1 achievement of 5-year-olds in the National Curriculum. Free training would be provided through dedicated provision, such as family literacy programmes for parents; full-time and part-time courses; and self-study, supported by **learndirect**. Above all, the policy would follow New Labour procedures elsewhere by setting targets and steering funding to achieve them. So, 'by 2004, our strategy will improve the literacy and numeracy skills of 750,000 adults in England', and the detail specifies ensuring provision for 130,000 job seekers, 10,000 public sector employees, 50,000 refugees and speakers of other languages, and 50,000 people who live in disadvantaged communities, among others.

It is fairly clear that the motivation for this New Labour work is a mixture: of ideology, in the sense that the policy pattern follows a model used elsewhere and has the same goal of tightening central government grip on the educational and training process; the correction of inequality, in that the policy specifically targets the disadvantaged; instrumental, in that the purpose of the policy is expressed in down-to-earth financial terms of the cost to the individual and to the country of not doing this. The motivation for the Conservative work of 1979-1997 is less clear; it also was ideological, in the sense of following, at least at the beginning, the tenets of Thatcherite education policy, and in later years, being accompanied by an ideological discourse; it was much less specific about its aims in correcting inequality and preferred the instrumental approach.

Clarity in the Civil Service: the Plain English Campaign

A widespread complaint in Great Britain, and indeed elsewhere, is that civil servants (and indeed, professional elites generally) seem unable to write clearly and simply but use 'gobbledygook', 'wooden language' (in French), and 'officialese'. The Treasury's invitation to Sir Ernest Gowers to produce guidance, originally for internal civil service documents, led to _The Complete Plain Words_ in 1954, constantly updated and widely available since to the public at large after its publication by Penguin. Its thirteen 'Elements' give Gowers' answers to the problems of writing, particularly by civil servants aiming to convey clear information in response to requests or complaints by the general public:

- be clear about what you are going to say before writing:
- begin by answering the question;
- confine yourself to the facts of the case;
- avoid pomposity;
- do not give the impression that you think the reader should be put to trouble to save you from it;
- use no more words than are necessary to do the job;
- keep sentences short;
- be compact;
- do not say more than is necessary;
- explain technical terms in simple words;
- do not use formulae;
- use precise words rather than vague ones;
- choose the common rather than the uncommon word.

But by the 1980s a whole culture change was in process in the civil service, and the aim of 'effectiveness' in conveying government policy became as important as 'efficiency' (Ager, 1996: 109-113). By this time, politicians themselves began to be interested in the question of civil service reform. Restructuring the civil service was indeed one of the aims of the Thatcher revolution. Eventually, the head of the service, Sir Robert Armstrong, defined the purpose of the civil service as being, quite simply, to serve ministers. This 'businesslike' definition arose to ensure that civil servants did not use their position to thwart aims which they might see as incorrect, unjust or immoral, but the effect was to change the emphasis from clarity to purposefulness. Prime Minister Thatcher wrote in 1988 'Plain English must be the aim of all who work in Government', introducing a short pamphlet on the topic, itself prepared by the Plain English Campaign in 1983 (*Making it Plain*, 1988). The Gowers recommendations now became:

- The first important thing is your state of mind. Your writing will be much easier to understand if you put yourself in the reader's shoes.
- Use shorter words.
- Use short sentences.
- Use sentences with active verbs.
- Use verbs instead of nouns created from verbs.
- Sometimes it's a good idea to address your readers as you and refer to yourself or the department as we.
- Use jargon and abbreviations only when you're sure the reader knows what they mean.
- Use a simple style.
- Organise your writing to help your readers.

The Plain English Campaign, founded in 1974 by Chrissie Maher and Martin Cutts with the intention of ensuring benefits claimants in Liverpool could understand official forms and leaflets, was seized on by Margaret Thatcher as a method of training the civil service to adopt competitive approaches and business ethos. After the PEC's opening stunt of shredding government forms in Parliament Square in 1979, a series of 'Inside Write' competitions was established with government support, with prestigious prizes for clarity and the reduction of officialese, accompanied by Golden Bull awards for the most convoluted and uninformative use of language. Theoretically at least, and sometimes in fact, the 'winners' of these awards were presented with their 'prizes' in public. One 1999 Golden Bull winner was the Employment Relations Act 1999:

a person carrying on an employment business shall not request or directly or indirectly receive any fee from a second person for providing services (whether by the provision of information or otherwise) for the purposes of finding or seeking to find a third person, with a view to the second person becoming employed by the first person and acting for and under the control of the third person.

The political approach mixed such punishment with the award of prizes and formal recognition of achievement in expression which reflected government priorities. One of the major achievements of the PEC was to ensure prestigious venues for their awards ceremonies, and the presence of senior government ministers and sometimes Royalty to present the prizes. Its Crystal Award, for plain expression in documents, is much prized by a range of organisations including not solely government and local authorities but also private enterprises.

Although the PEC was a campaign led by private individuals, it was much favoured by government and its approach went well with government priorities, during the Thatcher era and indeed since. Interestingly, it developed into an organisation offering training and assessment in writing, and is funded by the contracts it secures from both the civil service and from private sector organisations. It has established a range of contacts with similar organisations abroad in other English-speaking countries.

John Major's governments of 1990 to 1997, introducing Citizens' Charters, strengthened even more the 'businesslike', less inward-looking official style which adopted much of the rapidity and immediate style of the private sector's work in publicity. Even for internal administrative organisation and particularly documentation, private-sector jargon and linguistic constructions became familiar. The word 'quality' became widespread, particularly in the expressions 'quality assurance' or 'quality assessment'. The quality movement derived from pressure in the business world, where quality standards like ISO 9000 began to become a requirement for services. The revealing characteristics of the quality movement are that documents (and supposedly the actions they represent) follow a planning structure in a set sequence. This structure is then supposed to be known by all members of the organisation, who must comply with it. It is their familiarity with the plan, and the extent to which they all contribute to its achievement and accept the constant checking and restructuring that it implies, that can be checked (quality assurance) and tested (quality assessment). Assurance and assessment are conducted by external bodies.

It is for this reason that the following planning sequence can be identified in many official documents issued by a number of departments and organisations in a number of fields since the late 1980s and early 1990s:

Vision (a statement of the ideal outcome to be planned for)
Mission (the purpose of the plan)
Objectives (the outcomes and outputs to be expected from the plan,
    including precise targets, quantified as far as possible)
Plan (what is to be done, including methods)
Check (how the planner will know that the objectives and targets
    have been achieved)
Return (in theory, a check should be made at each stage of the
    sequence, with a return to the stage before if necessary).

This 'quality movement' continued after the return of the New Labour government in 1997, with the result that by 1999 the Cabinet Office had to provide guidance for civil servants on the range of quality schemes open to the public sector. The range included the Business Excellence Model, Investors in People, Charter Mark and ISO 9000. Each had its own awards and its own assessment processes, and even the relevant Minister had to concede there was 'no right route through the quality maze'. But the different parts of the public service were nonetheless expected to have no faith in their own processes, but to use at least one of these external organisations, use consultants to advise them how to present themselves, use external assessors to check they had done so, and adopt the language as well as the reality of the quality movement:

The Government is committed to improving and modernising public
    services ... That means high quality services which:
• put customers first;
• encourage access and promote choice;
• use new technology, especially IT, effectively;
• are open and accountable;
• work in partnership with others to ensure seamless delivery;
• use resources effectively;
• innovate and improve. (*Quality Schemes*, 1999)

Departments (no longer Ministries) have developed a new style and vocabulary for civil service language, with the result that traditional neutrality and objectivity has been replaced by discoursal features such as 'spin' (subtle interpretative discourse), 'style without substance' (a deliberate search for a striking form of expression, adopted for any initiative or even lack of it), 'imitations of business-speak' (a delight in adopting the latest buzz-words of the management gurus and business school language), and love of 'soundbites' (short, sharp phrases of a sentence or less which make impressive-sounding quotations for replay during television news). Thus, the NHS Plan of 2000 is both more businesslike in its style and more of an argumentative document than the traditional, colourless Civil Service report:

> The purpose and vision of this NHS Plan is to give the people of Britain a health service fit for the 21st century: a health service designed around the patient. (*vision statement*) ... In part the NHS is failing to deliver because over the years it has been underfunded. In particular there have been too few doctors and other key staff to carry out all the treatments required. But there have been other underlying problems as well. (*a series of short, sharp sentences*) The NHS is a 1940s system operating in a 21st century world. (*soundbite*) It has:
> - a lack of national standards
> - old-fashioned demarcations (*spin: why are these old-fashioned?*) between staff and barriers between services
> - a lack of clear incentives and levers (*business buzz-word*) to improve performance (*spin; assumes that business 'levers' work in the public service*)
> - over-centralisation and disempowered (*business buzz-word*) patients.
>
> (*bullet-point style, which does not add to the substance, but makes the expression crisp and enables the paragraph to have only one verb*). ...
> investment has to be accompanied by reform ... The Department of Health will set national standards ... (*objectives*) ... by 2004 patients will be able to have a GP appointment within 48 hours and there will be up to 1,000 specialist GPs taking referrals from fellow GPs. (*precise targets*).
> (Extracts from *NHS Plan Summary*, 2000)

Political Discourse

The rhetoric of radical Thatcherism and of Third Way Blairism reveals a subtler form of language planning, aiming at changing the way political debate is structured by changing the language practice in which politics is discussed.   Thatcherian discourse, revealing and shaping Thatcherian politics, was based on such phrases as *value for money, choice, standards* and on casting the concepts of monetarism in terms of the family budget (Phillips, 1998). The discourse combined three, somewhat contradictory, strands of Right-wing thinking: traditional authoritarianism, political and economic individualism, and a populist appeal to the ordinary person, particularly, as in many of the Prime Minister's own speeches, to the housewife. It is this type of mixture, itself often shocking to traditional Conservatives like Edward Heath and Harold Macmillan, that led to Thatcherism's unique view of the social world: 'there is no such thing as society'. Authoritarianism was bolstered by the adoption of hard-headed economics. Previously unthinkable solutions based on individualism became thinkable, aided by the size of the political majorities in the House of Commons. Such factors may have contributed to the brutality of expression that faced protests like the miners' strike and the poll-tax revolt. *Choice* appeared frequently in speeches. So did *enterprise* and *freedom*, and collocations, particularly *enterprise culture, value for money*. Populism meant the use of everyday vocabulary, even within a context of international finance or trade, so Margaret Thatcher's comparison of the national budget and the housekeeping requirement to *squirrel away* tins of groceries in reserve gave a new slant to the need to reduce public expenditure and taxes. Indeed, it could be said that discourse of this type led policy rather than the reverse, so the need for governments to invest and to deploy public resources in supporting industry where necessary, as in times of change, were lost simply because the ideologically-based language had no room for such concepts.

Under Prime Minister John Major from 1990 to 1997, 'Citizens' Charters' aimed at *empowering* the citizen as *consumer*. New Labour has built on Thatcherian discourse after 1997, adopting its populism, its themes like national renewal, responsibility, competition and governmental limitation, but replacing its inbuilt polemical need to define and if necessary create an adversary by a consensual, all-inclusive process of *going beyond* and *transcending* the left-right divide, combining *responsibilities* and *enterprise* with *rights* and *attacking poverty* (Fairclough, 1999). In these ways the Thatcher period has marked, perhaps permanently, political discourse in Britain.

Neither Thatcher nor Blair invented political discourse or spin doctors. Language in use necessarily incorporates a point of view, noticed most when it is one the listener or reader does not share. The language use of advertising and public relations is of course just as devious, and similarly locked in a specific universe of discourse. The language formulations of broadcast news or the written press, when they use 'neutral' expressions like *state terrorism* or *collateral damage,* reflect   ideological positions   just as much as those who describe *freedom fighters* and *weapons of mass destruction.* It is the task of supporters of one point of view or another to get the message across in their terms, and to ensure that their terms become accepted as though they were the neutral representations of truth they can never be, become hegemonic. To this extent, almost every public user of language attempts language planning, while it is axiomatic that governments and political parties will always attempt to influence the terms of debate. The whole field of political discourse and its analysis has become a central concern of political scientists, sociologists and economists as well as of linguists.

The Better English Campaign

Quite apart from such matters is the issue of 'Better English', the title of a short-lived semi-political campaign initially funded by the Department for Education and Employment from 1994. The issue was first raised after David Pascall, a senior oil company executive who became head of the Curriculum Council and caused considerable difficulties for Professor Cox who was trying to set up the National Curriculum for English, professed his belief that 'accurate English' was essential in education, and that 'understanding dialects and and accents was not a central purpose of the national curriculum.' (Guardian, 14.10.1994). Pascall's confusion between standard English and accurate English was mirrored by Gillian Shephard, Secretary of State for Education, who was outspoken in a newspaper interview as she condemned 'expression by grunt', the 'accelerated erosion' of the language and the spread of Estuary English. Her condemnation included television presenters, disc jockeys and pop musicians who encouraged such attacks on English. To counter this degradation of the language, Gillian Shephard launched a Better English Campaign, associating it with the 'final' version of the National Curriculum suggested by Sir Ron Dearing (see Chapter 8). Her introduction showed that one of the reasons for the campaign was to broaden the basis for approval of the revised National Curriculum, by 'losing' the detail of the changes such as introducing the grading of pupils in spoken English and tougher emphasis on grammar, spelling and punctuation.

The ability to communicate effectively in written and spoken
English is vital for people's life chances in general and their
career prospects in particular. Employers tell us again and again
that poor communication is one of the main reasons young people
fail to get jobs. ... This campaign is about bringing home these
messages and thereby promoting the use of good, effective
English in schools, the workplace and throughout the
community. ... Trevor McDonald has agreed to chair the steering
group which will lead this campaign. The group will include
people from business, education, the media, the unions, sport,
entertainment and voluntary bodies. ... an independent body of
bright energetic people who will make things happen ... My
Department will be providing £250,000 to pay for administrative
support and meet other costs for the first two years of the
campaign. Thereafter, the group will need to fund itself from
contributions from the private sector. The idea of setting up this
group grew out of discussions I have had over the last year with
a variety of people. (Department of Education and Employment
Press Release 227/95, 11.10.1995)

This semi-political campaign claimed to support the use and
teaching of standard English as a resource for all: 'For too long we have
been too slack in the treatment of English and we have impoverished
our children in the process'. The heady mixture of attacks on 'sloppy
English', insistence on stricter teaching of grammar, spelling and
punctuation, and encouragement of a vital skill without which young
people did not get jobs, was designed to raise support for Conservative
party educational policy on the National Curriculum by appealing to
prejudice, but the Campaign soon realised it would gain support only
from purists for such a retrograde approach. Trevor McDonald, in a
series of speeches and appeals, changed the tone and stressed delight
in the 'good' use of English as well as the 'hard economic case for better
English.'   Trevor McDonald, a black news-reader with ITN, who
himself had learnt to use standard English, would later co-chair the
Nuffield Languages Inquiry (see chapter 7).

People who cannot communicate effectively find life harder. ...
Poor communication skills ... have real costs in terms of putting
mistakes right ... ultimately, they mean lost orders and lost
customers. The involvement of employers in the Campaign is
crucial. ... We need to influence the climate within which
schools work. ... I hope that the Campaign will stimulate a

national concern to convince all young people that 'language is power'. We need to show the relevance of language skills to real life. ... We want to encourage enjoyment of English for its own sake. Those who learn to love language will also be more likely to use it effectively. ... newspapers, too, are important exponents of the written word. (Trevor McDonald speech to Northern Newspapers in Education, Summer School in York, reported by Department of Education and Employment 5.6.1996)

The Campaign tried to avoid charges that it was simply part of the Conservative party's policies by involving such groups and people as the Queen's English Society and Prince Charles in its work. Similarly, even the National Association of Teachers of English (NATE), one of the government's principal enemies in its policy for English, allowed Trevor McDonald space in its News to explain the Campaign's purposes. Indeed, the North East Branch Chair of NATE became a member of the steering group. The Campaign targeted less the general public than particular groups:

> We shall certainly be working through media with which young people are already comfortable, such as local radio, starting with an imaginative project in Manchester run by CSV Media and Piccadilly Radio. Cable TV companies are getting involved. There will be a pilot project in Bristol promoted by United Artists Communications, using television to develop communication skills across the curriculum. Channel One is running a competition in London to find the young video journalist of the year. The British Society of Magazine Editors is supporting the Campaign. ... The Newspaper Society, through Newspapers in Education, is also encouraging its members to support the Campaign. ... We have the support of key employer organisations, including the CBI, the British Chamber of Commerce, the Institute of Personnel and Development and the TEC National School. ... We are working with the Poetry Society Book Trust and _Times Educational Supplement_ ... Fellows of the Royal Society of Literature will also be supporting the Campaign. (_NATE News_, Summer 1996)

This grass roots approach to the Campaign should have ensured it a long life and a continuing importance. It must be said, however, that the Campaign's public profile gradually declined, and by 2001 neither the name nor the Campaign seemed to have survived: no address, no website, no mention in Department of Education information.

Motivation in resource-oriented language policy									
Identity sequence	Attitudinal structure								Ideal/objective
	Exc'nce		Vitality		Attract		Action		
	L1	L2	L1	L2	L1	L2	L1	L2	
Ideology									
Civil Service	3		3		2		3		cohesion /culture change
Political discourse	3		2		3		3		cohesion /electoral votes
Defend Identity									
Better English	3		1		3		3		cohesion /obligation
Improve use of Instrument									
Adult literacy	3		3		3		3		cohesion / improve

For an explanation of the Figure, see pp. 8-11 in the Introduction.
Note that, as with Figure 5.1 (p. 106 above), the motivation analysed here is that of the policy makers. L2 is not a relevant consideration in these cases. The L1 is English.

Fig 6.1 Motivation in resource-oriented language policy for the citizen

Chapter 7

Language as a Resource for the State

The United Kingdom is a major international economy and its ability in communication, whether in English as the international language of commerce or in other languages, is fundamental to its continuing success in the world. Managing and controlling these types of language use is an important task, recognised as such by successive governments. In this chapter we are concerned with LPP in creating and maintaining language resources whose main benefit will be for the state as much as for the individual citizen. Here, instrumentalism must be a strong motive for planners, but ideology, as we shall see, is never far away.

English Language Teaching and the British Council

English is a major international language (Crystal, 1997; Graddol, 1997; Maurais, 2001). Since we lack any kind of precise data on the number of users of languages worldwide, the statistics of the number of speakers of individual languages in the world are basically intelligent guesswork. Nonetheless, Graddol (p. 8) quotes the figures of Table 7.1 (in millions of speakers). Such tables are notoriously unreliable and dependent, firstly, on what a 'language' might be. 'Chinese', for example, although this is shown as a single entry in this table, is in fact a complex of spoken languages with a common written form. Hindi/Urdu, shown as one language, represents two divergent scripts and, generally, two or more very divergent communities, but has a largely common spoken form. The numbers given for Russian depend on estimates from the Soviet era, and are most likely optimistic. Secondly, the statistics are often composed simply of the population figures for a country, and the total population is simply assumed to speak the official language in its standardised form, to be equally proficient in it, and to speak no other language.

Table 7.1 First-language speakers of languages worldwide

	Language	engco model	*Ethnologue*
(1)	Chinese	1,113	1,123
(2)	English	372	322
(3)	Hindi/Urdu	316	236
(4)	Spanish	304	266
(5)	Arabic	201	202
(6)	Portuguese	165	170
(7)	Russian	155	288
(8)	Bengali	125	189
(9)	Japanese	123	125
(10)	German	102	98

First ten languages only. Figures in millions. engco is The English Company, Ltd. *Ethnologue* see Grimes, 1996.

Figures for all those who use English, in Table 7.2 below, relate to three types of speaker. In a primary circle of countries English is the first language; in a second extended or external circle, English has an important public role as second language; and in a third circle, of expansion, English is taught as foreign language. The differences between these three circles derive from history and are in a state of flux; language shift is occurring; and learners of English as a foreign language use it, if at all, at very different levels and to a very different extent. The nature of use, too, means that many users have a linguistic repertoire consisting of a number of languages, all of which they use, in different circumstances and for different purposes: the vernacular at home, Hindi in the office and English for commercial reasons.

Table 7.2 Speakers of English worldwide

L1 speakers		L2 speakers		FL speakers	
US	227	Nigeria	43		
UK	57	India	37		
Canada	20	Philippines	36		
Australia	15	US	30		
New Zealand	3	Papua New Guinea	28		
South Africa	3	Palau	16		
Ireland	3	Pakistan	16		
Trinidad	1	South Africa	10		
Total	375	Total	375	Total	750

List shows main countries only; totals are for all countries. Figures in millions, as for Table 7.1. Tables 7.1 and 7.2 adapted from Graddol, 1997: 8-11.

The Future of English

When we come to measure the future of languages and the relationships between them, statistics become even more difficult to defend. Since birthrates in the primary circle of English language users are generally low, the future for English will depend on users in the second and particularly the third circles where birthrates are much higher. In the third circle however, education is often not provided after the primary school; foreign languages are not always taught; and the major role currently allocated to English as a foreign language is by no means a certain indicator of future trends.

English will be important more and more as an international language. This fact has a number of consequences. English as an international language is not the first language of its speakers, and indeed its first speakers are unlikely to be those who determine the nature of the English actually used. The vocabulary, grammar and style of the international second language is that appropriate to the elites who use it: the 'globalese' of trades and industries, including non-sectoral ones like marketing and finance, is unlike the intimate and everyday vocabulary, the occasionally complex grammar and the family style which is appropriate to first speakers. For globalese, what matters is a fairly technical vocabulary, an approximate grammar particularly slanted towards the present and the future, and an interactive style. Even when this globalese is used for cultural productions such as films and novels, the language is special. The language of the novels of Japanese and Anglo-Indian novelists is subtly, and occasionally strikingly, different from that of the American epic novel or the British film, whether based in working-class Sheffield or upper-class Notting Hill. The global English of the future may look and sound quite different from that of the native speaker of the language.

The second major consequence derives from the inevitable existing or future oppression of many languages, and indeed cultures, by the fact that English has taken over, is taking over or will take over the majority of speech domains they formerly occupied, particularly those at the public level which are the most prestigious. In the same way that political or economic domination can breed resentment and rejection, linguistic domination can provoke resentment and sometimes retaliation against English language and sometimes English speakers. English, like French, German and Russian in different parts of the world and at different times, can be regarded as a legitimate target for freedom fighters, nationalists and defenders of endangered languages.

It is for these and other reasons that Graddol is somewhat cautious about the future for English. He assesses the likely effect of such factors as population growth, migration, urbanisation and the habits, preferences and needs of a growing middle class across the world. While in 1995 English had the second largest number of first-language speakers, his view is that by 2050 the position will have changed, with Hindi/Urdu taking its place. Arabic, too, will be rising in numbers. French and Japanese are likely to remain fairly static (Table 7.3).

Table 7.3 Estimates of native-speaker numbers in 2050 (millions)

	Language	Native speaker numbers
(1)	Chinese	1384
(2)	Hindi/Urdu	556
(3)	English	508
(4)	Spanish	486
(5)	Arabic	482

Source: adapted from Graddol, 1997: 27

The Graddol report was written for the British Council, and we would do well to recall that anticipating competition and a declining future provides a sensible basis for requesting further and greater funding for an expansion of activities aimed at spreading British language and culture abroad, even though the Graddol Report itself was an academic, not a cynical exercise.

Why should English be so widespread? Some commentators, Graddol among them, allege that English has certain characteristics which make it intrinsically an excellent choice. English is a hybrid and permeable language, made up of a mixture of Germanic and Latin roots in both vocabulary and grammar. It can transform elements from other languages, which it borrows with ease. It transforms other languages, to which it lends elements easily. Secondly, it is easy to learn, being easier in this respect than German or French: the cost of acquiring it is low. Thirdly, it is now a useful language and a valuable addition to economic capital for individuals as well as states, simply because of its history in these roles. English has developed a wide vocabulary in a wide range of domains ranging from politics to technology, from culture to gardening, and is thus usable and useful in any area of modern life. It is particularly valuable in diplomacy, of major importance to states; and in economics, of major importance to individuals. English is already widely taught and understood, and since it is already known to many, expenses involved in learning it are easily recouped. Finally, whatever may be the truth of such beliefs - and since many of them are subjective they are not amenable to factual discussion and even less to proof - the facts remain that English is the language of the world's largest and most powerful economy (the USA) and of another one in the top five (the UK); and that it is widely used by the world's second largest (Japan). It cannot be avoided; there is no alternative.

One particular aspect of the spread of English abroad is the situation in regard to the European Union. EU citizens agree that English is the most useful language and that it is the best choice to act as a common EU language (*Eurobarometer* 54, 15.02.2001). Some EU countries do not welcome this, nor the increasing selection of English as the language to use in EU institutions. The 'case' against English relies on statistics such as those concerning the drafting language of internal Commission documents (Table 7.4).

Table 7.4 Drafting language of European Commission documents (%)

Year	French	English	German	Others
1986	58	26	11	5
1989	49	30	9	12
1991	48	35	6	11
1997	40.4	45.4	5	9.2
1998	36.7	49.6	not known	

It is statistics such as these that have led to calls, by France in particular, for a European language policy aimed at protecting language diversity. Such calls essentially try to ensure that languages other than English receive priority, and that their speakers, nationals of countries other than the UK, retain significant roles within the Union bureaucracy. The consequences and the ramifications of this opposition to English are far-ranging, and potentially expensive. They include insisting on a full range of languages for every meeting of bureaucrats, which has the effect of maintaining the enormous cost of interpreting and translating. They include proposals for a European language policy, which would involve a Union-wide agreement for each schoolchild to learn two foreign languages including English where that is not the native language: a more costly affair for the UK than elsewhere. At a wider level than the purely linguistic, proposals for a European language policy are coded demands for allocation of senior posts by nationality rather than by merit, and it is in this sense that French newspapers were horrified by the retirement of French-speaking Jacques Delors from his post of Commission President and his replacement, eventually, by Romani Prodi and many English-speaking functionaries including Neil Kinnock. Neil Kinnock's reform of the administration of the Commission was treated by many French newspapers as a rejection of French norms and practices by 'Anglo-Saxon' ones, and as clear indications of a British take-over. The English language, in official Europe, is a hot political potato.

The British Council

Matters such as the present spread of English and the future situation of the language have been dealt with to this point as though they are mainly questions of linguistics. But the growth of English has not come about through linguistic factors alone. Since English is so widespread, British language industries make considerable money, about five billion pounds in the year 2000, much of which is derived from the export of English Language Teaching (ELT). ELT is conducted by both private providers, of whom there are many, including language schools and publishers, and by a non-departmental public body, the British Council. The British Council, although nominally an independent organisation, has long been extensively funded through the Foreign Office and the Ministry for Overseas Development. Under Margaret Thatcher, the British Council's ELT had to be self-financing and indeed the Council itself was nearly closed down in 1983 in the midst of the Thatcherian reform of the civil service and review of bodies which cost money. This was an apparent rejection of any role for the state in the global language situation, as well as a major misunderstanding of the role of cultural diplomacy. Such ignorance of the outside world and penny-pinching refusal to accept the costs of policy did not last long. De-facto arrangements, including 'contracts' and 'agencies', enabled the continued funding of the British Council's external role in ensuring that the UK might be viewed favourably, not merely by industrialists but also by states, organisations and private citizens who appreciate the worth of Shakespeare and British film as well as the language.

The British Council had been set up as a deliberate political act by the government of the day, in 1934 (Ager, 1996: 113-7). Its language teaching was deliberately expanded in 1954, again as a government act. Although, following the 1983 issue and continued difficulties throughout the period of Conservative governments, it was restructured in 1993, it survived. The 1997 Graddol report was commissioned by the Council as part of its 'English 2000' initiative, started in 1995, and was both a bid for increased funding and an external review of how best to maintain ELT. Its conclusions, that 'British English language services' might indeed have a future, were conditional on 'careful strategic planning, far-sighted management, thoughtful preparation and focused action' - in themselves a clear condemnation of the Conservative government's hasty and ill-thought-out policies of the 1980s, but at the same time an indication of the care needed in making bids for further official support (Graddol, 1997: 62). In 2000, half the Council's income (i.e. about £M170) was derived from selling services such as project management, UK-based training, English language courses, and examinations. Its ELT is thus a significant part of Council activity, a fact of which the new British government was reminded in a simple way. After being 'told off by the Mayor of Shanghai for failing to promote English abroad' (*Guardian*, 29.10.2000), Prime Minister Tony Blair got the message and provided £5 million extra for British Council English-language initiatives in 1998 - a minor amount but an indication of a change of attitude. It is this 'Blair initiative' that has made ELT initiatives more aggressive, and that has led to realisation both that cultural diplomacy is of major importance for Britain's future role in the world and that the English language is a major asset.

Like other parts of the civil service the British Council has its own mission statement, although its website simply calls this 'the work of the British Council'. This follows the 'quality' pattern outlined in the previous section, with the usual lack of modesty such documents require, and with the obligatory bullet points:

> Our aim
> The British Council's purpose is to enhance the United Kingdom's reputation in the world as a valued partner. ... We aim to be recognised as the world's most effective cultural relations organisation.
> Our objectives
> - to project the United Kingdom's creativity, cultural diversity and recent achievements, and to challenge outmoded stereotypes of the UK abroad;
> - to build the UK's role as a leading provider of educational and cultural opportunity for people overseas;
> - to promote wider and more effective learning of the English language overseas, especially as a means of influencing young people's views of the UK;

How we work
The British Council is international in operation and internationalist in outlook. ... we cooperate closely with the British Embassy or High Commission and other relevant UK organisations as part of a coordinated UK public diplomacy strategy. ... We try to present a generally positive picture of our country but we do not hide its problems, nor do we censor what is said by the many people whom we bring together. ...   The Foreign and Commonwealth office provides us with a core grant-in-aid and our objectives and main performance targets support their policies. ... We earn approximately half our revenues from selling services such as project management, UK-based training, English language courses, and examinations. (shortened: see www.britcoun.org)

The British Council, and ELT generally when provided by Western countries, have been heavily criticised by some for a 'colonialist and imperialist' language teaching programme and methods which support 'the totalitarian tendencies - of local nationalist groups and Western multinational agencies - through uniformity of thought and communication', and prevent 'the struggle of communities for empowerment' (Canagarajah, 1999: 197). The extent to which access to English empowers the wealthy and disempowers the poor is arguable, as is the extent to which a knowledge of English (alone) acts as the gatekeeper to social advancement in the relevant societies. Access to education itself clearly does act as gatekeeper, in developing as in developed societies. But attacks on the 'imperialism' (Phillipson, 1992) of the British Council, and indeed on the 'global triumphalism' of ELT providers generally, are hotly rejected (Crystal, 2000). Such opposition to English and to the British Council may stem from a variety of causes, including a rejection of an international role for the UK; a similar rejection of the far more powerful influence of the USA, the main user of English today; local politics, including the politics of language; religious opposition to Westernisation and to commerce; as well as to the deeply felt concerns about social justice which inspire commentators such as Canagarajah and Phillipson. Partly, such opposition to English may derive from or be strengthened by the way in which undisputed statistics are presented, the sometimes unconscious triumphalism of apparently neutral experts. Even commentators like Graddol often present international comparisons of languages in the form of 'language hierarchies' for example. The major languages of international communication are shown on top of a pyramid even though they have fewer speakers than many others. Such major languages are often called 'the big languages' or some similarly oppressive term, while national languages are relegated to the bottom of the heap. Presentations like Figure 7.1 are so provocative that most of the contributors to a special issue of the Canadian journal _Terminogramme_ (Maurais 2001) on 'geostrategies' for languages devoted time to decrying the implications of such hierarchies, not merely for languages but for their speakers.

The big languages
ENGLISH   FRENCH

Regional languages

ARABIC	CHINESE	ENGLISH
FRENCH	GERMAN	RUSSIAN
	SPANISH	

National languages
Around 80 languages serve over 180 nation states

Official languages within nation states
Around 400 languages worldwide

Local vernacular languages
The remainder of the world's 6,000+ languages

Source: Graddol, 1997: 13
Figure 7.1 The world language hierarchy.

For these and other reasons British Council, and UK, policy towards cultural diplomacy and towards ELT have stressed the ethical dimension in their undertakings. The British Council's fourth objective is 'to position the UK overseas as a committed partner in tackling key reform agendas and promoting sustainable development'. The jargon involved: 'committed' partner, 'reform agendas', 'sustainable development' is sensitive to the needs of the mainly Third World countries in which projects are undertaken. Projects are

> based on the principles of cooperation, mutual respect and shared benefit ... We work on ways of strengthening civil society, especially in the areas of governance, human rights, the rule of law and the role of the media. ... We help develop systems that

promote individual opportunity and improve the quality of life. (www.britcoun.org)

Moral concerns such as these are reminiscent of other British LPP actors over the years. They are not predominant in the Council's description of its activities. But since the Council has a leading role for British ELT providers, one of Graddol's recommendations is that ELT providers of all kinds should cooperate in order to undertake 'more careful brand management', ensuring that the provision of services 'relates to the wider image of Britain as a leading-edge provider of cultural and knowledge-based products'.

Overall, the British Council presents itself as an honest broker:

> We achieve our purpose by creating opportunity for people worldwide. We give them access to unbiased information, we enable them to share knowledge and expertise across cultural boundaries, and we help them to acquire new knowledge, skills and qualifications. *In everything we value individuals, promote internationalism and demonstrate integrity*. (www.britcoun.org. Italics in the original.)

In terms of motivation for its, and hence the UK's, LPP in this area, there is a mixture of at least three of the motives we have identified. The moral and ideological concern that underlies 'ethical ELT' is clear; the instrumental motivation of improving financial returns, both for ELT itself and also for the country at large, is equally obvious; and the maintenance and defence of the British identity, of representing what the UK is and the values it represents, is a key factor. The main motive, however, is (the manipulation of) image: to ensure that the view of British identity that others hold is as positive as possible.

Foreign Languages in Education

Traditionally, schools in the UK have taught French as the main foreign language, followed by German. For many years after the Second World War, teachers and planners alike considered that foreign language learning should be restricted to children of higher ability, yet also claimed considerable advantages for this element of the curriculum: it 'enhanced career possibilities, cultural enrichment, linguistic understanding and character development' (Hornsey, 1983: 1). Much of the professional discussion until the 1980s aimed at increasing the numbers of pupils studying modern foreign languages (MFL). Proposals were made to change what was taught, how and how it was examined. In terms of the languages, calls were made for an increase in study of languages other than French. There were repeated calls for new teaching methods, many of which were based on the Direct Method, itself first proposed in the 1900s. The 'audio-visual revolution' encouraged teachers to use new recording devices and 'tape-slide' systems were heavily promoted, as were, later 'language laboratories' consisting of banks of tape recorders which could be centrally controlled and gave practice in 'learning drills'. The examining bodies were asked to develop oral tests of speaking and listening ability, and to change their advanced syllabuses to allow teachers to study aspects of civilisation other than literature. Many changes were indeed made: the principal planners were in practice two: commercial publishers and the Examination Boards. The publishers catered for a market where purchasing decisions were made by each school in pursuance of its own decisions on curriculum and methods. The Examination Boards were all-powerful, since they also responded not to central planning but to individual schools, albeit with pressure from Local Government and from Her Majesty's Inspectorate, part of the Ministry of Education.

Changes in this situation were to come about as a result of membership of the European Union, and the educational rationalisation and reform of the 1980s under the Conservative government of the time. The process took some considerable time: there were many and vocal objections, and the planners, increasingly centralised on the Department for Education and Science, took ten years to bring about a shift from the 'secret garden' of the curriculum to the National Curriculum with its precision, its detail and its testing processes. The first changes that took place concerned the teaching of foreign languages in the primary school, which had become widespread after the war. This 'experiment' led to the publication of *Primary French in the Balance* in 1974 (Burstall *et al*), a research report which questioned the value of such early teaching. This government-funded study was seized on by education authorities as a way of closing primary school languages, thus saving money. It took until 2002 before the Secretary of State for Education proposed that primary schools again teach foreign languages. The second change coincided with the development of comprehensive education, fostered by the Labour government of 1965 even though many local education authorities had introduced it before. Comprehensive education led to a much larger percentage of children studying a language at age 11: 25% in 1965, 89% in 1977 (Hawkins, 1983: 100). In the National Curriculum of 1994, at the stage of centralisation of planning, a foreign language became compulsory for all to age 14, although this requirement was removed in 2002. One could probably fairly say that the fifty years from 1950 to 2000 had seen language planning in foreign language education move from a local to a national concern, while the power of pressure groups and other external forces grew, as we shall see.

Membership of the European Union decrees that the official languages of member countries must be taught by the education system. The implementation of this policy in the first version of the National Curriculum introduced in 1989 led to considerable pressure from groups who supported non-European languages, principally those of the larger ethnic communities in the UK, and who had ensured that their languages were taught more and more within local communities and at primary level, but wished to see them taken more seriously at secondary level and within the examination system. The debate that followed led to a solution in which, provided that schools first offered a European language, they could then also offer other languages such as community languages. This policy was implemented in the UK in 1991 through a working party revising the initial suggestions for the National Curriculum, and at the same time foreign language learning became compulsory for all children aged 11-15, to Key Stage 3 (Ager, 1996, 148-53). The Appendix (p. 189) shows the numbers of examination candidates per foreign language at GCSE level (age 16) in 2000, from which it will be seen that while French and German are still the most taught languages, Spanish is strong and the next strongest is Urdu, just in advance of Italian. The next important group is made up of the community languages Chinese, Bengali, Punjabi and Gujerati, with Russian following. The territorial languages Welsh and Irish are strong although localised in their respective countries, with Welsh having over 13,000 students of whom 4,157 take the language as a first language, while Irish has over 2,000 students.

The issue of the numbers studying a foreign language in the education system had not been solved by these decisions. The Nuffield Report of 2000 (McDonald & Boyd, 2000) detailed the decline in the numbers studying languages, particularly at A level, (see Appendix), and the low esteem in which a knowledge of foreign languages was held in the country. It savagely criticised the lack of a coherent national strategy for the use and promotion of foreign languages, particularly in education but also in working life, and noted a rapid decline both in the numbers of children taking examinations in languages and an even more rapid decline in the numbers of students entering universities for higher education. The Report's fifteen recommendations were ambitious, but at the same time severely practical. They reflected a wish to see both long-term and short-term actions; were addressed to the national level, rather than to local initiatives; and recognised the diversity of reasons for language learning which their working groups had suggested.

(1) Develop a national strategy for languages as a key skill

(2) Appoint a languages supremo

(3) Raise the profile of languages in the UK

(4) Establish-business-education partnerships

(5) Provide schoolchildren with a sound basis for language learning for life

(6) Invest in an early start

(7) Raise the quality of provision for languages in secondary schools

(8) Ensure wider participation beyond school

(9) Promote languages for the majority of 16-19 year-olds

(10) Develop a strategic approach to languages in higher education

(11) Develop the huge potential of lifelong language learning

(12) Intensify the drive to recruit more language teachers

(13) Exploit new technologies to the full

(14) Ensure policy is reliably and consistently informed

(15) Establish a national standards framework for languages.

The initial Department for Education and Employment response of February 2001 noted existing policies such as the institution of over 100 specialist Language Colleges at secondary level since 1997, the National Languages for Export Campaign and the National Languages for Export Award Scheme, and official support for the European Year of Languages in 2001. The Nuffield Foundation continued strong support for the topic however, with grants of £200,000 for research in the area. In November 2001 the next stage in the governmental response to the Nuffield Report was the creation of a Steering Group to take the matters forward. Chaired by a minister, it consisted of twenty people: four representatives from the renamed Department for Education and Skills (DES), including one from the Office for Standards in Education and a newly appointed DES National Adviser for Languages; one each from the Foreign and Commonwealth Office and the Department for Trade and Industry; a representative from CILT, from the Central

Bureau for Educational Visits and Exchanges and the Languages National Training Organisation, all departmental bodies; one each from the National Institute of Adult and Continuing Education, the National Association of Language Advisers, the Nuffield Foundation, the University Council for Modern Languages, which is the professional umbrella body for subject associations and teacher organisations in higher education, and the Association for Language Learning, which is the professional association for language teachers across the country and across the different sectors of education, although its main membership is from secondary schools; three head teachers, a university, and a college representative. Reporting to this Steering Committee a National Languages Working Group includes a similar mix of representation from government, sponsored bodies and representatives of educational sectors. Together, these groups could be said to represent a major part of the interest network for foreign language teaching in the country.

The Council of Europe and the European Union had set up a joint initiative to celebrate the 'European Year of Languages' in 2001 across Europe. A number of promotional events were devised, including a 'Language Challenge' to be undertaken by public figures and others and awards and prizes for achievement in language learning such as the European Award for Languages. The international Year had four aims:

- to raise awareness of Europe's rich linguistic heritage
- to make the widest possible public aware of the advantages of competence in another language
- to encourage lifelong learning of languages
- to publicise information about the learning and teaching of languages.

The main agency and coordinator in the UK was the Centre for Information on Language Teaching and Research (CILT), a department-sponsored public body set up in the 1960s, and the only subject-oriented body supported by the Department for Education and Skills. CILT has financial support from other organisations and also acts as support for a number of language-related schemes across the country. Its financing is based on a mixture of public funds and the bids it submits for various language-related initiatives, themselves mostly public, typical of such public bodies since the 1980s. This mixture means that much of its information-related function relies on selling publications, reports and relevant papers rather than providing them free to the public, which again is the British interpretation of freedom of information and typical of information dissemination across Whitehall. CILT has a Scottish equivalent, and the Directors of the two CILT organisations have taken on more and more central roles in language policy formation in the UK in recent years, since a time in the early 1980s when the then Minister for Education, Keith Joseph, in his desire for radical moves and rejection of 'expert' advice, nearly closed the organisation down.

As part of the European Year of Languages in 2001, an 'Agenda for Languages', prepared by CILT, was produced for a conference in October 2001 (King and Johnstone, 2001). The _Agenda_ was produced as the next stage in the response to the Nuffield Report. The document, in which the interdepartmental group was involved and which may form the basis for the new Steering Group's work, aimed to affect 'education, employment and civil society' and hence cover much more than the straightforward task of improving the teaching and availability of foreign languages as a resource for the country. The document was presented as the basis for a comprehensive UK policy for languages, and was treated as such by a number of commentators and advisors from other countries. The document

> provides a vision of languages and language capability as basic
> life skills. It offers key messages which we believe are capable
> of being widely shared within the particular and diverse context
> of the UK:
> • communication is the key
> • languages are a precious resource
> • multilingualism is better
> • a language policy is not a luxury.

The first message is aimed at peace and prosperity. Communication is the key for individuals to understand their own identity; for communities to avoid isolation, xenophobia and racism; for economies to prosper and survive, and for societies to ensure political progress, peace and prosperity both within Europe and globally. The second message is that languages are a resource to be valued; although the UK is rich in languages the majority of its people are linguistically impoverished. The third message is that only through multilingualism can we really understand and appreciate the stranger, and multilingualism is better for countries and states, for business, for social inclusion and tolerance, and for individuals in their sense of self and their openness to the world. The fourth message is that languages and language capability are basic life skills to which all citizens should have entitlement.

This outline of an ideological basis for a national policy is addressed to three actors: education; civil society; and commerce and industry. Overall, 'the opportunity is to make a significant breakthrough on this issue which is crucial to our national prosperity, our well being and our place in the world.' The breakthrough is not intended to be sudden or complete: 'the Nuffield Inquiry spoke of a 20-year agenda' and supporting documents for the Agenda note that 'the next fifty years is a crucial period for British language policies and practice'.

In terms of language policy and planning for the UK the document is important, if only because it clearly marks out the ground, provides a very clear ideological statement of purpose for the agenda, and equally clearly indicates the nature of a number of forthcoming problems in the implementation of any policy. Problems, faced and possibly solved, are five.

Firstly, there is mention several times of 'governments in constituent parts of the United Kingdom'. Far from being a single national policy for the UK, there is a strong likelihood of a separation of languages policy, to be conducted 'in England through the work of the Languages National Steering Group, in Scotland through the Ministerial Action Group on Languages, and in Wales by the production of a draft strategy for languages.' Whether this separation bodes well for future policy across the UK only time will tell. The danger, of course, is that while Scotland, Wales and Northern Ireland, which is strangely missing from the document, have specific responsibility for their own territorial languages through their roles in relation to the European Charter for Regional and Minority Languages, England has taken on no such role. Education is a devolved responsibility, too!

Secondly, the agenda is directed at two outcomes, both dependent on a view of language as 'closely bound up with cultural and individual identities': economic prosperity and social inclusion. These are two central political responsibilities, and politicians are often ideologically divided on them. This policy is a political statement, intended for a political audience, and based on a political ideology which Margaret Thatcher would probably have found repellent. It is a policy for its time, despite its repeated mention of the long-term scale. Indeed, its mention of 'our vision of a United Kingdom' is one with which New Labour can be expected to be very content, and which indeed most politicians who do not share the Thatcherian belief that 'there is no such thing as society' can be expected to support. But if, and when, the Conservative Party returns to power, particularly if it remains a Euro-sceptic party, the policy may not seem so attractive.

Thirdly, the practical implementation of the policy, sketched in outline at this stage and in this document, hints at 'entitlement' in education 'to enable learners to develop their own mother tongue or dialect ... to develop all learners' competence in a range of styles of English appropriate for educational, work-based, social and public-life purposes'. This presentation neatly shifts from the 'Resources' approach of the Nuffield Inquiry and Report to the 'Rights' approach of the Australian National Languages Policy of 1987.

Fourthly, it encapsulates and neutralises the battle between the 'dialectologists' and the 'standard English' supporters which wrecked the push for a satisfactory and languages-wide policy background for languages in the National Curriculum. In this respect, it is intended to obtain the support of the languages specialists, particularly those in education and academe.

Fifthly, the role of CILT and the input from the Nuffield Foundation demonstrate the renewal of a feature of the British approach to policy-making which was important before the Thatcher period and which much of that period was devoted to destroying: the desire of government to involve a number of 'outsiders' in both developing policy lines and also in seeking ways to implement them. The reliance on policy networks, both for the creation of policy and for much of its implementation, was a characteristic of British action in many fields. Thatcherian destruction of policy networks has been charted in e.g. Richardson, 1993. In the language field, too, the policy network suffered (Ager, 1996: 147-53). The destruction of networks did not take place because government, both politicians and civil servants, were necessarily lacking in ideas, but because the British tradition of amateurism was regarded as inefficient in most fields, with the notable exception of agriculture. After Thatcher, a conscious desire to involve civil society directly in policy matters regained importance, and networks were widely restored. The approach can be seen in at least two other features of the language field: the desire to ensure wide consultation before any practical solutions are proposed for problem areas, and the desire to make policy in education for a wide spectrum of interests, particularly involving the business world. Since the collapse of the first, brutal attempts at imposing the National Curriculum, the education authorities of the country have never felt it possible to devise an education policy and practice in which the specialists and the ministry itself had the final say. To this extent, ideology as a motive appears rarely: it is apparently replaced by instrumentalism or even simple managerialism. But managerialism, the desire to run things smoothly, is a method, itself used to ensure that ideologically-based policies are implemented with little opposition. In the 'Agenda for Languages', however, the triumph of ideology is clear, while the mechanism for implementing it, the Steering Group, is the concrete realisation of the policy network approach to managerialism.

Motivation in Resource-oriented Language Policy

The six areas of language policy that we have reviewed in chapters 6 and 7 present a rather mixed picture insofar as motivation is concerned. We have divided them into resources for citizens and individuals, and resources for the state. This division is occasionally artificial. Improving adult literacy, as is fairly clear from the rhetoric and the actual proposals of all British governments since the early 1970s, has been a matter of improving life skills, not solely for the sake of the individual and his own economic betterment, but for the better health of the economy at large. True, the rhetoric has been accompanied by the occasional cultural comment, but the vast majority of the discourse surrounding the improvement of literacy has been directed towards functional literacy, the negotiation of social and economic traps, and towards enabling individuals to obtain better employment. Clarity in the civil service, too, has a number of aims: it may help the state but is also a cultural acquisition for the individual, as indeed the sales of Gowers' _Plain Words_ show. Political discourse and its development affects both the party activists whose personal skills are honed and the general public whose ears are attuned to fine distinctions and subtleties of interpretation which reflect policy shifts and the construction of new orientations. On the face of it, the Better English campaign intended to improve the life chances of every citizen; the rhetoric in which it was often presented made it clear that business and the state could only benefit by greater care and attention to expression. On the other hand, those policies we have considered to be mainly oriented towards generating resources for the state, representation abroad and foreign language learning at home, have undoubted advantages for individual citizens as well. Indeed, it has long been clear to educational planners that parents are keen for their children to have access to foreign language learning from an early age.

Attitudinally, the impression is given in planning for adult literacy of a strong belief among planners in the excellence of the instrument, English; that (standard) English is the means of communication for all domains; that English is itself attractive, and that action is essential. The overall social ideal, whether we consider resources for the state or for the citizen, to which planners aspire is social cohesion, enabling citizens to participate in all aspects of social and economic life, even though the subsidiary objective is that of improvements for the economy.

'Clarity' in the civil service, and the related aims of planners to introduce new thinking among public servants, are both directed towards an ideological acceptance of new political thinking. Planners may not have thought of civil service language as necessarily attractive, but in all other aspects of the attitudinal structure the scores will have been high. The overall objective was efficiency in the public service, aimed at ensuring delivery of the political message. Political discourse, too, reflects the strength of ideological concerns in the construction of planners' self identity. While the nature of the discourse may have differed between Thatcher and Blair, the planners' aims were the same: attitudinally, the structure is the same, with high scores in all aspects except possibly that of the vitality scale. The overall ideal was to achieve cohesion through hegemony, or the unconscious adoption by the public of the particular discourse proposed by the relevant politicians. A subordinate objective was to obtain electoral votes and to conserve support, by much the same means.

The Better English campaign was more redolent of old-fashioned purism, even though it strove strenuously to avoid becoming linked to Blimpish attitudes and outdated beliefs in social correctness. The overall ideal, again, was social cohesion, with a subsidiary objective of common acceptance of an obligation or duty towards better speech. Here the identity creation stage was closer to that of defending identity rather than to establishing it. English Language Teaching abroad seems to reflect an overall identity stage of image manipulation: planners wanted to ensure favourable reception of their view of Britain. Here, attitudes reflect a very similar structure to that of the Better English Campaign, with perhaps a slightly stronger belief in the appropriateness of English for use in all domains of life. The subsidiary objective of competition with other countries was never far from planners' purposes, although the superordinate ideal may have been the search for a favourable image. Finally, the Nuffield Languages Inquiry and subsequent moves towards improving skills in Modern Foreign Languages present an overall instrumental motive, again despite many protestations that the aims were more cultural and educational. Planners' attitudes reflected strong approval of both

English and of foreign languages, although action in regard to English was no part of the plan. The ideals, and the subordinate objectives, were mixed, ranging from improving competition to desires for social change and, in some cases and for some languages, the need for recognition of the importance of languages and relevant societies.

The six issues fit rather uneasily together on our chart (Figure 7.2). It may be for this reason that policy on resources is by no means clear, and has changed so much from government to government and from time to time.

Motivation in resource-oriented language policy									
Identity sequence	Attitudinal structure								Ideal/objective
	Exc'nce		Vitality		Attract		Action		
	L1	L2	L1	L2	L1	L2	L1	L2	
Ideology									
Civil Service	3		3		2		3		cohesion /culture change
Political discourse	3		2		3		3		cohesion /electoral votes
Image									
ELT	3		2		3		3		competition / seek favourable
Defend Identity									
Better English	3		1		3		3		cohesion /obligation
Improve use of Instrument									
Adult literacy	3		3		3		3		cohesion / improve
MFL	3	3	3	3	3	3	1	3	(mixed)

For an explanation of the Figure, see pp. 8-11 in the Introduction.

Note that, as with Figures 5.1 and 6.1, the motivation analysed here is that of the policy makers. Except in the case of Modern Foreign Languages, L2 is not a relevant consideration. In the case of Modern Foreign Languages, 'L2' applies to those foreign languages whose teaching is thought appropriate for inclusion in the National Curriculum..

Figure 7.2 Motivation in resource-oriented language policy

Chapter 8

Language as a Political Problem

Language planning and policy has in recent years been at the centre of at least three major examples of political LPP in Great Britain: the teaching of standard English in schools; multiculturalism; and the devolution of power to Scotland, Wales and Northern Ireland. The issues are complex and sometimes interrelated, as is particularly the case with the first two. The issues reflect both political ideologies and the close connection between these and cultural attitudes. They show particularly the extent to which language acts as a prime site in the desire to influence the symbolic status of a community. All three reveal how language planning and policy can be deliberately used by planners to resolve, or sometimes simply to sharpen, a problem which has many other aspects than language behaviour.

Standard English and the National Curriculum.

The mainstream teaching of English in Britain had been the subject of innumerable British government reports prior to the introduction of the National Curriculum. In the twentieth century these included the Newbolt Report of 1921, the Bullock Report of 1975, the Swann Report of 1985, and the Kingman Report of 1988. The National Curriculum, introduced by the Education Reform Act of 1988, brought with it the establishment of national learning and achievement targets, and national assessment of schools, as opposed to local control of education. For the first time, national programmes and national standards of achievement were set up for four Key Stages of education: ages 5-7, 8-11, 12-14, and 15-16 with tests at the end of each stage. Most importantly, there would be a national curriculum of subjects to be taught. No longer would the curriculum be determined by individual Local Education Authorities, head teachers or the requirements of the many different Examination Boards.

As part of this major reform, the syllabus for each subject to be included in the national curriculum was determined by a working party, composed of selected experts and civil servants. The composition of these working parties was determined by ministers, and although they theoretically contained members of the relevant interest groups, the selections were finally determined on a political level. The English syllabus was developed by a committee working with Professor Brian Cox of Manchester University. Professor Cox, one of the organisers of the pressure group the National Council for Educational Standards, was a leading contributor to the *'Black Papers'*, a series of pamphlets attacking what their authors considered to be the decay of English language teaching, and teaching generally, through poor teacher training, political indoctrination in courses and permissiveness in approaches to education. Much of the blame was allocated to sociolinguists and educators whose views were basically that language varieties are of equal worth and of equal linguistic validity; that the linguistic differences between them, as in Bernstein's 'restricted' (working class) and 'elaborated' (middle class) codes, made them markers of social difference; that it was no part of the purpose of education to denigrate working class children because of their accent or dialect; and that thus social and regional dialects should be encouraged and valued in the school (see e.g. Bernstein 1971, Halliday *et al* 1964). Among significant contributors from the opposite point of view were Dr Rae, headmaster of Westminster School, and Dr John Honey who in 1983 wrote *The Language Trap*, into which working-class children dropped through not being obliged to learn standard English. The Cox Report, published in 1989, did not slavishly follow the earlier Kingman Report of 1988, whose purpose had been to determine a 'model' of English for the curriculum. Nonetheless, Professor Cox was left in little doubt about the political nature of his task. The draft that was submitted to the Education Secretary, Kenneth Baker, was by no means the final version as published in 1989. It became necessary to ensure that political views, both of the Conservative politicians and of educationalists, were taken into consideration even in the detail. One reason why many Conservative politicians, not merely the Minister, at first sympathised with the Report was that they were completely ignorant of the fine distinctions that had been drawn between standard English and southern English, and between the possible pronunciation of standard English in any accent, and RP. After the Report was published criticism came from both Left and Right, from educationalists but also from politicians.

> The left argued that children who speak dialect at home could not be expected to speak standard English, which they regarded as middle class, and that it was improper to make this an essential attainment target in a national curriculum. The right thought that we were too soft on primary school children, who should be expected to speak and write standard English as soon as they arrive in the classroom. (Cox, 1991: 26)

Language became the site of major political controversy as the New Right social engineering agenda was driven through, against the vocal opposition of teachers and language experts. Right-wing approval for (its own view of) standard English, and for teaching methods aimed at bringing 'order' into both what was taught and how it was taught, attacked the 'new orthodoxy' of linguistic relativism and the 'permissive' educational methods of the 'trendy 60s' (see also the discussion of standard language and language ideologies in Chapter 2).

A particularly influential contribution was Marenbon's *English, our English*, a pamphlet produced by the Conservative think-tank, the Centre for Policy Studies, in 1987, and which, with *The Language Trap*, may have been the impetus for the change from implicit to explicit language policy in the UK.

Standard English is a difficult term to define, as we have seen. At the time of the controversy, at least four different meanings for the term were called upon. Standard English was seen firstly as an objectively describable norm, as essential for the proper use of language as a standardised currency is for monetary exchanges. Secondly, standard English was seen as of high quality, prestigious and morally right: good English and not bad English. Thirdly, standard English was seen as the common possession of all, as the social glue essential for a cohesive society. Fourthly, it was the badge of the middle classes and of southern England: the language of the elite. Both political Left and political Right used whichever definition suited them.

Although ostensibly about language, the issue was presented, particularly by Education Secretary Kenneth Baker, as one of morals and standards. Kenneth Baker attacked the liberalisation of the 1960s, when 'social scientists propagated excuses for the inexcusable', values became relative and the result was 'escalating delinquency, political violence, attacks on free speech, rising divorce and illegitimacy, truancy in schools and vandalism' (Williamson, 1990: 257). These beliefs, based on a 'Tory reading of morality and history', founded the new proposals for the teaching of history and English in the 'shared values which are a distinctive feature of British society and culture' as

Keith Joseph, one of the main Tory philosophers and practical politicians of the time, put it in 1984. The government's aim was to combat the moral decline of the 1960s by emphasising British history and a proper pride in the nation's institutions, symbolised through the use of the standard language. It was this issue, and this association, that characterised the language policy of Conservative governments during the 1980s and early 1990s.

The Conservatives, and later, Honey in his book *Language is Power* (1997) in which he defends most of the 1980s LPP, suggested that teachers and linguists wished to allow schools to promote such varieties as Creoles, Black English, and the regional dialects, in both speech and writing, and to accord them the same status as standard English in the educational process. A powerful and ideologically-based linguistic school was said to have grown up, claiming that all languages and dialects were equally good, and devoted to disparaging standard English.   In return, attacks on Conservative party LPP questioned the clarity of thought, the accuracy of the linguistics, and the (political) ideology it was said to reveal (Milroy & Milroy, 1985; Crowley, 1989).   Marenbon, Honey and others were accused of not understanding simple differences between written and spoken language, between the meanings of 'standard'. They ignored the historical reality of dialects as well as their relationship to their speakers, whether regionally-based or ethnic groups.   They equated dialects with language corruption, and inserted confusion into the debate in replacing technical linguistic distinctions by a class-based hatred for minority and powerless groups. Above all, their policy was ideological and class-based.

How pernicious, then was Conservative party LPP? The issue has been much discussed and analysed (see for example Cox, 1991; Crowley, 1989; Cameron, 1995: 78-115; Thompson *et al.*, 1996: 102-6; Ager, 1996; Honey, 1997; Bex & Watts, 1999; Holborow, 1999; Milroy, 2001). Generally, the majority of language experts and educationalists tend to regard LPP of this time as misguided and excessive. There is of course no objective way of deciding whether Conservative LPP was 'right' or 'wrong'. At the time, one criticism was that it lacked both linguistic and political authority. In linguistics, there is little to be said, despite the heated debates which continue. Linguistics by itself cannot provide a simple answer to the question as to whether the standard language, and its dialects , should be taught in schools, and if so how and when. Arguments over the advantages or disadvantages of bilingualism - or, in this case, bidialectalism - still rage, although most opinion tends today to agree that bilingualism is an advantage for the individual and indeed for society. Political science is clear that in a democracy where brute force alone is an insufficient guarantor, the political authority of a government derives from its consistency, credibility and legitimacy. The government was consistent throughout the debate; its credibility and legitimacy among the general population were absolute, as shown by the reelection of the Conservative party, by large majorities, between 1979 and 1992. There is hence absolutely no doubt that this policy did not offend the British public in this period, nor that the Conservative party was (politically) fully justified in pursuing it. The issue symbolised the contrast between the macro policies of what was thus the ideologically consistent, credible and perfectly legitimate government and the micro policies, generally opposed to Conservative ideology, of authority figures in the classroom and particularly of their professional associations and leading thinkers.

One of the most interesting aspects of the 'great grammar crusade' is the extent to which professional linguists were involved and to which what had previously been basic assumptions of linguistics were put on public trial. To this extent, the process followed the pattern of Thatcherite 'handbagging' of established interest groups and professionals, and was by no means an unusual exercise in that context. History teachers, and indeed economists, are other professional groups that suffered much the same fate. It was part of the process of radical social engineering of the new Right that the basic assumptions of linguists and teachers should be branded as political ideologies, and attacked on these grounds. On the wider level, 'the struggle that rages around the English curriculum is about identity and authority ... the prosperous are nervous about the poor' (Alan Howarth, then Conservative MP, reported in *The Guardian*, 15.10.1994). Indeed, it was not until 1994 and after the involvement of a well-known 'fixer', Sir Ron Dearing, bearing the message that standard English should be seen as a resource to which the socially deprived should be given access, that the classroom opposition to the teaching of and in this variety weakened.

The change of government in 1997 changed some, but not all, of this approach to standard English in the National Curriculum. If anything government instructions, curriculum specifications and the insistence on teaching spoken standard English have become even more evident as changes have been made in the detail. The requirement now is that 'since standard English, spoken and written, is the predominant language in which knowledge and skills are taught and learned, pupils should be taught to recognise and use standard English'. That this should be so is worthy of examination, particularly if the case is being made, as we are doing here, that Conservative party education and language policy was politically inspired and ideologically driven. Why did the Labour Party not completely reverse this policy in 1997, as it did reverse the policy on territorial languages?

The answer lies partly in the Third Way beliefs of New Labour, and partly in the point, many times repeated, that the educational professions were keen not to go through yet more turmoil. The government decided rather to implement its National Literacy Strategy, targeted at the primary school, and to stress the implementation of targets - for example of 80 percent of pupils aged 11 (Key Stage 2) reaching the expected standard in 2002 - rather than revising the general approach. Indeed, while 70% of pupils reached the expected standard in 1999, only 54% did so in writing and the accusation remained that there was much to do to raise achievement in the schools. As a consequence, the structure of the National Curriculum, the central role of English and of standard English within it remain, as do the programmes of study and the attainment targets. These latter are arranged in eight levels for the four skills of speaking and listening, for reading and for writing, with an additional level for exceptional performance. Pupils are expected to work within the level descriptions 1-3 at ages up to 7; between 2 and 5 at ages up to 11; and between levels 3 and 7 up to age 14. The expectation, too, is that by age 14, at the end of Key Stage 3, pupils should have achieved levels 5 or 6. Standard English is mentioned only in the level descriptors for speaking and listening; and is mentioned first at level 3 ('They are beginning to be aware of standard English and when it is used'). Better use of spoken standard English is then correlated with improvement in the levels:

> Level 4. ... They use appropriately some of the features of standard English vocabulary and grammar.
> Level 5. ... They begin to use standard English in formal situations.
> Level 6. ... They are usually fluent in their use of standard English in formal situations.
> Level 7. ... They show confident use of standard English in situations that require it.
> Level 8. ... They show confident use of standard English in a range of situations, adapting as necessary.

Exceptional performance. ... They show assured and fluent use of standard English in a range of situations and for a variety of purposes. (www.nc.uk.net)

Official attitudes towards English are revealed both in general paragraphs and in detailed points in the curriculum descriptions.

The importance of English

English is a vital way of communicating in school, in public life and internationally. Literature in English is rich and influential, reflecting the experience of people from many countries and times. In studying English pupils develop skills in speaking, listening, reading and writing. It enables them to express themselves creatively and imaginatively and to communicate with others effectively. Pupils learn to become enthusiastic and critical readers of stories, poetry and drama as well as non-fiction and media texts. The study of English helps pupils understand how language works by looking at patterns, structures and origins. Using this knowledge pupils can choose and adapt what they say and write in different situations.

The English literary heritage is determined by specification of authors who must, or who may be, studied by all pupils during Key Stages 3 and 4 (examples for major drama writers, only, are given in full below).

Pupils must study drama by major playwrights. Examples ... include: William Congreve, Oliver Goldsmith, Christopher Marlowe, Sean O'Casey, Harold Pinter, J. B. Priestley, Peter Shaffer, G. B. Shaw, R. B. Sheridan, Oscar Wilde.
Pupils must study works of fiction by two major writers published before 1914 selected from the following list ...
Pupils must study works of fiction by two major writers published after 1914. Examples ...
Pupils must study poetry by four major poets published before 1914 selected from the following list ...
Pupils must study poetry by four major poets published after 1914. Examples ...
Pupils must study recent and contemporary drama, fiction and poetry. Examples ...
Pupils must study drama, fiction and poetry by major writers from different cultures and traditions. Examples ...
Pupils must study a range of literary non-fiction and print and

ICT-based information and reference texts. Examples of non-fiction and non-literary texts ...

At Key Stages 3 and 4, for speaking and listening, pupils are taught about language variation:

Language variation
a . the importance of standard English as the language of public communication nationally and often internationally
b. current influences on spoken and written language
c. attitudes to language use
d. the differences between speech and writing
e. the vocabulary and grammar of standard English and dialectal variation
f. the development of English, including changes over time, borrowings from other languages, origins of words, and the impact of electronic communication on written language.

These topics, and the requirement that at Key Stages 3 and 4, pupils should read 'texts from different cultures and traditions', are almost the only relics of a component in the early draft of the National Curriculum submitted to Education Secretary Kenneth Baker on 'Language Knowledge in the National Curriculum'. This component did not survive Mr Baker's views on what was appropriate, and junking the documentation and course materials provided for it cost over £M15 in 1989 (Ager, 2001: 47-9). But current Labour Party implementation of the National Curriculum for English has accepted most of the points about the importance of general access to standard English, and the necessity for teaching it, that were made by Kenneth Baker, Keith Joseph and others. In this area, despite the importance of ideology as a motive for Conservative LPP, the Labour Party approach has made little change.

Multiculturalism

The standard English problem was closely related to the issue of multiculturalism in schools and in society generally, again a bone of contention between Left and Right (Tomlinson, 1993; see also Chapter 1 for a description of UK ethnic communities, and Chapter 5 on the issue of the maintenance of non-indigenous languages). The multicultural problem poses the same issue as multilingualism in a state like the UK: how far should one culture predominate or should a plurality of cultures be the norm? Is assimilation and integration preferable to recognition of difference and mosaicity? Should the state language,

English, be a requirement for citizenship, or should the state accept
that citizens may use any of many languages? It is not just
multiculturalism that is at issue here: the ideologically-based design
of society is the crucial theme for modern political parties.
Particularly since the 1950s, it is the opposition between the primacy
of civil society and that of the state which has been at the heart of
politicians' views on social organisation, in Britain as elsewhere. If
civil society is to triumph, then social diversity has to be accepted and
indeed fostered. Pluralism, including political pluralism, has not
merely to be accepted but encouraged, and the numerous communities,
categories and groups making up society have to be recognised and
encouraged to participate while retaining their identities. If, on the
other hand, the nation-state is to predominate, then assimilation to an
overarching ideal will require that such groups dissolve their separate
essences in the common good. This approach means that the state is
conceived as made up of individuals, who collectively allocate power
to the state to rule on their behalf. But the components of the state are
individuals, not groups, and groups of any sort whether communities,
trade unions, social classes or pressure groups must have no special
privileges or roles, and are, at least theoretically, of no importance to
the state as such. The models of the overarching state, France to the
fore among them, contrast with the 'Anglo-Saxon' ideal of the plural
and multicultural mosaic (see Allum 1995: 97-106).

Not that the contrast is simply between a French view of the state,
with citizens (supposedly) freely embracing unity, a single cohesive
model of organisation; and a British or American view of pluralism,
with citizens (supposedly) freely embracing diversity. In France there
is little doubt that groups (farmers, state employees) and communities
(regionalists, some religions) possess power, and the state manages
these and the conflicts between them by a mixture of clientilism and
confrontation. The American melting pot (Glazer & Moynihan, 1963)
was strongly assimilationist, and recent globalisation, led by American
capitalism, aims at as strong economic and cultural assimilation in
many ways as any statist ideology. In Britain, the contrast between a
Right-wing social cohesiveness through a social design based on a
unified monarchy whose subjects accepted common practices, and a Left-
wing cultural pluralism through the acceptance of social diversity, has
developed at the turn of the millennium into Margaret Thatcher's
'there is no such thing as society' and Tony Blair's communitarianism.
But neither of these was taken to extremes; there remains in both an
acceptance of both social cohesion and diversity. The differences are

ones of degree.

The Labour party, in its manifesto for the 2001 elections (*The Choices for Britain*), was clear about its priorities:

> There is such a thing as society. We are not isolated individuals. We are responsible for our own actions but we have a duty to each other too. Labour's ambition of a responsible society with stronger communities ... We have consistently worked to promote equality and social justice. ... we will introduce citizenship education into the national curriculum in 2002.

The basic tenet of the multicultural approach is that society should allow communities to exist and retain their own cultural preferences, habits and traditions, and should not oblige them to assimilate to mainstream cultural assumptions. Multiculturalism implies mosaicity, differing aims and purposes as well as histories and approaches, and is the direct opposite of a coherent, cohesive, society with a single world outlook. As part of the multicultural approach, society is expected to tolerate a range of religions, cultures and languages. This ideological background was seen by both Left and Right as fundamental in the issues of the National Curriculum as it developed in the late 1980s, and has become of greater importance as race riots continued and as international terrorism struck in 2001.

Insistence on teaching standard English in schools was seen in the 1980s by the multicultural Left as symbolising a rejection of the languages, varieties, accents and cultures not merely of traditional dialect areas but of ethnic groups including those speaking English-based Creoles, and hence as a rejection of such social groups themselves. The, possibly deliberate, confusion around this issue was further confounded by the belief that ethnicity, membership of social category, personal wealth, and willingness to obey the law were closely related, so prime minister Thatcher condemned multicultural education ('what is multicultural mathematics?', she is reported to have asked) while many opponents declared that the real intention of the governments of 1979 to 1990, and indeed later, was to marginalise ethnic groups, the poor, and the North by regarding them as in effect criminal. The debate thus lacked clarity, to say the least; neither side understood the other or wished to understand it, and the issue rapidly descended to a shouting match. Interestingly, the governmental desire to define identity by specifying who were the social outsiders added race, ethnicity and language use to what had traditionally, in Britain, been a matter of social class, of geography and of (type of) school.

But even during this period there existed at least a 'remedial' policy of making provision for some of the obvious problems facing immigrants and the offspring of former immigrants. One of the main vehicles for this has been through 'Section 11 Grant', a fund which was set up in 1966 by the Local Government Act, providing 50% funding for Local Authorities, schools and further education colleges 'to help members of ethnic communities to overcome barriers of language or culture, and thereby to play a full part in the social, economic and political life of the country'. In its first year the grant totalled £1.4M; grant was paid at 100% from 1969-70; the largest annual provision was in 1990-91, at £131.2M; in 1994, 55% of the grant was transferred to the 'Single Regeneration Budget', aimed at urban renewal (figures as allocated, not adjusted for inflation). The largest single use of the grant was to employ teachers or bilingual assistants to teach English as a second language in schools.

The Linguistic Minorities Project (LMP: Stubbs, 1985) was a major attempt to discover basic facts about multilingualism in Britain. The project was funded by the Department for Education and Science between 1979 and 1983, involved 150 bilingual interviewers, a sample of nearly 2,500 adults and thousands of children, and was followed by further research funded by the Economic and Social Research Council between 1983 and 1985. LMP investigated eleven linguistic minorities in three cities (London, Bradford and Coventry) and concentrated on mother tongue teaching. By the time it reported, its perhaps naive acknowledgement that 'a book about the other languages of England is therefore indirectly a book about the dominant language and values in England'; its admission that its objective was to put the other languages of England on the educational and political agenda; its belief that the social meaning of different languages and varieties, and educational policy and practice, derive from 'complex historical, political, economic and social processes in the wider society'; and its advocacy of change in these, were seen as direct attacks on the Conservative party's educational policy of the time, and as one more proof of the 'enemy within' in the home institution, the University of London's Institute of Education. The LMP, and with it bilingualism, sociolinguistics and minority languages, came to symbolise a major battle area for the struggle between Left and Right until at least 1994.

The 1997 Labour government was based, among other things, on ideas of multiculturalism and communitarianism which received their probably most outspoken presentation in the speech by Prime Minister Tony Blair to the Labour Party Conference of October 2001. This ideological climate led to policy from 1997 on, aimed at 'neighbourhood renewal' and at a considerable effort at improving race relations, both through the consequences of the MacPherson Report of 1999 into the death of Stephen Lawrence on 22nd April 1993 and through a range of anti discrimination measures. A Social Exclusion Unit was set up in the Cabinet Office to improve government action by producing 'joined-up solutions to joined-up problems' (see www.cabinet-office.gov.uk/seu). In its work, the Unit found that 'while many people from ethnic minority communities were prospering, as a group they are disproportionately disadvantaged and this disadvantage cuts across all aspects of deprivation'. Minority ethnic communities suffered a double disadvantage: while they were concentrated in deprived areas and thus suffered from the problems that affect everyone in such areas, they also suffered 'overt and inadvertent racial discrimination; an inadequate recognition and understanding of the complexities of minority ethnic groups, and hence services that failed to reach them and their needs; and additional barriers like language, cultural and religious differences'. As a consequence (see SEU, 2000: chap. 3),

> The government is determined to make Britain a successful multicultural country and is committed to promoting and improving race equality. It is pursuing these goals through a range of mechanisms, including:
> - extending the direct and indirect racism provisions in the Race Relations Act 1976 to cover public functions not previously covered and to create a statutory duty on public authorities;
> - to promote race equality;
> - introducing race equality targets in the civil service and various public services;
> - establishing race consultative and advice fora like those set up by the Home Secretary, the Secretary of State for Education and the President of the Board of Trade;
> - negotiating European legislation that will outlaw discrimination on grounds of ethnic origin and race in all fields in which the European Community has competence.

Language, and ability in English, was seen by different groups in two distinct and conflicting ways in this situation: as positive, a means of accessing the labour market and a necessary help to assimilation and economic advance; or as negative, a cultural imposition, indicative of a patronising approach and potentially racist. Here, as in the issue of the maintenance of indigenous languages, information was lacking.

A report was published in 2000, following the Moser report of 1999 on basic skills, to set out the Labour party's thinking on the provision of teaching in English for speakers of other languages, widely known as ESOL (Grover, 2000). Provision of classes in English had indeed long been provided as part of initiatives on basic skills (see Chapter 6 above), but the specifics of provision for ESOL had often been lost or subsumed as part of EFL (English as a Foreign Language) or in classes for basic skills including literacy.

The range of potential ESOL learners was defined as:

- settled communities, principally, although by no means exclusively, from the Asian sub-continent and Chinese from Hong Kong;
- refugees, who subdivide into
(a) asylum seekers. ... In recent years the highest number of applications for asylum have been from persons from the former Yugoslavia and Sri Lanka;
(b) settled refugees with exceptional leave to remain (ELR) or full refugee status
- migrant workers, mostly from elsewhere in Europe.
- partners and spouses of students from all parts of the world who are settled for a number of years.

Within these groups the needs varied greatly, and one of the greatest problems lay in the lack of comprehensive, reliable data on numbers and existing abilities. A 1995 report for the Basic Skills Agency estimated a figure of 450,000 with poor command of English, while an earlier estimate for the Department for Education and Employment thought the figure was nearer one and a half million. In 1998, 54,000 people were granted British citizenship; applications for asylum were 46,000. Both figures have increased since.

Enrolments in ESOL classes in 1997-8 were as in Table 8.1. Most of these were in classes whose sole purpose was ESOL , but the earlier introduction of 'language support' classes means that some at least, between 20% and 40%, were in courses for other subjects and had access to supporting classes in English. There were long waiting lists for classes in inner city areas, and the increases in numbers of asylum seekers since 1995 meant that provision for long-established groups had been cut. There was little provision in the workplace and some, but insufficient 'outreach' provision. Up to 25% of students dropped out of courses during the year; Inspectors' reports in 1998-9 showed that 'the standard of provision in this area is a cause for concern when compared with the standard in other programme areas'; qualifications available were poorly understood; some classes were too large and contained very mixed levels of ability and prior knowledge; needs were very variable; teachers were often not trained for language work. Many of the students were highly skilled professionals in their own countries, but the provision of courses was mainly in colleges' 'basic skills' programmes aimed at students who had achieved little at school.

Table 8.1 Enrolments in ESOL classes

Further Education college	56,415
Training Organisation	1,628
Local Education Authority	28,033
Voluntary Organisation	497
Employer	60
Prisons (estimated)	5,000
Other	3,966
Total	95,599

Grover's Report continued with a number of recommendations, most of which were accepted by the government for implementation within its new organisational systems and structures. By 2001, however, little had changed apart from the change of names and the creation of the Learning and Skills Council, an overarching body with 72 regional LSCs, which will bring together all educational and training provision for over-16-year-olds. This restructuring may, eventually, go some way towards simplifying the complex maze of institutions, qualifications and programmes available. The problems that existed at the time of the report, however, were in the fields principally of standards, where there was a lack of higher level certification; curriculum, where the main issue was the lack of specific provision for a range of learners and for oracy as well as literacy; accreditation, where one of the main problems was that cultural differences put many learners at a disadvantage; funding, where the existing situation was too complex; and quality assurance, where teacher training needed to be differentiated from that for basic skills teachers.

The multicultural policy of New Labour has hence consisted of anti-racist proposals on the one hand and the continuation of ESOL classes on the other. The issues come together in the larger, ideological one of 'belonging': citizenship, employment and communication are closely related. The growth of self-imposed segregation, caused by the natural desire of individuals to live with families and friends, led to what four reports on the race riots of 2001 in Oldham, Bradford and Burnley decided had become single-race ghettos, together with considerable resentment at this from nearby districts. Commenting on these reports, Home Secretary David Blunkett urged new migrants to take part in programmes in which they are taught English language. Indeed, he was moved to urge ethnic minority communities to 'abide by British norms of acceptability', and accept that social cohesion was a 'two-way street':

> We need to be clear we don't tolerate the intolerable under the guise of cultural difference. We have norms of acceptability, and those who come to our house - for that is what it is - should accept the norms, just as we would have to do if we went elsewhere.

David Blunkett was attacked for such 'racist' views by many political friends (reported in _The Times_, 10.12.2001):

> Children born and brought up here feel themselves to be British, are proud to be British and I don't think they need any lessons from anybody about their patriotism and Britishness. (Mohammed Sarwar, Labour MP for Glasgow)
> insensitive ... sensational ... disturbing. (Shahid Malik, member of the Labour Party National Executive)
> This is a total red herring ... There is no evidence of any immigrant coming to this country who has no intention of integrating with the society here. (Iftakhar Khan, project organiser with the Forum Against Islamophobia and Racism)

How far should UK citizenship require knowledge of English? New citizens have to prove that they have a 'grasp of English', but beyond this there has been constant and continuing pressure to require all aspirants to citizenship, including spouses joining them, to learn the language. Right-wing groups generally consider such a requirement as strengthening the status of the nationality requirement and preventing those without UK nationality having access to social resources and support, in some cases going as far as to see such a policy as preventing or reducing immigration. Left-wing supporters see the policy as 'ensuring that new citizens have proper access to mainstream society and the labour market', and particularly 'that ethnic minority women are not denied their civil rights by their own menfolk', as Home Office Minister Lord Rooker put it in 2001. The provision is part of the Nationality, Immigration and Asylum Bill being discussed by Parliament in late 2002. The ideological battle is likely to run and run.

The Territorial Languages and the European Charter for Regional or Minority Languages

Wales was formally united with England in 1536; Scotland in 1707, and Ireland in 1800, in each case after a history of battle and settlement dating from shortly after the Norman Conquest. Since unification, there has been a considerable degree of common action, population mixing and movement, a lack of barriers to social advancement in the UK on grounds of nationality, while UK prime ministers, members of parliament and social leaders have come from non-English backgrounds for centuries, and allegations of internal colonialism on the centre-periphery economic model are not always easy to uphold. All four countries have a closely entwined history, their economies can barely be disentangled, and their cultures have influenced each other. Yet sufficient of the former separate political identity has remained in cultural differences, including to a certain extent language, to ensure that political devolution could be strengthened in 1998 with the passage of Acts that effectively transferred responsibility for many matters, including education, to the Scottish Parliament, the Welsh Assembly and the Northern Ireland Assembly.

The aim of Plaid Cymru, the Scottish National Party and Sinn Fein, the three main nationalist parties, throughout the twentieth century has been independence or at least autonomy, including linguistic autonomy, from England. Until very recently, the UK's formal acceptance of such aims, and of documents like the European Charter for Regional or Minority Languages represented a major political problem for the Westminster executive, in a country where the issue of citizens' rights in Northern Ireland ran through every aspect of public life and armed struggle had been taking place with the Irish Republican Army, closely connected to Sinn Fein, since 1922. It was not until the IRA ceasefire, eventually followed by the British-Irish Agreement, that 'normal' politics could start to address the problem issue. The same type of problem had affected Wales, where Welsh activists had attacked an RAF station in 1936, the Welsh Language Society had burned holiday homes in Wales in the 1960s and protest at English influence, although nowhere at the Irish levels, had continued since. Generally speaking, the Conservative party had supported ideas of cohesiveness and unity, while the Labour party had given support for greater local and regional control of affairs and argued for less domination from London.

Formal devolution in all three countries occurred shortly after the

Labour election victory of 1997. Soon after, the UK government signed the European Charter for Regional or Minority Languages, and ratified it as a Convention in March 2001 (see Appendix). Each devolved authority - Parliament or Assembly - is responsible for implementing the Convention, and substantially for its own language policy, so that the actual format adopted in each of the three countries is different, both in the specific language(s) referred to and in other ways. The Charter is drawn up in five parts:

> Part I: General provisions;
> Part II: Objectives and Principles;
> Part III: Measures (from which a selection may be made, with a minimum of thirty-five paragraphs including three on education and cultural activities and one each on judicial matters, public services, media, economic and social life;
> Part IV: Application, including a periodical report to the Council of Europe;
> Part V: Final Provisions.

The ratification document is a UK document, and specifies different paragraphs in Part III for each of the UK's territorial languages. These have been chosen to reflect the different situation of each language, so that for example Welsh has signed up to more, and more detailed, paragraphs for the economic and social life section of Part III than have the other languages. UK commitment to support for translation, media and public services differs, too. As part of the UK's acceptance of the Charter the UK appointed, on 4th October 2001, Emyr Lewis as the UK representative on the Council of Europe Committee of Experts whose duties include inspection of the reports submitted by the contracting countries. One aspect of the Convention that is not finally concluded is the position of Cornish, a language that had died in the nineteenth century and has since been revived by activists.

A language question ('Can you understand spoken Gaelic (in Scotland), Welsh (in Wales), Irish (in Northern Ireland), speak, read or write it?') appeared in the 2001 Census forms, themselves separate for each country. The forms for England blandly stated that 'this question is not applicable in England'. Indeed, the 'myth of homogeneity' of the 'White' UK population, criticised in the 1991 Census when citizens were asked if they were 'White', will be only slightly affected by the formulations for England and Wales in 2001, which add 'Irish' and 'Any other White background' (Aspinall, 2000). Although in Scotland citizens may select 'Scottish', 'Other British',

'Irish' or 'Any other White background', neither the Welsh nor the English can declare their nationality anywhere.

Wales

Welsh language activism had been dormant since the 1940s (Grillo, 1989: 95). The 1942 Welsh Courts Act allowing Welsh to be used in legal proceedings had followed the trial of two activists in which they refused to testify in English. A broadcast in 1962, following the 1961 Census results showing further decline in Welsh speaking, was followed by the creation of the Welsh Language Society, a campaign of demonstrations and disobedience, an official report and the 1967 Welsh Language Act, passed just two years before Prince Charles was inaugurated as Prince of Wales in Caernarvon. This Act proposed the principle of 'equal validity' for English and Welsh in Wales. Its 1993 successor formalised this and set up a Welsh Language Board, funded at £M1.861 in 1994-5.   The Welsh Language Board was decried by language activists at the time as falling far short of the official status for Welsh they wanted. They feared that it would lack adequate powers of compulsion to bring about the state of 'natural bilingualism' they wanted. Indeed, the main method proposed to support Welsh was for the Board to require public bodies to set up Welsh Language Schemes, rather than to impose its own.

The legislation was the result, partly, of intense pressure group activity.   Indeed, 'as the Welsh Office expanded its competences since its foundation in 1964 it may be argued that a distinct Welsh lobbying community has grown up. ... The Welsh language lobby is unique to Wales and can be perceived by sections of the non-Welsh-speaking public as a powerful interest group - a "taffia". ' (A. Thomas, 1997). Significant, too, was the fact that at General Elections Conservative Party seats declined from 14 in 1983 to 6 in 1992.

The statistics on Welsh language use from the 1991 Census show that 508,000 people aged over three years could speak Welsh (17.9% of the population). As we noted above in Chapter 1, the statistics show a consistent decline since 1921, when 37.1% of the population spoke Welsh. It took about two years after the 1993 legislation to set up the Welsh Language Board. The Board set up an LPP strategy on the basis of the positive findings of a 1996 attitude survey (see Chapter 1): that 71% supported Welsh throughout Wales; that 75% agreed that Welsh should have the same status as English; that services should be available in Welsh; that Welsh-medium education should be widely available. As a result, the strategy aimed at

- increasing the numbers of Welsh speakers, targeting
  - children and young people
  - parents and the extended family
  - adults who learn Welsh
  - support systems
- providing opportunities to use the language, considering
  - the public sector
  - the voluntary and private sectors
  - increasing opportunities socially and in the workplace
  - information technology and backup support
- changing the habits of language use, considering
  - promoting the use of the language by young people
  - using the language when receiving or providing services
  - the role of the media
- strengthening Welsh as a community language.

The Board started by publishing guidelines for language schemes and negotiating with bodies and organisations to implement these, starting with public services and the larger local councils. Many public services are now available in Welsh, including job services and benefit offices; local councils; health services; income tax and VAT; in court services, including being arrested by the police; post office; main banks and, in some cases, commercial organisations, together with the 'Working in Welsh' scheme. In all these cases, 'services available' usually means that written forms and documents are provided, although in some cases, as with doctors, Welsh-speaking intermediaries are available, as a right, if asked for. The provision is not, quite, the automatic right the Welsh Language Society claims, which aims at a 'naturally bilingual' society throughout Wales. Few Assembly Members use Welsh in debates or committees, although members have the right to do so, and the Assembly itself had not finally agreed its Welsh Language Scheme with the Board by late 2001. On the other hand, the Chief Constable for Northern Wales appointed in 2001 took Welsh lessons on appointment and aims to increase the proportion of Welsh speakers in the police above the 30% at the time of his appointment. Welsh language schemes have been agreed in the case of many councils large and small, the National Parks, Fire Authorities, train services, voluntary bodies like the Royal National Institute for the Deaf and Age Concern, with Universities and with central government such as the Home Office and the Ministry for Agriculture, Fisheries and Food and its successors. The schemes involved here have been developed with the help of the Welsh

Language Board, and in some cases have gone through a number of versions before the Board has been satisfied.

Devolution and the creation of the Welsh Assembly in 1998 meant that Welsh became the responsibility of the Welsh Assembly. LPP is part of the responsibility of the Welsh Minister for Culture, Sport and the Welsh Language. The Welsh Language Board is now formally classified as an Assembly Sponsored Public Body (ASPB), one of those with which the Ministry works, the others being the Arts Council, the Sports Council, the National Library, and National Museums and Galleries. In all these areas, including language, 'the Assembly's policies are largely delivered by the ASPBs'. In support of this, the Assembly allocated £M6.33 for the year 2000-1 to support for the Welsh Language Board.

Generally speaking, the Board's work since has followed the outline strategy established in 1996, with additional emphasis and resources since devolution in 1998. The Board has basically positive things to do, aimed at encouraging and promoting the language; and some negative tasks as well, particularly its policing role in establishing and monitoring Welsh language schemes in both official and non-official bodies and organisations. For this latter role, it has some teeth, although nothing like the draconian powers of the French Délégation Générale aux Langues de France. While in other parts of the United Kingdom policy is limited to support for the territorial languages, in Wales the Board has the power to require bodies to institute Welsh Language Schemes, and is involved in such actions as the recruitment of Chief Constables and the staffing aspects of County Councils. One other intriguing aspect of the LPP work involved has been the creation of community language initiative organisations, the Mentrau Iaith, twenty of which were funded by the Board in 2000/2001. These organisations were first set up in 1991, aiming to identify local language planning needs, take part in cooperation with other Mentrau and their sponsors, act as information and resource centres, and promote the use of Welsh in as many areas as possible, particularly in community services and the voluntary sector. In essence, these organisations are local Welsh Language Boards, staffed mainly by enthusiastic young volunteers aiming at enhancing the use of Welsh in their communities. A report on their activities in 2000-2001 found they had generally had a 'positive influence', despite a somewhat alarming lack of training for the role, and, while they had a good understanding of their local area, they lacked adequate expertise, research and consultation to enable them to conduct efficient surveys and planning.

LPP in Wales has concentrated on status planning, particularly on promotion to ensure that the language is used in the higher level domains, and on acquisition planning. Despite fairly constant calls for corpus work, for example in complaints on the 'degradation' of the language by borrowing from English, by Dafydd Elis Thomas in 1994, and the continuing funding of corpus work such as dialect surveys, literary language and spell checkers, the Welsh Language Board has only moved to consider corpus planning as a whole in 2001. The topic is sensitive: cultural nationalists aim to preserve the language untouched, particularly by English, but the encouragement to learners and particularly to young learners has to enable them to devise and use new vocabulary for new things and new concepts, and if the overriding aim of Welsh LPP is to create a bilingual society there is no way that the Welsh language can be kept isolated from English or from modern life.

While monolingual advertisements in Welsh for posts in Welsh organisations do now appear even in publications circulating outside Wales; Welsh is widely heard on the broadcast media; and many official documents, if they affect Wales, are printed in both Welsh and English; the Welsh Language Society remains unconvinced and still encourages protest. For the Society, in its August 2000 document calling for a new Welsh Language Act for a new century, the 1993 Act is 'legislation which marginalises the language' and represents 'Tory ideology which has no place in the 2000s'. The Society's political position puts it among those who see 'Tory legislation' as being elitist, and see language as the battle flag for the fight against injustice (Chapter 1): 'the fight for the Welsh language is ... part of the wider struggle to create a world that is fairer and more equal'. The 1993 Act 'was an Act to create a Quango'; its ideology was a neo-liberal one, setting no obligations on the private sector since for it, 'the market rules over other social forces'. The Society points out that by contrast to legislation on sexism and racism, there is no nation-wide compulsion involved for bodies to set up language schemes, which themselves are expensive since they are all different. The Society favours compulsion for four reasons: Welsh is a core value for Wales; there is a need to modernise 'outdated legislation'; language legislation has strong symbolic force; and 'reliance on goodwill has not brought a Welsh language service in the case of banks, building societies, mobile phone or software companies. In effect relying on goodwill means relying on language campaigners'.

Ratification of the European Charter in 2001 has brought formal undertakings into play, and the detail of these is noted in the Appendix. They are wide-ranging and cover most, if not all, the demands of the moderate language lobby. To stress the point that pressure to sign the Charter came mainly from Welsh-language activists, the first UK representative nominated to the Council of Europe Expert group which receives reports on the situation in regard to language minorities from signatory countries, was from Wales.

The motivation for LPP in Wales has to be considered in two ways. The motive for the UK government to pass the 1967 Act was mainly a simple response to pressure, or perhaps a sympathetic response to such feelings of despair as those expressed in Saunders Lewis' 1962 lecture on *The Destiny of the Language.* Or perhaps they responded to the call to revolution in that lecture, and hoped to mollify the revolutionaries. The 1993 Act is a much clearer response on the part of a political party which had lost considerable ground in Wales (and Scotland), and felt it necessary to demonstrate its support for Welshness in the hope of regaining political support. The matter was not regarded as crucial nor even as very important for the UK government, and no great fears were expressed over the possible loss of unity; indeed, even in 1980 the Secretary of State for Wales could rather dismissively 'start from the assumption that it is the will and wish of the people of Wales that the language should survive ... and that they will breathe new life into it'. For the Welsh activists, however, the matter was very clearly one of the defence of identity. Dafydd Elis Thomas, the first Chairman of the Welsh Language Board and President of Plaid Cymru from 1984 to 1991 gave a BBC talk in 1994 quoting approvingly the words of Prince Charles, Prince of Wales: 'having a proper sense of pride in one's own cultural heritage and a sense of belonging to a discrete community are surely vital ingredients ... of human societies'. Lord Elis-Thomas then pointed out that the Act 'will affect an important part of our public life in Wales, that part which more than anything else differentiates us as a nation from other nations, namely the use of the language'. He agreed that the fate of the language lay with the people of Wales, and that its future would depend on promotion of the language and 'the enhancement of the status of the Welsh language which will come in the wake of the implementation of the Welsh Language Act'. These clear indications of the identity motive, although building on cultural and economic nationalism, clearly fall within the realm of political nationalism and hence the ideological drive.

Scotland

In Scotland, although the Scottish Office had made some moves towards language support before devolution in 1998, the creation of the Scottish Parliament and added funding for Gaelic meant that the language has a better chance of surviving and of being more used than before. Official language support before devolution was indeed quite strong: Gaelic versions of important documents were regularly produced, particularly if they specifically affected Gaelic, such as the 5-14 curriculum guidelines and the 1994 Inspectorate report on Gaelic education. The Education (Scotland) Act of 1980 had required Gaelic to be taught in Gaelic-speaking areas; specific grants for Gaelic organisations and education had been made since 1986 and amounted to nearly £2M in 1994/5; Gaelic road signs had been authorised since 1981; and the Broadcasting Acts of 1990 and 1996 required support for Gaelic-language broadcasts, so that £8.7M had thus been provided for the Gaelic Television Fund in 1994/5.   Comunn na Gaedhlig was set up in 1984 as the official Gaelic Development Body with support from public funds.

The 1991 Census statistics indicated that Gaelic was spoken by 69,510 people, 1.4% of the Scottish population. The Gaelic-speaking areas are the Western Isles, the Highlands and Argyll, with an urban concentration in Glasgow. In education, in 1999, pre-school Gaelic-medium groups had around 2,000 pupils; 1,831 were in primary education with 232 in secondary, while there were 50 candidates in Gaelic for proficient speakers and 138 for Gaelic for learners at the Higher Grade (age 17). There is general agreement that the use of Gaelic is declining, since there were 210,677 speakers in 1901 (5.2% of the population).

LPP initiatives in Scotland have responded to political priorities since 1979, when the newly elected Conservative government discovered that its popularity in Scotland, as in Wales, had dropped considerably. McKee (1997) indeed places the basis for the revival to the period from 1965 to 1985, when institutions were established such as the Gaelic College (Sabhal Mor Ostaig) on the Isle of Skye, the Highlands and Islands Development Board, the Gaelic Books Council and the playgroups organisation CNSA (Comhairle nan Sgoiltean Araich). In schools, 1965 saw a boost to the implementation of Gaelic education in primary schools, even though the Education (Scotland) Act of 1918 had already placed a duty on education authorities to provide for 'adequate teaching of Gaelic in Gaelic-speaking areas'. Bilingual education developed through the 1970s. In 1984, when the agency Comunn na Gàidhlig was established to coordinate activities, it concentrated at first on education. The, mainly localised, initiatives that followed through the 1980s and 1990s were crowned with devolution in 1998, and since then initiatives have been taken nationally as well as locally. Nonetheless, the largest year-on-year increase in resources for Scottish Gaelic had taken place in 1990, with the 1990 Broadcasting Act and its grant of £M9.5, paid from 1992-3. The Gaelic Television Fund was set up in 1990 to finance the making of television programmes in Gaelic, providing about 200 hours annually.

Policy changed and strengthened in 1998 after devolution, as responsibility for the language and its development transferred to the Scottish Parliament. The Columba Initiative, aimed at fostering linguistic ties between the Gaelic-speaking communities in Scotland and Ireland, was set up in 1997 and is publicly funded. _Gaelic: Revitalising a National Asset_ (MacPherson 2000), a report on the public funding of Gaelic produced as a background to the signing of the European Charter in 2000, and noting the precarious situation of the language, insisted that it remain a National Priority. The ratification of the European Charter itself in 2001 meant that Gaelic could now be used in civil proceedings if witnesses or others wished, as opposed to the previous policy of using Gaelic only if the individual concerned could prove they had no English. Mostly, policy has taken the line of better resource policy with allocations of official money to support Gaelic cultural and linguistic organisations, broadcasting and education. For 2001-2, the planned sums involved were: Gaelic education £M3.439; cultural grants £M0.739; and broadcasting £M8.5, a total of £M12.678. Gaelic has been used since devolution as a debating medium in the Scottish Parliament, subject only to the approval of the Presiding Officer, notably in the debate on the future of Gaelic on 2nd March 2000, although its use is rare. Even the Scottish National Party, a 'democratic left-of-centre political party committed to Scottish independence', still makes no specific mention of Gaelic in its manifesto Platform 2001.

The general analysis is that although things have improved since 1980,

> it is a tribute to its tenacity, if not a miracle, that Gaelic has survived thus far. ... The visibility and public profile of the language have been substantially increased through the process (of additional resource provision), and the political and cultural ramifications of these developments have unquestionably been significant. ... There has been a serious lack of strategy to this

'renaissance', and fundamental questions have been sidestepped. ... Resources have been allocated unevenly, with some fields receiving disproportionate funding and others being severely neglected. (Macpherson, 2000)

Systematic language planning, promoted in Macpherson 2000, is likely to follow the outlines proposed in that report, as well as calling on international resources such as those of the European Bureau for Lesser-Used Languages and policy experts such as Professor Lo Bianco of Australia. In this sense, action is likely to aim firstly at stabilising the language at its present level ('secure status') and move in ten years time to expand it; to concentrate planning in the Gaelic Development Agency; to massively increase funding; and to take emergency action in the educational field. To do this, it is suggested that securing and promoting Gaelic in its heartland must be a key objective in the 'Vision' of Gaelic as a 'foundation stone in the building of a new Scotland, a robust and self-assured community with economic and social stability and pride in its linguistic and cultural identity'. Motivation for Gaelic is hence a matter of aiming at reversing language shift, at first if not mainly in the remaining small Gaelic-speaking area, and is closest to the cultural nationalism seen also in Wales than to the political battle of Northern Ireland. Wider motivation, and particularly the connection between Scottish identity and the Gaelic language, is not a main motivating factor for the majority of the Scottish population.

Northern Ireland

The Government of Ireland Act 1920, followed by the creation of the Irish Free State in 1922 and the Republic in 1948, meant the restoration of an Ireland independent from the British crown after a long and bitter struggle crowned by the 1916 uprising. The Irish language was an important symbol in this process. In 1922, Article 4 of the Constitution of the Free State declared Irish to be the National Language, also recognising English as co-official. Article 8 of the 1937 Constitution of the Republic states that Irish is the primary official language because it is the national language, and the provision has been maintained since. Irish language policies have thus been in place since the 1920s. The language is treated by the state not as a minority language but as the 'real' native language of Irish citizens, and it hence enjoys the highest status. But the language itself had to be remade. By the 1920s it had fallen out of use in elite circles, and had to be recreated from the rural dialect of the socioeconomically disadvantaged. To this extent it is an artificial language. Surprisingly, there is no general Language Law, although one was being prepared in 2001 (see ÓhIfearnáin, T, 2000: 94-7). Knowledge of Irish was, and indeed still is required of civil servants in the Republic, and all children had and have compulsory lessons, so the language is now strongest in the urban middle-income bracket, although the Irish-speaking communities in the Gaeltacht, from whose dialect the language had been recreated, are still rural and still poor. As a result of nearly a century of language planning, the 1991 Census gave a figure of 32.5% of the population as Irish speakers. Despite the high status, despite the language planning, Irish remains, not merely a minority language, but indeed in an endangered state for a number of reasons, and 'state agencies in the 1980s and 1990s (were) speaking more of survival than revival' (Riagáin, 2001: 209).

Northern Ireland, formally part of the United Kingdom, is a different case. Language has long been a symbol of the religious and political differences between the two main communities there (Crowley, 1999). Striking indications of this include renaming streets with Irish names and flying the Irish tricolour in parts of Belfast, and the publicity given to Irish in the Hunger Strikes of 1981 by Republican prisoners. The aim of devolution after 1997, insofar as it affects Northern Ireland, was to institute closer ties between the Republic of Ireland and Ulster, and the main result has been to create cross-border bodies and councils to oversee practical ways of working together. The North-South Ministerial Council thus enables political ministers and administrative civil servants from both Republic and Northern Ireland to meet, discuss their area of expertise and align policy if this seems appropriate. In the case of language, a North/South Language Body was set up following Article 2 of the British Irish Agreement to support Irish, Ulster Scots and Ullans 'across the island of Ireland'.

The 1991 Census question on Irish produced a figure of 45,338 people claiming to speak Irish of a total population aged over three years of 1,502,835 (3%) (quoted in Northover and Donnelly, 1996: 47). An alternative way of presenting the figure is to note that of the 1,502,835 people over the age of three, 39,725 did not reply to this question and 1,320,657 did not know Irish, giving a maximum of 182,178 people (12%) who might have some knowledge of Irish although the more normal figure given elsewhere is 142,000 (9.5%). The raw returns were:

    Can speak Irish: 45,338
    Can read Irish: 5,887
    Can write Irish: 1,340
    Does not know Irish: 1,320,657

Language choice has become a badge of differentiation, and the Northern Ireland agreement and subsequent policy have stressed the LPP decision on language in the attempt to act 'fairly' between the communities. The North/South Language Body has two parts, one for Irish and one for Ulster-Scots; consists of 24 members appointed by the North-South Ministerial Council, 16 for Irish and 8 for Ulster Scots; has two Chairpersons, one of whom is the Chair of the Irish Language Agency and the other that of the Ulster-Scots Language Agency, and is intended to 'understand the desirability of exploring joint projects'. The Body is intended to provide advice for both administrations, public bodies and other groups; undertake support of projects, grant-aid bodies and groups as necessary; and undertake research and promotional campaigns. The two separate Agencies, working for this controlling Body, are the active components, and while the Irish Language Agency absorbs the functions of the Irish government bodies the Bord na Gaeilge (Board for Gaelic), An Gum (publishing) and An Coiste Téarmaíochta (Terminology Development), the Ulster Scots Agency (Tha Boord o Ulstèr-Scotch) has been newly formed and allocates its operations and resources for 2001-2, the start-up year, in four areas: linguistic development (£K565.5), culture (£K262.5), education (£K432.5) and promotion (£K187.5). The total resources for 2001-2, of £M1.45, gave programme expenditure of £K895, divided into support for the Linguistic Dictionary and Development surveys; for cultural support grants; for the School of Ulster-Scots Studies and other educational programmes and materials; and a promotional programme. The practical programme of support for linguistic work, cultural groups and educational programmes is thus aided by a strong promotional programme, and the essentially political nature of language support can be gauged from the list of opportunities and challenges that the Agency saw for itself at the outset of its work:

Opportunities
(a) to promote a greater sense of identity of the Ulster-Scots community;
(b) to play its part in supporting the strategic objectives of the two sponsoring departments, north and south of the border;
(c) to promote the Ulster-Scots language, culture and history throughout the Island of Ireland and beyond;
(d) to play a significant role in the pan-European recognition of minority languages and human rights;
(e) to learn from the experience of other minority languages

Challenges
(a) to maintain the aims of the Agency in an environment of possible political instability;
(b) lack of public awareness;
(c) erosion of the language;
(d) the academic linguistic debate, locally and in Scotland;
(e) the future of the Scots language.
(www.ulsterscotsagency.com, consulted 09.11.01)

Motivation for language support and LPP in Northern Ireland is fairly clearly a matter of political ideology. Identity politics are at the heart of the support for both Irish and for Ulster Scots in the province. The involvement from the Westminster politicians, although clearly driven by a recognition of the strength of this, derives rather from a recognition of the need to correct inequality - even though this is itself part of the ideology of New Labour. The provisions accepted for the European Charter (see Appendix) are fairly clear that political motivation lies behind the paragraphs chosen: they are far fewer in number than for Welsh, and contain some striking exclusions, mainly to do with contacts and developments across the border. Such developments lie clearly within the province of the Anglo-Irish agreement, and the treaty specifically excludes such points as cross-exchanges and joint action across borders.

Motivation in Problem-solving Policy

The three problem areas we have reviewed in this chapter indicate that language planning and policy in Great Britain has responded to quite sharp political problems. Legislation has been passed in all three areas. The sharpest ideological and political battles have turned around the first issue, that of standard English and the National Curriculum. Here, the political ideology of the Thatcher governments of the 1980s claimed moral foundations. Margaret Thatcher's values of personal responsibility, the family and 'rolling back the frontiers of the state', she maintained, were rooted in the spiritual redemption of Christian tradition.   It is hardly surprising that the attitudinal structure of planners reflected high scores in the three scales of excellence, attractiveness and need for action on language, but perhaps somewhat lower ones in vitality: the recognition that there were some domains of use where standard English had not yet achieved full acceptance.   The overall ideal was cohesion or even elitism, ignoring social diversity in the process. This particular problem area is probably the one that has been most studied in relation to LPP in Britain, and the one where it is clearest that the major motivation relied on a particular ideological stance.

The two other cases reflect New Labour's developing concern with language planning, and its relationship with deep-seated ideological differences. New Labour understood that its own ideology involved a different stage in identity creation from the rather stultifying and backward-looking defence of identity. The correction of social inequalities is a long-standing concern of the political Left. Multiculturalism, for those approving Britain's social mosaic approach to social structure, reflected positive attitudes for English as well as other languages; a recognition that English was important because it was used in all domains although other languages clearly were not and never would be; nonetheless a belief in the attractiveness of all languages equally. The desire for action, however, applied only to English. Overall, the ideal was to improve social cohesion by recognising the identity of groups other than the English L1 speakers, but not through their languages.

In the case of the European Charter, also, the main stage in identity formation was to correct social inequality. There is little doubt that behind the saga of the recognition of the territorial languages lay a number of political and ideological battles. Among these were the recognition that Scotland and Wales had become areas where normal political differences between the two main British political parties were no longer at the forefront of politics. In effect, both countries had become no-go areas for Conservative politicians, and two General Elections had returned no or a minute number of Conservative MPs to Westminster. It was clear, too, that politics had in both cases, but particularly in Scotland, been to a large extent taken over by issues of independence or autonomy for the countries themselves. National policy issues at the UK level were of less and less relevance; local and regional issues such as the future of Scotland's oil, the future of the fishing industry or the inward investment from Japanese car manufacturers were of much greater significance. Here, attitudinally, the strong showing of English was matched by rueful recognition of lesser standing for excellence and for vitality for L2s, although it was accepted that both were attractive. What characterised this problem area was the realisation of the need for action in support of the L2, in all parts of Great Britain except England. The ideal planners demonstrated was a need to improve and recognise local identities.

Northern Ireland is not quite the same problem. Political battles had turned round ideas of independence and autonomy, and ideological differences were based on social inequalities. But the situation is special, complicated by numerous factors such as religion and does not reflect a simple Left/Right opposition of motivation. The overall political situation has a long history, well known and kept alive in Northern Ireland. Attitudes towards languages are dictated by political preferences, themselves nourished by community differences. For LPP planners in the UK, although the same solution has been adopted through acceptance of the European Charter, the attitudinal and motivational structures are quite different. Figure 8.1 summarises the overall situation for all three countries, but these differences should be borne in mind.

Motivation in problem-solving policy									
Identity sequence	Attitudinal structure								Ideal/objective
	Exc'nce		Vitality		Attract		Action		
	L1	L2	L1	L2	L1	L2	L1	L2	
Ideology									
Standard English	3		2		3		3		cohesion / elitism
Correct Inequality									
Multiculturalism	3	3	3	1	3	3	3	1	cohesion / mosaicity
European Charter	3	2	3	1	3	3	1	3	cohesion / devolve the issue

For an explanation of the Figure, see pp. 8-11 in the Introduction.

Note that, as with Figures 5.1, 6.1 and 7.2, the motivation analysed here is that of the policy makers. The L1 in each case is English. In the case of both Multiculturalism and the European Charter, the L2 applies to whichever language is 'confronting' English: this might be Welsh or Gujerati, for example.

Figure 8.1 Motivation in problem-solving policy

Chapter 9

British Language Policy and Planning in Perspective

Our investigation of examples of (mainly) governmental language-related actions in Britain aimed at seeing whether these could fairly be called language planning and policy. One thing is immediately clear: if these are examples of LPP, they do not follow a single overall design. They apply to different areas of governmental action, ranging from a concern with economic success to the status issue of the territorial languages; even over the last twenty-five years of the twentieth century they have responded to different ideologies of the political parties, as with the quite different political discourses of the 1980s and the late 1990s; some are long-term, like literacy and anti-discrimination, while others, like the Better English Campaign, have been ephemeral. There is no overarching grand ideal or single problem like that of the defence of French in France. British LPP could be characterised, firstly, as bitty and piecemeal. Alternatively, as pragmatic and practical. In this, language policy seems to reflect policy in many areas.

This conclusion explores the three evaluative approaches we indicated in the Introduction: international comparisons; issues of motivation; and the relationship between language and power.

International Comparisons

The question we raised in the Introduction was the nature of the contrasts with France that the absence of an English Academy implies. We have seen (Chapter 3 and 4) that this country has resisted the establishment of an Academy, in 1714 as in the 1920s, for political reasons. Far from 'bubbling up out of the British character', this resistance is constantly attacked. In newspapers, readers' letters about language matters, and particularly about 'correct' English, are far and away the most numerous. If anything, 'we', the British people, would welcome an Academy with open arms; it is 'they', the elite and the politicians, who resist it. What prevents and continues to prevent its establishment was, historically, Whig distrust of central (Royal) power and its extension. The continuing force of this attitude is shown in defending civil liberties, in political dislike of taking on difficult problems, in British cautiousness about cultural issues, in dislike of elites. There is, too, the lack of a powerful incentive such as that which provokes French linguistic ire: the negative power of Americanisms. France is the most obvious contrast with Britain (Ager, 1996, 1999 and 2001). It has a long history of official support for the standard language going back to the 1539 Royal declaration that French should be used in drafting and administering the law, even though the British equivalent dates from 1362.   The French Revolution of 1789 consecrated French as the language of Reason, of Liberty and of the Rights of Man, and started the process by which French has come to be seen as the embodiment not of Frenchness alone but, at the same time, of universal human rights, of democracy and justice: the 'Republican Values'. Politicians and most French citizens, of Right and Left alike, see the language as a vital part of French identity, and its protection as a duty for all democrats and indeed for humankind.   French was formally declared to be the language of the Republic in a Constitutional amendment in 1992. French is now protected by the Toubon Law of 1994, particularly against Americanisms. There is an extensive mechanism of Terminology Committees in each ministry, and neologisms must be approved by the French Academy, a state-supported body originally formed in 1634, a century before Swift's abortive attempt in Britain. The Academy's decisions are legally binding on the civil service. The Academy's technical work is carried out in the Culture Ministry by the Délégation Générale aux Langues de France (DGLF), for which there is no British equivalent, and whose predecessor was set up by de Gaulle in 1966. The Délégation, with a coordinating role in France covering both corpus and status issues affecting French, the regional languages and 'immigrant languages', has teeth: it provides an annual report to Parliament, has a large budget and, significantly, the ability to conduct or support court cases aimed at enforcing the Toubon Law and at ensuring the use of French rather than other languages in commerce and advertising. Its main role is in behind the scenes activity aimed at convincing professional organisations of the need to protect French and French interests from the invasion of American English. It is because of the philosophical and political pedestal on which French was and is placed that the battle for regional language rights has been much fiercer in France than Britain and much more central to politics, despite the violence of the Irish Republican Army and, to a lesser degree, of the Welsh Language Society. Regionalists supporting Corsican in Corsica, Dutch in Nord-Pas-de-Calais and Picardie, German in Alsace and Lorraine, Occitan/Provençal, Catalan, and Basque in the South, Breton and Gallo in the Northwest, as well as the languages of Tahiti and New Caledonia, both officially regarded as parts of France, are accused not merely of trying to fragment or 'balkanise' the state, but of attacking the very idea of democracy and with it, of cultural advancement and intellectual worth. Like Britain, France signed the European Charter for Regional or Minority Languages in 1998, but immediately found that the Constitutional clause prevented its ratification. The clause had not been changed by 2002, and is still invoked, for example to outlaw state support for the Breton private bilingual schools.

Status and acquisition policy are hence clearly defined in France. There is a single grand ideal: the defence of French has been a theme of successive governments for most of the twentieth century. Currently, the Délégation, keenest in pursuing protectionist commercial policies and media regulation under the cover of cultural protection, represents a tough and consistent implementation, strongly supported by most of the political parties. Nonetheless, one must wonder whether the apparently draconian corpus language policy is anything other than symbolic. The rules on using French and particularly the official vocabulary are constantly ignored; written French in technology, commerce and the media adopts more and more Anglicisms; everyday French itself is changing under the influence of both Arabic and Portuguese, filtering into the language through inner-city slang.

Contrasts with Britain include the lack of a British grand design and single ideal for LPP; the lack of a tough policy of implementation, except perhaps in the field of rights and discrimination; a much weaker British approach to language in the Civil Service; and the lack of official support for technical language work, although this is changing in the devolved countries. Similarities include concerns with literacy; the powerful policy in education, even though this is extremely recent in Britain and centuries-old in France; the 'hands-off' approach to non-territorial language maintenance. Interestingly, France, the cradle of Human Rights, probably has a less powerful anti-discrimination language policy than Britain's. This may be at least partly due to linguistic reasons: whereas the use of 'he' can be discriminatory in English, 'il' refers, not to the sex of an individual but to the grammatical gender of the noun. It is for this reason that, contentiously, the French Academy has consistently ridiculed gender discrimination in language as not applicable to French.

Power struggles have resulted in official language policies, mostly different from Britain's, in all the world's other main countries using English as their principal language (India, the USA, Canada and Australia - but not New Zealand) (Herriman and Burnaby, 1996). At Independence, India's hopes were that English could be dispensed with in fifteen years. At this point in time English was seen by many as being a mark of servitude, of colonial and not of Indian identity. Indeed, the main issue for Congress politicians was the establishment of an Indian identity which would clearly mark the difference between the years of British rule and their hopes for an independent democracy. The situation is an enormous contrast with Britain: more than 1,600 languages, 33 of them with at least a million speakers each. Hindi, using the Devanagari script, and Urdu, using the Persian-Arabic script, were two main languages with a degree of commonality, and a mixed form (Hindustani) had been used for many years both by the civil service and indeed by Congress politicians. But the religious splits meant that Hindi was the language and became the symbol of the Hindus, while Urdu played a similar role for the Muslims. The battles which followed Independence led to the formation of Pakistan and then Bangladesh, meaning that Hindustani could not be adopted as a national language for India. Urdu became the national language of the 'enemy' Pakistan, although it remained a main language within India too. Hindi, the main language for the remaining North, could not act in the same way for India, since it was not the main language for the centre or the South. The enormous size of India and the British inheritance meant that the civil service and indeed public services had to use a common language, and brutal necessity dictated that this should continue to be English. As this brutal necessity became clearer, another linguistic difficulty emerged in the management of the state: if Hindi were to become the national language, non-Hindi-speakers would be automatically disadvantaged, even in the administration of states where Hindi was not the main language or was not spoken at all. As a result, it became clear that policy would have to require many citizens to know English, Hindi and the official state language, together possibly with others according to regional practice. In some states, citizens could need as few as two languages; in others, the need was for at least three and possibly several more. The country hence needed a formal language policy, enshrined in official documents and practice, rather than the covert planning of British rule. India's language policy has been and still is a subject of contention, and aims above all at balancing the interests of India's many language communities. Language policy is defined in the Constitution and its important eighth Schedule, and has been summarised as '3 plus or minus 1' (Ager, 2001: 25-30). Hindi is the official language of six states and the first language of at least two hundred million people. Urdu is the official language of two states and the first language of over twenty million people (in India). Other states have an official language for the state. In Karnataka, for example, a Marathi speaker must know Marathi, Hindi, English and the state's official language, Kannada. An interesting development since Independence is that English has been adopted through necessity, but that it is itself changing and developing, acquiring a distinctive Indian flavour not merely in pronunciation and intonation, but also in grammar and vocabulary. It has been conquered by those who were conquered, and is as a consequence losing the image of colonialism that it once had.

The contrast with Britain is threefold: that multilingualism and multiculturalism are foundation stones in India but not in the UK; that an overt policy is the only answer in India but has not been so until recently in the UK; and that language battles have been much more violent in India than in the British Isles, are not solely political but also economic, but are currently of less importance in India while they are growing in importance in the UK. Despite the growth of Hindu nationalism and the strength of feeling about this and other languages, if India is to remain one country a degree of tolerance towards other communities and other languages is an absolute requirement. Incorporating language policy in the formal Constitution and its Schedules means that there is reliance on textual formulations, and that as a consequence legislation on language is not so new as in Britain. Finally, the violence of the Indian language battles has been strong and occasionally bursts out again, but generally these are matters of the past. The Welsh situation and particularly that of Northern Ireland look old-fashioned from the Indian standpoint. Also, they look perilous: while Welsh is defended in Wales and Irish in Northern Ireland, there is no nationwide protection. Civil servants serving the UK national government are not expected to be multilingual.

Canada has faced the Quebec issue by officially declaring itself bilingual: citizens have the right to demand services in either English or French, and civil servants receive training in both languages. But implementation of this policy is variable, and the provinces themselves do not always follow it. Quebec itself declares the province to be monolingually French, while the western provinces give lip service only to French. Language maintenance programmes for Native Canadians and for immigrant groups are patchy in Quebec, and indeed it was this patchiness and the refusal to consider the situation of groups other than French speakers that have several times defeated referenda for the political autonomy of Quebec. The main contrast with the UK lies in the extent to which Quebec language policy is single-mindedly determined to protect what it sees as a language under attack. French is indeed under pressure in Canada, particularly through the presence of a large and powerful neighbour, the USA, but also from the rest of English-speaking Canada which often tends to see French as a Quebec issue rather than a national one. This places French in the perilous position of being a core value for Quebeckers, and a language policy as being a means of defence for them against powerful and oppressive majorities. Quebec language laws are thus much more defensive and more absolute than the European Charter, and the intensity of the political situation of Welsh, Irish or Scottish Gaelic is nowhere near so great as that for French. On the other hand, the battle over French has marginalised the position of other languages apart from English in Canada, and the position of the indigenous languages is generally poorly protected.

For Canada as a whole, the province of Quebec is important; by contrast, for Britain as a whole, none of the countries other than England is so powerful that its language must be recognised across the country. Canada and Britain share another area for comparison. The UK is a member of the European Union, while Canada, together with Mexico and the United States, forms the North American Free Trade Agreement area. While this is not as political or as all-embracing a union as that in Europe, it nonetheless has linguistic consequences, and Quebec in particular could be forgiven for considering it a major danger for French in north America. In fact, Quebec's attitude is quite different: it has welcomed NAFTA and sees greater links with the USA as being a reinforcement for the Quebec economy, eventually enabling the province to seek autonomy if not complete independence from the rest of Canada. It sees no danger for French: 'the Treaty remains, from the Quebec point of view, a way of promoting cultural and linguistic diversity, while in the other provinces where the same language is spoken as in the US, American culture is likely to dominate' (Morris, 2001). For Canada as a whole, the language issue has been, is, and is likely to remain a problem so major it could lead to the break-up of the country. For Britain the situation is quite different. The UK has generally been careful to keep out of discussions on a possible language policy for the EU, if only because it seems inevitable that English will dominate internally as it already does externally. Only if it looks likely that this language policy by default were to falter would Britain allocate any importance to language matters in the EU.

Australia instituted an official National Policy on Languages in 1987 under Labor, defining the use of English as the required language for all, advocating support for Aboriginal and Torres Strait Island languages, requiring that education provide a language other than English for all, and ensuring equitable and widespread language services including media provision. In education particularly, this had major consequences for teacher employment and for revising the teaching of foreign languages. Most of the policy has been implemented with less enthusiasm as multiculturalism has waned under a more conservative government, although the change from teaching mainly French as the first foreign language to mainly Japanese has remained. Indeed, already in 1991 the policy became one for 'Australia's Language', the title of the White Paper of that year, and the NPL became the ALLP: Australian Language and Literacy Policy. The original NPL had a number of characteristics which mark it off as quite different from the British approach to foreign languages in 2001. Firstly, the policy was solidly backed by all the interested parties, ranging from ethnic pressure groups to teachers of foreign language, of English as a first and as a second language and to media interests wishing to develop new television and broadcasting services. Secondly, the main political push came from ethnic groups, which, in Australia as in Britain, are unlike American ones in that they limit their concerns mainly 'to issues that affect ethnic communities as ethnic communities, such as ethnic broadcasting, ESL programmes, or similar issues' (Ozolins, 1993: 258). Neither of these characteristics is true of UK policy in any of our twelve examples. In the UK, pressure came from the territorial languages for agreement to the European Charter and, quite separately, from the foreign language teaching profession, mainly in universities for the Agenda for Languages. There was little pressure from media interests. In the UK, too, both solutions have remained separate from each other. The UK has a number of language policies, and, perhaps because its economy is already powerful, does not see languages as an essential skill for its economic wellbeing. There is perhaps one similarity: the NPL was a political document, prepared by experienced politicians who carefully analysed the best way to get their message across. In the UK, both the Agenda and the European Charter are political solutions, demonstrating a degree of political understanding of what is needed for policy issues to lead to successful outcomes.

The USA has a long and respectable history as the 'melting pot' absorbing migrants from many countries and many language backgrounds. It has done so by and through its use of English, reshaping the names of Central Europeans as they immigrate and insisting on such symbols as the Magna Carta in the creation of its historical 'myth'. In recent years it has been slowly coming to terms with the existence of its Hispanic underclass, many, but not all, of whom are recent migrants from South and Central America. Although citizens often need Spanish in order to deal with' the local shops, garbage collectors, plumbers, realtors and financial negotiators, and many Californian City Hall telephonists simply pull the plug when English speakers call, many states have instituted 'official English' policies and there is a strong 'US English' movement. Sometimes, as in Arizona, such policies go too far: there, it was struck down when it was used to sack Spanish speakers from state employments. There remain nonetheless many states in which this policy has been adopted, and their main aim is generally to reinforce the melting pot approach and to retain prestige for English. There is a strong movement, too, supporting official English throughout the whole of official life in the USA, pressing for a   Constitutional Amendment to declare the language official for the United States. The 'protection' of English as the official language is a live issue in school Boards as well as in the national political sphere. By contrast to the UK, language is often a hot political issue.

Two main lessons arise: firstly the lack of formal LPP for the official language in the UK. France has its Constitution and its Toubon Law; India its Constitution and Constitutional Schedule; Canada its Official Languages Act of 1969; Australia its Language Policy; the USA its state language legislation. In Britain the legislation lies mainly in two domains: the Welsh Language Act and the ratification of the European Charter, neither of which affects English; and legislation for the National Curriculum, which does. The second lesson is the lack of a single overriding language-related issue in the UK: English is in no danger; devolution and minority rights have not been a central issue until recently. British LPP has responded in different ways to the issues of rights, resources and problems it has encountered.

Motivation in British LPP									
Identity sequence	Attitudinal structure								Ideal/objective
	Exc'nce		Vitality		Attract		Action		
	L1	L2	L1	L2	L1	L2	L1	L2	
Identity (personal)									
Identity (social)									
Ideology									
Civil Service	3		3		2		3		cohesion /culture change
Political discourse	3		2		3		3		cohesion /electoral votes
Standard English	3		2		3		3		cohesion/ elitism
Image									
ELT	3		2		3		3		competition/ favourable
Insecurity									
Maintain Identity									
Non indigenous langs	3	1	3	1	3	1	1	1	cohesion / ignore issue
Defend Identity									
Better English	3		1		3		3		cohesion /obligation
Maintain inequality									
Correct Inequality									
Sexism	2		3		2		3		cohesion/ change corpus
Other discrimination	2		3		2		3		cohesion/ change corpus
Multiculturalism	3	3	3	1	3	3	3	1	cohesion/ mosaicity
European Charter	3	2	3	1	3	3	1	3	cohesion/ devolve the issue
Integrate									
Improve use of Instrument									
Adult literacy	3		3		3		3		cohesion / improve economy
MFL	3	3	3	3	3	3	1	3	(mixed)
Despair									

Figure 9.1 Motivation in British language policy

Motivation in British LPP

During the period 1975-2001, the twelve acts of language policy that we have reviewed in this book seem to relate to different stages of identity creation and maintenance. To present these motivations in the way that we did in Ager (2001) implies a chart like Figure 9.1, in which we have incorporated Figures 5.1 (p. 106), 6.1 (p. 122), 7.1 (p. 131) and 8.1 (p. 172). For an explanation of the basis for the Figure, see pp. 8-11 of the Introduction and note that 'corpus' is used in its LPP meaning.

Political ideology has clearly been an important stage in the identity sequence. Three of our examples seem to be directly inspired by this: discourse change in both the Civil Service and in politics, and the battle over standard English that so enlivened the late 1980s and early 1990s. In these three cases, the attitudinal structure of the planners seems to reflect a general acceptance of the excellence of English, with some reservations in the latter two issues about its vitality or the degree of its actual use in domains the planners wished to influence. Its attractiveness, except perhaps in the case of the Civil Service where 'clarity' rather than beauty was the aim, was accepted, while in all three cases action was clearly called for. The overall ideal which lay behind planners' action seems to be that of social cohesion, while the more specific objectives planners aimed for included culture change in the Civil Service, the search for electoral gain and a desire to ignore, or even repress, growing social diversity by stressing the importance of the elite's language.

Image creation, the presentation of the identity to others, is obviously important when English is being taught abroad. Here, the ideal, by no means specific to Britain, is the desire to compete with other languages and nations. The objective is to seek a favourable image for the country, often difficult in the case of a language with the history of English world-wide. It goes without saying that English is regarded as excellent and attractive.

In the other issues we have dealt with, the stage in identity creation and maintenance which is involved is not quite so clear. The defence of identity, and its most obvious manifestation in nationalism, has not been a motive of great concern to the British political Establishment, at least in relation to England and English. Nonetheless, in the case of the Better English Campaign, which rather fizzled out and was by no means regarded as a key element even in the Conservative Party, the motive was to maintain identity against the 'attacks' from the social barbarians who would misuse it. The maintenance of non-indigenous languages has also not been an issue high on the agenda of any political party, and while the search for social cohesion may be the ideal, the general lack of enthusiasm for action at national level seems to imply objectives of simply wishing to ignore the question. By contrast, issues of discrimination, collected together under our heading of 'correcting inequality', have attracted considerable political concern. The correction of gender inequalities has been taken seriously, and the planners here have been strongly encouraged to take action by vocal and enthusiastic pressure and interest groups. In the case of discrimination on grounds of gender, race or disability though, action does not seem to have been simply forced by pressure. There has been a genuine desire to change and improve society. The debates on multiculturalism have opposed supporters of mosaicity in society with those who preferred more obvious social cohesion through assimilation. The ratification of the European Charter shows a growing realisation that the forced unification of 'Great Britain' from the fourteenth century on has not been a success, and that the cultural identities of Scotland, Wales and Ireland had not been suppressed. Although we have considered 'social cohesion' as an overall ideal in most cases, it must be remembered that the term is understood very differently on the political Right from the political Left. 'Social cohesion' is in any case an eminently political and ideological ideal. We could well have included all these cases under our 'ideological' stage.

Interestingly for those who regard Britain as a nation of shopkeepers, concerned only with financial advantage, two of our other issues have clear connections to improving the skills of the population at large. Adult literacy is not promoted just to help individuals, but also to ensure a better work force, while it may be because the aims of teaching more modern foreign languages and teaching them better are somewhat clouded, that policy in this area has itself so often seemed woolly, unsure of itself and has rarely been followed though with any consistency. The sole aim that has been regularly put forward is that of improving the country's record in exporting.

The one word that seems to recur in the discourse of language planners in Britain at various times in the past had been 'moral'. From the moral concerns of Swift and Dr Johnson to those of nineteenth century educators and colonialists, worry about the potentially destructive effects of bad language as well as about the corrupting consequences of poor grammar has been a recurring leitmotif. The term has not fallen out of use. Nor is its use specific to the Thatcherite radicalism of the 1980s. It was indeed a main feature of the standard English debate in the 1990s. But it also inspired the New Labour government's aim to create a 'prosperous and fair society, in which all individuals have an opportunity to fulfil their potential'. Even the Agenda for Languages of 2001, too, sets a high moral tone throughout (King & Johnstone, 2001).

From this discussion we may conclude that a strong sense of duty, of ideological concern about the health and wellbeing of the nation, inspires much of British language planning. This sense of morality seems to be ideologically founded. It is however, interpreted quite differently by the two main political parties. On a rather more cynical level, one could point out that while the ideal has often been social cohesion, this, for political parties, is often tantamount to aiming at calming things down and reducing the pressure on themselves. The three quite distinct and only marginally related problems outlined in Chapter 8, those which have marked the change of British LPP from a covert to an overt language policy, are all ideologically marked. The policies represent the result of opposing political ideologies and are struggles between competing political approaches. The standard English issue was raised, almost as a battle flag to be followed by all true believers, in Conservative party moves for educational reform. Multiculturalism, too, acted as an issue of high political sensitivity for both main political parties at the time, and even though the parties had opposing views, each claimed the moral high ground. Devolution, seen as a simple issue of natural justice, has consistently been an aim for the Labour party, and has been just as consistently opposed by Conservatives.

But the same is true for almost all the other issues dealt with in this book. From literacy to clarity in the civil service, from campaigns for better English to antisexism, morality and ideology have coloured the discourse of planning and inspired the actions to be taken. It may be that this motivation is indeed discoursal, rather than real, and it is healthy to keep a degree of cynicism when analysing all the works of politicians; but the extent to which this is the key motivation for Britain is remarkable.

Language and Power

At the extreme some see language planners, indeed all authorities as evil, motivated by the desire to dominate and oppress, while others seem to consider them as angelic, determined to prevent a collapse of linguistic, social, political and moral order. Tollefson's attacks on LPP in *Planning Language, Planning Inequality* (1991), in which the possession of power is seen as inherently selfish, are countered by Honey's (1997) *Story of Standard English - and its Enemies* supporting 'the ability of a common standard language to function as a form of "social cement" in modern nation states'. Tollfeson said that language policy is never about language, but always about power. The three most recent pieces of legislation in language policy in the UK (the National Curriculum, the Welsh Language Act and the ratification of the European Charter for Regional or Minority Languages) reflect this. Each represents the result of an ideological battle and a power struggle. For some, these battles are between one social class and another: the elite versus the rest. For others, the battle is geographical: between England and the other countries, or between London and the South-East on the one hand, and the rest of the UK on the other. The battle could be economic: by improving access to standard English, planners improve the life chances of the socially deprived. The battle is certainly ideological: between the Conservative party, which 'won' the National Curriculum battle, and the Labour party, which 'won' devolution.

There is a distinction to be made between 'top-down' planning and 'bottom-up' planning (cf Kaplan & Baldauf, 1997: 196-213). Top-down planning is that exemplified in the status planning involved in instituting Gaelic-language debates in the Scottish Parliament: it is the elite, the state, or another authority which proposes the change, for social, economic or ideological reasons. Bottom-up planning is that reflected in language choices made by the population: preferences for Cockney over standard English; for maintaining the use of Gujerati; for discoursal choices preferring 'Blair language' to 'Thatcher language', or adopting Americanisms. Top-down planning tries to create a demand for verbal resources such as a new language or a different discourse; bottom-up planning is such a demand, forcing a redistribution of the supply of such resources. To this extent, language planning in the UK represents bottom-up planning much more than top-down planning. It is the demand, particularly in Wales, for the greater use of Welsh in the public domains which led to the Welsh Language Act; it remains to be seen whether the top-down planning in Scotland will actually result in greater use of Gaelic.

In the Introduction (p. 2) we raised a number of questions, all of which relate to the issue of power in society:

(1)   Who are the democratic 'we'?
(2)   How have 'we' ruled ourselves?

(3)   How 'natural' are the mysterious 'forces of change'?
(4)   What is meant by 'dogma and prejudice'?
(5)   What is meant by 'unfettered freedom'?

We are a diversified people. Chapters 1 and 2 have explored the dimensions of diversity: territorial, and becoming more and more significant, ethnic origin; the confusion over British and English identity, with a general conclusion that, even in the other countries of the United Kingdom, Britishness remains a significant identity feature. There are changes in issues of identity caused by membership of the European Union and by increasing immigration. We are the elite and the rest; the planners and the planned. Of this two-part Marxist division, the most significant element is the second. Not for nothing has the Whig interpretation of history remained significant: there remains the dislike for the grand gesture and the symbolic policy. Planning proceeds by fits and starts. The all-embracing language law is not for the British.

How have we ruled ourselves? In language matters, as indeed elsewhere, there has been a long dominance of England and English over the rest of the UK, as Chapter 3 has shown. The hegemony of London, of Parliament, of a national media industry has meant that regional political and linguistic life in England is all but extinct. Which is not to say that dialects and accents have been extinguished: merely that they are reserved for private domains. Regional languages, even those with strong pressure groups like Cornish, have little rallying power. Chapter 3 has also shown the falsity of the idea that we, the populace, have ruled ourselves, free from (linguistic) authority. Not for nothing was Dr Johnson called a language Dictator; the very idea of Britain was a piece of spin produced by James I; the insertion of English into the other countries of the UK was a deliberate act; education at secondary level, at least until 1945, was a restricted resource as was standard English.

Are the mysterious forces of change natural? Yes and no. Language has changed in mysterious ways: the pronunciation of the Queen has changed drastically over the fifty years of her reign. But social pressure has had a major effect on changes in our verbal repertoire and on our use of English. So too has political change: the public discourse of the late Nineties and early Noughties is quite different from that of the Eighties (Chapter 6), while the status change for Welsh, Scottish Gaelic, Ulster Scots and Irish has been the result of political change. Top-down management of language behaviour has also resulted, through the National Curriculum, in improved test results in English as elsewhere in GCSE and at A level (Chapter 8). The jury may still be out on whether the Agenda for Languages will have significant effect on the teaching and learning of foreign languages in Britain (Chapter 7).

Dogma and prejudice are present as ever. The public, writing to the Press, is as dogmatic and sometimes ill-informed as ever it was; its purism remains absolute (Chapter 4). Prejudice remains in some language usage; Americanisms are still anathema to some. But there are changes: the public seems if anything more enamoured of language authority than it used to be: Fowler, Gowers and Partridge are sold in large numbers; the style guides in the Press refer to them; correspondence with the Press reveals a concern with clarity. Anti-discrimination language planning has been accepted; racist and sexist language have generally disappeared (Chapter 5).

So is the freedom of language users in the UK fettered? Will LPP control them, or will language users remain free to say what they want how they want? To an extent, the question is misguided. Language usage has never been unfettered. Social constraints, the requirements of discourse, the need for effective communication have always constrained the use of language except in poetry. Dictionaries, and the language usage industry, have added to the social pressure and epitomised it. U and non-U language, and the class-based usage behind them, have represented a recurring strand in British linguistic history. But freedom depends on having the resources to be free: the verbal resources available to the citizen have been increased by LPP actions (Chapter 6), despite an unsuccessful attempt to direct the 'proper' use of English in the Better English Campaign.

Is there a British language policy? As with most things, the answer is yes and no. Yes in the sense that top-down management of language behaviour has occurred and is present in the UK. There is language legislation: the Welsh Language Act; the ratification of the European Charter for Regional or Minority Languages and the subsidiary legislation associated with it; anti-discrimination legislation on gender, race, disability, with more to come; and the National Curriculum specifications of language(s) to be taught, how, and how they will be tested. Yes, there is considerable language control through such mechanisms as the control of public discourse. But no, there is no British language policy, in the sense that there is no piece of legislation called Control of English, no official declaration that English alone may be used as the medium of education, no legislation requiring that the media broadcast songs in English, no law declaring that asylum seekers will only be addressed in English and must make nands in English (although they must show a knowledge of one ui tne *ipso facto* official languages of the country if they wish to obtain naturalisation). There is no legislation requiring scientific terms to use English (although the British Standards Institution does have a terminology section which approves the use of some terms rather than others).

A society's structure, attitudes and language practices reflect just as powerful a policy as any documented, overt and symbolic statement (see Thompson, Fleming & Byram, 1996: 99). The lack, until recently, of symbolic texts and laws in Britain does not mean that there has not been a very clear, well-defined and well understood official approach to language, so much a part of British society that it did not need a 'language police'. Margaret Thatcher's approach to the use of the standard language was not exclusively hers. Everybody knew that the territorial languages could not be given official status since that would imply devolution. Milroy and Milroy's two types of complaint have a long history, and the answers have often been official. Britain has, and has always had, language policies.

But Britain is now discovering a formal and explicit language policy, as we have seen. Elmes' (2000:108) belief, that 'attempts to prescribe the spoken English of Britain are today doomed to failure. People will do what they want, whether it is 'correct usage' to do so or not ... It is above all usage that largely determines the shape of the language today' is manifestly incorrect as far as discriminatory language, 'bad' language and political discourse are concerned. But 'usage', too, does not come from nowhere. People do not speak, write or indeed drive as they want, replacing 'correct usage' by linguistic anarchy. Influences from social and economic priorities have always played a major part in British language policy. 'Usage' is itself the result of these influences. More and more, political ideologies and authorities are openly shaping a formal, declared, symbolic as well as practical UK language policy.

Appendix

Forty most common Languages in London Schools 1999					
English	608500	French	5600	Luganda	800
Bengali,Sylheti	40400	Spanish	5500	Ga	800
Panjabi	29800	Tamil	3700	Tigrinya	800
Gujarati	28600	Farsi	3300	German	800
Hindi/Urdu	26000	Italian	2500	Japanese	800
Turkish	15600	Vietnamese	2400	Serbian/Croatian	700
Arabic	11000	Igbo	1900	Russian	700
English creoles	10700	French creoles	1800	Hebrew	650
Yoruba	10400	Tagalog	1600	Korean	550
Somali	8300	Kurdish	1400	Pashto	450
Cantonese	6900	Polish	1500	Amharic	450
Greek	6300	Swahili	1000	Sinhala	450
Akan	6000	Lingala	1000	Numbers rounded to the	
Portuguese	6000	Albanian	900	nearest 50	
SOURCE: Community Languages Bulletin 7, 3 Autumn 2000					

Census 2001 ethnic group (England)	Census 2001 forms available in	Population 2001	Population estimate 2020	GCSE entries 2000
WHITE				
British	English	50986000	49000000	666793
Irish		2092000	3000000	2608
Any other White background			?	Welsh: 1st lang 4157; 2nd 9166
	Albanian/Kosovan			
	Croatian			
	Farsi/Persian			255
	French			341011
	German			133612
	Greek			652
	Italian			5625
	Polish			266
	Portuguese			485
	Russian			1791
	Serbian			
	Spanish			49981
	Turkish			943
MIXED		239000		
White and Black Caribbean				
White and Black African				
White and Asian				
Any other Mixed background				
ASIAN OR ASIAN BRITISH				
Indian	Hindi	984000	1200000	
	Gujarati			1374
Pakistani	Punjabi	675000	1250000	1649
	Urdu			6723
Bangladeshi	Bengali	257000	460000	1933
Any other Asian background		242000		
BLACK OR BLACK BRITISH				
Caribbean		529000	1000000	
African	Somali	440000	700000	
	Swahili			
Any other Black background		305000		
CHINESE OR OTHER ETHNIC GROUP				
Chinese	Chinese	149000	250000	2233
Any other	Japanese	219000		636
	Vietnamese			
	Arabic			1307
TOTALS		57100000	57860000	
Sources:	Census Forms	ONS	Parekh 2000:374	CILT Yearbook

The Decline in the Numbers studying Modern Foreign Languages in the UK

'There are lies, damned lies and A-level statistics' (_Independent_, 15.8.2002). The same caution should perhaps apply at other levels of the examination and indeed to the education system in the UK. The statistics below are for England and Wales, where the examinations are the General Certificate for Secondary Education (GCSE) at approximate age 16, the Advanced Subsidiary (AS level) at age 17 and the Advanced Level (A level) at age 18. Scotland and Northern Ireland are not included, as the examination system is quite different. The nearest approach to full and accurate statistics on pupil numbers, numbers studying particular languages, examination entries and passes are available in the CILT Yearbook, published annually. The following figures are those available on the Qualifications and Curriculum Authority's website (qca.org.uk) on 22nd August 2002, or from CILT.

Different conclusions can be drawn. At A level, there has been a decline in England and Wales overall and in proportionate numbers studying foreign languages, since 1996. For some years, the decline is part of a general decline in numbers of pupils at that age in the population, although the decline has exceeded any such general decline in pupil numbers. For individual languages (e.g. Spanish) there has on the contrary been an increase. Between 2001 and 2002 entries dropped for French by 13%; for German by 17%; and increased for Spanish by 0.8%. Other subjects, too, have been in decline: entries for mathematics at A-level fell by 18.6% between 2001 and 2002.

The decline at A level was not matched at GCSE level. This is partly due to the effect of the National Curriculum requirement for a foreign language. Individual languages have again increased or decreased in different proportions over the years since 1996.

Changes at A level (number sitting the examination))

	1996	1997	1998	1999	2000	2001	2002
All langs	59343	48752	46316	42335	N/A	N/A	33722
French	27487	25881	23579	21333	18341	18079	15614
German	10726	10440	10228	9677	8718	8575	7013
Spanish	5232	5606	5644	5876	5702	5743	5572
Urdu	N/A	1184	675	637	742	485	N/A

N/A not available or unconfirmed

In 1992, the A-level entry figures for French were 31261; for German 11338; for Spanish 4720. Over the ten years 1992-2002, the percentage changes are French -50%; for German -38%; for Spanish +18%.

Changes at GCSE level (number sitting the examination)

French	347160	335997	337577	342227	344305	347007	338468
German	134286	134604	134286	137011	134356	135133	126216
Spanish	42553	43468	47406	49329	51264	54326	57983
Urdu	N/A	7222	6779	6348	6723	6423	N/A

N/A not available or unconfirmed.

Over the five years 1996 to 2000, the increases are minimal except for Spanish (French +0.8%; German +0.05%; Spanish +20%).

The European Charter for Regional or Minority Languages.

The Charter will be implemented in Wales, under the aegis of the Welsh Assembly (Division of Culture, Sport and Welsh Language); in Northern Ireland, under the aegis of the Department for Culture, Arts and Leisure (Linguistic Diversity Branch), and in Scotland through the Ministerial Action Group on Languages. The full version of the Charter is available at www.local.coe.int. The provisions which apply from March 2001 under devolution include the following paragraphs and sub-paragraphs of Part III of the Charter, provisions which vary from country/language to country/language.

Part III
Article 8 - Education
1. a i: to make available pre-school education in Welsh;
   a iii: to make available preschool education, or a substantial part of it, in Irish and Ulster Scots, to those pupils whose families so request and whose number is considered sufficient;
1. b i: to make available primary education in Welsh;
   b iv: to make available primary education, a substantial part of it, or to provide for teaching within primary education, in Irish and Ulster Scots to those pupils whose families so request and whose number is considered sufficient;
1. c i: to make available secondary education in Welsh;
   c iv: to make available secondary education, a substantial part of it, or to provide for teaching within secondary education, in Irish and Ulster Scots to those pupils whose families so request and whose number is considered sufficient;
1. d iv: to make available technical and vocational education, a substantial part of it, or to provide for teaching within technical and vocational education, in Welsh, Irish and Ulster Scots;
1. e iii: to encourage and/or allow the provision of university or other forms of higher education in, or of facilities for the study as university or higher education subjects of, Welsh, Irish and Ulster Scots;
1. f ii: to offer Welsh, Irish and Ulster Scots as subjects of further and continuing education.
1. g: to make arrangements to ensure the teaching of the history and the culture which is reflected by Welsh, Irish and Ulster Scots;
1. h: to provide the basic and further training of the teachers required to implement those of paragraphs (a) to (g) accepted (for Welsh, Irish and Ulster Scots);
1. i: to set up a supervisory body responsible for monitoring the measures taken and the progress achieved in establishing or developing the teaching of Welsh and for drawing up periodic reports of their findings, which will be made public.

Note that Paragraph 2, which 'allows, encourages or provides teaching in the regional languages' 'in territories other than those in which the regional languages are traditionally used' is excluded.

Article 9 - Judicial authorities
1. undertake, in respect of those judicial districts in which the number of residents using Welsh justifies the measures specified below, according to the situation of

this language and on condition that the use of the facilities accorded by the present paragraph is not considered by the judge to hamper the proper administration of justice:

a: in criminal proceedings:
  ii: to guarantee the accused the right to use Welsh, if necessary by the use of interpreters and translations involving no extra expense for the persons concerned.
  iii: to provide that requests and evidence, whether written or oral, shall not be considered inadmissible solely because they are formulated in Welsh, if necessary by the use of interpreters and translations involving no extra expense for the persons concerned.

b: in civil proceedings:
  ii: to allow, whenever a litigant has to appear in person before a court, that he or she may use Welsh without thereby incurring additional expense; and/or
  iii: to allow documents and evidence to be produced in Welsh; if necessary by the use of interpreters and translation.

c. in proceedings before courts concerning administrative matters:
  ii: to allow, whenever a litigant has to appear in person before a court, that he or she may use Welsh without thereby incurring additional expense;
  iii: to allow documents and evidence to be produced in Welsh; if necessary by the use of interpreters and translations.

d. to take steps to ensure that the application of subparagraphs (i) and (iii) of paragraphs (b) and (c) above and any necessary use of interpreters and translations does not involve extra expense for the persons concerned.

2. b: undertake not to deny the validity, as between the parties, of legal documents drawn up within the country solely because they are drafted in Welsh, and to provide that they can be invoked against interested third parties who are not users of Welsh on condition that the contents of the document are made known to them by the person(s) who invoke(s) it;

3.: undertake to make available in Irish and Ulster Scots the most important national statutory texts and those relating particularly to users of these languages.

Article 10 - Administrative authorities and public services

1. Within the administrative districts of the State in which the number of residents who are users of regional or minority languages justifies the measures specified below and according to the situation of each language, undertake, as far as this is reasonably possible:

a i: to ensure that the administrative authorities use Welsh;
a iv: to ensure that users of Irish or Ulster Scots may submit oral or written applications in these languages;
b: to make available widely used administrative texts and forms for the population in Welsh or in bilingual versions;
c: to allow the administrative authorities to draft documents in Welsh, Irish or Ulster Scots.

2. In respect of the local and regional authorities in whose territory the number of residents who are users of regional or minority languages is such as to justify

the measures specified below, undertake to allow and/or encourage:

- a: the use of Welsh within the framework of the regional or local authority;
- b: the possibility for users of Welsh, Irish or Ulster Scots to submit oral or written applications in these languages;
- c: the publication by the regional authorities of their official documents also in Welsh;
- d: the publication by local authorities of their official documents also in Welsh;
- e: the use by regional authorities of Welsh, Irish or Ulster Scots in their assemblies, without excluding the use of English;
- f: the use by local authorities of Welsh, Irish and Ulster Scots in debates in their assemblies, without excluding, however, the use of English;
- g: the use or adoption, if necessary in conjunction with the name in English, of traditional and correct forms of place-names in Welsh, Irish or Ulster Scots;

3. With regard to public services provided by the administrative authorities or other persons acting on their behalf, undertake, within the territory in which regional or minority languages are used, in accordance with the situation of each language and as far as this is reasonably possible:

- a: to ensure that Welsh is used in the provision of the service;
- c: to allow users of Irish and Ulster Scots to submit a request in these languages.

4. With a view to putting into effect those provisions of paragraphs 1, 2 and 3 accepted , undertake:

- a: to provide translation or interpretation as may be required (for Welsh, Irish and Ulster Scots);
- b: recruitment, and, where necessary, training of the officials and public service employees required (in Welsh).

5. to allow the use or adoption of family names in Welsh, Irish or Ulster Scots at the request of those concerned.

Article 11 - Media

1. undertake, for the users of regional or minority languages within the territories in which those languages are spoken, according to the situation of each language to the extent that the public authorities, directly or indirectly, are competent, have power or play a role in this field, and respecting the principle of the independence and autonomy of the media:

- a i: to ensure the creation of at least one radio station and one television channel in Welsh;
- d: to encourage and/or facilitate the production and distribution of audio and audiovisual works in Welsh, Irish or Ulster Scots;
- e i: to encourage and/or facilitate the creation and/or maintenance of at least one newspaper in Welsh, Irish or Ulster Scots;
- f ii: to apply existing measures of financial assistance also to audiovisual productions in Welsh, Irish or Ulster Scots;
- g: to support the training of journalists and other staff for media using Irish or Ulster Scots.

Note that specifically excluded are:

1 a iii: to make adequate provision so that broadcasters offer programmes in Irish or Ulster Scots;

1 b ii: to encourage and/or facilitate the broadcasting of radio programmes on
          a regular basis (in Irish and Ulster Scots);
2: to guarantee freedom of direct reception of radio and television broadcasts from
neighbouring countries in a language used in identical or similar form to Welsh,
and not to oppose the retransmission of radio and television broadcasts from
neighbouring countries in Welsh. ... further undertake to ensure that no
restrictions will be placed on the freedom of expression and free circulation of
information in the written press of a language used in an identical or similar form
to Welsh. The exercise of the above mentioned freedoms, since it carries with it
duties and responsibilities, may be subject to such formalities, conditions,
restrictions or penalties as are prescribed by law and are necessary in a
democratic society, in the interests of national security, territorial integrity or
public safety, for the prevention of disorder or crime, for the protection of health
or morals, for the protection of the reputation or rights of others, for preventing
disclosure of information received in confidence or for maintaining the authority
and impartiality of the judiciary.
This paragraph is specifically excluded for Irish and Ulster Scots.
3. undertake to ensure that the interests of the users of Welsh are represented or
taken into account within such bodies as may be established in accordance with
the law with responsibility for guaranteeing the freedom and pluralism of the
media.
Article 12 - Cultural Activities and Facilities
1. With regard to cultural facilities and activities especially libraries, video
libraries, cultural centres, museums, archives, academies, theatres and cinemas, as
well as literary work and film production, vernacular forms of cultural
expression, festivals and the culture industries, including inter alia the use of new
technologies ... undertake, within the territory in which such languages are used
and to the extent that the public authorities are competent, have power or play a
role in this field:

   a: to encourage types of expression and initiative specific to Welsh, Irish
         and Ulster Scots and foster the different means of access to works
         produced in these languages;
   b: foster the different means of access in other languages to works
         produced in Welsh by aiding and developing translation, dubbing, post-
         synchronisation and subtitling activities;
   c: foster access in Welsh to works produced in other languages by aiding
         and developing translation, dubbing, post-synchronisation and
         subtitling activities;
   d: ensure that the bodies responsible for organising or supporting
         cultural activities of various kinds make appropriate allowance for
         incorporating the knowledge and use of of Welsh, Irish and Ulster
         language and culture in the undertakings which they initiate or for
         which they provide backing;
   e: promote measures to ensure that the bodies responsible for organising
         or supporting cultural activities have at their disposal staff who have a
         full command of Welsh, Irish and Ulster Scots as well as of the
         language(s) of the rest of the population;
   f: encourage direct participation by representatives of the users of
         Welsh, Irish and Ulster Scots in providing facilities and in planning
         cultural activities;

g: encourage and/or facilitate the creation of a body or bodies
       responsible for collecting, keeping a copy of and presenting or publishing
       works produced in Welsh;

h: if necessary create and/or promote and finance translation and
       terminological research services, particularly with a view to
       maintaining and developing appropriate administrative, commercial,
       economic, social, technical or legal terminology in Welsh, Irish and
       Ulster Scots.

2.: In respect of territories other than those in which Welsh, Irish or Ulster Scots
are traditionally used, if the number of users justifies it, to allow, encourage
and/or provide appropriate cultural activities and facilities in accordance with
Paragraph 1 above.

3. : to make appropriate provision, in pursuing cultural policy abroad, for Welsh,
Irish and Ulster Scots and the cultures they reflect.

Article 13 - Economic and Social Life

1. undertake, within the whole country,

a: to eliminate from legislation any provision inhibiting or limiting
       without justifiable reasons the use of Welsh in documents relating to
       economic or social life, particularly contracts of employment, and in
       technical documents such as instructions for the use of products or
       installations;

c: oppose practices designed to discourage the use of Welsh in connection
       with economic or social life;

d: to facilitate and/or encourage the use of Irish and Ulster Scots by
       means other than those specified in the above sub-paragraphs.

2. With regard to economic and social activities, undertake, insofar as the public
authorities are competent, within the territory in which Welsh is used, and as far
as is reasonably possible:

b: in the economic and social sectors directly under their control (public
       sector), organise activities to promote the use of Welsh;

c: ensure that social care facilities such as hospitals, retirement homes
       and hostels offer the possibility of receiving and treating in their own
       language persons using Welsh who are in need of care on grounds of ill-
       health, old age or for other reasons;

e: arrange for information provided by the competent public authorities
       concerning the rights of consumers to be made available in Welsh.

Article 14 - Transfrontier Exchanges

Note that both paragraphs are specifically excluded for Northern Ireland (i.e.
application and conclusion of agreements to foster contacts; and facilitate and
promote cooperation across borders by regional or local authorities).

Devolution

Legal provisions concerning language

The Scotland Act 1998 implemented devolution and set up the Scottish Parliament.
Language provisions were included in UK Statutory Instruments 1999 No 1095:
Rule 7.1 (1) The Parliament shall normally conduct its business in English but
members may speak in Scots Gaelic or in any other language with the agreement of
the Presiding Officer. (2) Any person addressing the Parliament on the invitation
of the Parliament in accordance with Rule 15.3.5, may do so in any language other

than English with the agreement of the Presiding Officer.

Rule 8.2 2. (and 8.5. 2a) A motion shall be in English. (An amendment shall be in English)

The first debate in Gaelic in the Scottish Parliament took place on the second of March 2000.

In Wales, the major legislation is composed of the Welsh Language Act 1993 (c. 38), the Government of Wales Act (1998 c. 38) and the ratification of the European Charter for Regional and Minority Languages (see above). The Welsh Language Act has three parts: The (Welsh Language) Board; Welsh Language Schemes; and Miscellaneous. The key provision is Part I, 3 (1): 'The Board shall have the function of promoting and facilitating the use of the Welsh language.' In paragraph (2) of this section, the Board is given specific advisory functions for the Secretary of State, for 'persons exercising functions of a public nature', and for 'those and other persons providing services to the public'. In paragraph (3) of this section, the Board 'may do anything which is incidental or conducive to the performance of its functions', although it requires Treasury approval to 'make a grant or loan, to give a guarantee or acquire or dispose of any interest in land'. In Part II, 'every public body to which a notice is given under Section 7 below' has to prepare a scheme specifying the measures it proposes to take' to 'give effect, as far as is appropriate to the circumstances and is reasonably practicable, to the principle that in the conduct of public business and the administration of justice in Wales the English and Welsh languages should be treated on a basis of equality'. There is a major reservation: In paragraph (21) of this part 'references in this Part of the Act to public bodies do not include references to any person acting as the servant or agent of the Crown'. The paragraph continues to make it clear that there is nothing against any such person adopting a Welsh language scheme. In Part III the main provisions are for legal proceedings, where Welsh may be spoken by 'any person party, witness or other person who desires to use it', subject to notice, and any necessary provision for interpretation shall be made accordingly'. Provision is also made for the use of Welsh in 'documents relating to Welsh companies'.

From time to time Statutory Instruments (e.g. 1999 No. 1100) specify the public bodies involved in Welsh Language Schemes.

The Government of Wales Act 1998 sets up the Welsh Assembly and specifies the functions devolved to it. These include culture, and the 'National Assembly has inherited the responsibility for a wide range of cultural policies. These include policies towards the arts and sport; libraries, archives and museums; the Welsh language and publishing; and film' ... 'The Assembly's policies in the cultural field are delivered largely by the Assembly Sponsored Public Bodies and other organisations which are funded by us' (National Assembly website: www.wales.gov.uk). These include the Welsh Language Board.

Legislation for Northern Ireland derives from the British-Irish Agreement of 10th April 1998 and the Multi-Party Agreement of the same date annexed thereto. Statutory Instrument 1999 no 859 specifies the setting up of various implementation bodies, to include one for language to be known as the North/South Language Body. The provisions of the European Charter applicable to Northern Ireland are set out above.

References

Ager, D. E. (1996) *Language Policy in Britain and France. The Processes of Policy.* London: Cassell Academic.

Ager, D. E. (1999) *Identity, Insecurity and Image. France and Language.* Multilingual Matters 112. Clevedon: Multilingual Matters.

Ager, D. E. (2001) *Motivation in Language Planning and Language Policy.* Multilingual Matters 119. Clevedon: Multilingual Matters.

Alladina, S. & Edwards, V. (1991) *Multilingualism in the British Isles.* (2 vols.) London: Longman

Allum, P. (1995) *State and Society in Western Europe.* Cambridge: Polity Press.

Amis, K. (1997) *The King's English.* London: Harper Collins.

Amis, M. (2000) *War Against Cliché.* London: Jonathan Cape.

Aspinall, P. (2000) The challenges of measuring the ethno-cultural diversity of Britain in the new millennium. *Policy and Politics* 28 (1),109-18.

Bailey, R. W. (1991) *Images of English. A Cultural History of the Language.* Cambridge: Cambridge University Press.

Baker, C. (1992) *Attitudes and Language.* Multilingual Matters 83. Clevedon: Multilingual Matters.

Barbour, S. (2000) Britain and Ireland: the varying significance of language for nationalism. In S. Barbour & C. Carmichael. (eds) *Language and Nationalism in Europe.* (pp. 18-43). Oxford: Oxford University Press.

Barbour, S. & Carmichael, C. (eds) (2000) *Language and Nationalism in Europe.* Oxford: Oxford University Press.

Baugh, A.C. & Cable, T. (2002) (5th ed) (1st ed 1935) *A History of the English Language.* London: Routledge.

Bernstein, B. (1971) *Class, Codes and Control. Vol 1: Theoretical Studies towards a Sociology of Language.* London: Routledge and Kegan Paul.

Bex, T. (1999) Representations of English in twentieth century Britain: Fowler, Gowers and Partridge. In T. Bex & R. J. Watts (eds) *Standard English: the Widening Debate.* (pp. 89-109). London: Routledge.

Bex, T. & Watts, R. J. (eds) (1999) *Standard English: the Widening Debate.* London: Routledge.

Bryson, B. (2001) (3rd ed) (1st ed 1983) *Penguin Dictionary of Troublesome Words.* London: Penguin.

British Social Attitudes. (Annual). London: Sage.

Bryson, B. (1990) *Mother Tongue.* London: Penguin.

Bullock, A. (1975) *A Language for Life. Report of the Committee of Inquiry under the Chairmanship of Sir Alan Bullock.* London: Her Majesty's Stationery

Office.

Burchfield, R. (1981) *The Spoken Word: a BBC Guide*. London: BBC Publications.

Burchfield, R. (1985) *The English Language*. Oxford: Oxford University Press.

Burstall, C., Jamieson, M., Cohen, S. & Hargreaves, M. (1974) *Primary French in the Balance*. London: National Foundation for Educational Research.

Cameron, D. (1990) Demythologizing sociolinguistics: why language does not reflect society. Reprinted in N. Coupland, & A. Jaworski, (eds) (1997) *Sociolinguistics. A Reader and Coursebook* (pp. 55-67). London: Macmillan.

Cameron, D. (1995) *Verbal Hygiene*. London: Routledge.

Cameron, D. (1998) (2nd ed) *The Feminist Critique of Language. A Reader*. London: Routledge.

Canagarajah, A. Suresh. (1999) *Resisting Linguistic Imperialism in English Language Teaching*. Oxford: Oxford University Press.

Carney, E. (1992) *History of English Spelling*. London: Routledge.

Carter, R. (1999) Standard grammars, spoken grammars; some educational implications. In T. Bex & R. J. Watts (eds) *Standard English: the Widening Debate*. (pp. 149-66). London: Routledge.

Chambers, J. K. (1995) *Sociolinguistic Theory. Linguistic Variation and its Significance*. Oxford: Blackwell.

Cheshire, J. & Trudgill, P. (eds) (1998) *The Sociolinguistics Reader. Vol 1: Multilingualism and Variation. Vol 2: Gender and Discourse*. London: Arnold

CILT. (Annual) *CILT Direct Languages Yearbook*. London: Centre for Information on Language Teaching and Research.

Coates, J. (1993) (2nd ed) *Women, Men and Language*. London: Longman.

Cooper, R. (1989) *Language Planning and Social Change*. Cambridge: Cambridge University Press.

Coulmas, F. (1992) *Language and Economy*. Oxford: Blackwell.

Coupland, N. (2000) Sociolinguistic prevarication about 'standard English'. *Journal of Sociolinguistics* 4 (4), 622-34.

Coupland, N. & Jaworski, A. (eds) (1997) *Sociolinguistics. A Reader and Coursebook*. London: Macmillan.

Cox, B. (1989) *English from 5 to 16*. London: National Curriculum Council.

Cox, B. (1991) *Cox on Cox: An English Curriculum for the 1990s*. London: Hodder and Stoughton.

Crowley, T. (1989) *The Politics of Discourse. The Standard Language Question in British Cultural Debates*. London: Macmillan.

Crowley, T. (ed) (1999) *Language and Politics in Ireland. A Critical Reader: 1366-1922*. London: Routledge.

Crystal, D. (1987) *Cambridge Encyclopedia of Language*. Cambridge: Cambridge University Press.

Crystal, D. (1997) *English as a Global Language*. Cambridge: Cambridge University Press.

Crystal, D. (2000) On trying to be Crystal-clear: a response to Phillipson. *Applied Linguistics* 21 (1), 415-23.

Davies, A. (1999) Standard English: discordant voices. *World Englishes* 18 (2), 171-86.

DEE. (2000) *Skills for Life*. London: Department for Education and Employment.

Economist, The. (1991) *The Economist Style Guide*. London: The Economist Business Books.

Edwards, J. (1994) Group rights v. individual rights: the case of race-conscious policies. *Journal of Social Policy* 23 (1), 55-70.

Elis Thomas, D. (1994) *A Life for the Language. Annual Radio Lecture*. Cardiff: BBC Cymru Wales.

Elmes, S. (2000) *The Routes of English. Vol. 2*. London: BBC Education Production.

Eurobarometer. (Series). Brussels: European Commission Public Analysis Sector.

Fairclough, N. (1999) *New Labour, New Language?* London: Routledge.

Fasold, R. (1987) Language policy and change: sexist language in the periodical news media. In P. Lowenberg (ed) *Georgetown University Round Table on Languages and Linguistics 1987*. (pp. 187-206). Washington DC: Georgetown University Press.

Fennell, B. (2001) *A History of English. A Sociolinguistic Approach*. Oxford: Blackwell.

Fishman, J. (ed). (2001) *Can Threatened Languages be Saved?* Multilingual Matters 116. Clevedon: Multilingual Matters.

Fowler, H. W. (1968) (2nd ed, revised and updated by Sir Ernest Gowers) (1st ed. 1926) *Modern English Usage*. Oxford: Oxford University Press.

Giles H. & Powesland, P. F. (1975) *Speech Styles and Social Evaluation*. London: Academic Press.

Glazer, N. & Moynihan, N. (1963) *Beyond the Melting Pot*. Cambridge, Massachusetts: MIT Press.

Gowers, Sir E. (1954) *The Complete Plain Words*. London: Her Majesty's Stationery Office.

Graddol, D. (1997) *The Future of English? A Guide to Forecasting the Popularity of English in the 21st Century*. London: Glenton Press.

Greenbaum, S. (1990) Whose English? In C. Ricks and L. Michaels (eds) *The State of the Language*. London: Faber and Faber.

Grillo, R. (1989) *Dominant Languages. Language and Hierarchy in Britain and France*. Cambridge: Cambridge University Press.

Grimes, B. F. (1996) *Ethnologue: Languages of the World*. Dallas: Summer Institute of Linguistics.

Grover, D. (2000) *Breaking the Language Barriers. Report of the Working Group on ESOL, under the Chairmanship of D. Grover*. London: Department for Education and Employment.

Halliday, M. A. K., McIntosh, A. & Strevens, P. (1964) *The Linguistic Sciences and Language Teaching*. London: Longman.

Halsey, A. H. and Webb, J. (eds) (2000) *Twentieth Century British Social Trends*. London: Macmillan

Harris, M. (Working Party Chairman) (1991) *Modern Foreign Languages in the National Curriculum*. London: Department for Education and Science.

Hawkins, E. (1983) Language Study for the Slower Learner. In G. Richardson (ed) *Teaching Modern Languages*. (pp. 99-128) London: Croom Helm.

Herriman, M. & Burnaby, B. (eds.) (1996) *Language Policies in English-dominant countries*. The Language and Education Library 10. Clevedon: Multilingual Matters.

Hoggart, R. (1957) *The Uses of Literacy: Aspects of Working Class Life with special reference to Publications and Entertainments*. London: Chatto and Windus.

Holborow, M. (1999) *The Politics of English: a Marxist View of Language*. London: Sage.

Honey, J. (1983) *The Language Trap: Race, Class and the Standard English Issue in*

British Schools. Kenton, Middlesex: National Council for Educational Standards.

Honey, J. (1997) _Language is Power: the Story of Standard English and its Enemies_. London: Faber.

Hornsey, A, W. (1983) Aims and Objectives in Foreign Language Teaching. In G. Richardson (ed) _Teaching Modern Languages_. (pp.1-18) London: Croom Helm.

Images. (1986) _Images of Women: Guidelines for Promoting Equality through Journalism_. London: National Union of Journalists.

Isajiw, W. (1993) Definitions and dimensions of ethnicity: a theoretical framework. In Statistics Canada and Bureau of the Census. _Challenges of Measuring an Ethnic World: Proceedings of the Joint Canada-United States Conference on the Measurement of Ethnicity. 1992_. Washington, D. C.:US Government Printing Office.

Jespersen, O. (1982) (10th ed) (1st ed 1905) _Growth and Structure of the English Language_. Oxford: Basil Blackwell.

Jowell, R., Curtice, J., Park, A., Thomson, K., Jarvis, L., Bromley, C. & Stratford, N. (2002) Politics and Political Parties. In A. Park, J. Curtice, K. Thomson, L. Jarvis & C. Bromley (eds) _British Social Attitudes. The Eighteenth Report_. (pp. 59-75). London: Sage.

Kaplan, R. B. & Baldauf, R. B. (1997) _Language Planning. From Practice to Theory_. Multilingual Matters 108. Clevedon: Multilingual Matters Ltd.

King, A. S. & Reiss, M. J. (eds) (1993)_The Multicultural Dimension of the National Curriculum_. London: The Falmer Press.

King, L. & Johnstone, R. (2001) _An Agenda for Languages_. London: Centre for Information on Language Teaching and Research.

Kingman, J. (1988) _Report of the Committee of Inquiry into the Teaching of the English Language_. London: Her Majesty's Stationery Office.

Labov, W. (1966) _The Social Stratification of English in New York City_. Washington, D. C. : Center for Applied Linguistics.

Lakoff, R. (1975) _Language and Woman's Place_. New York: Harper and Row.

Larsen, H. (1997) _Foreign Policy and Discourse Analysis_. London: Routledge.

Lewis, Saunders. (1962) _The Destiny of the Language. (Tynged yr Iaith)_. Annual Radio Lecture. Cardiff: British Broadcasting Corporation Radio Cymru.

Lowenberg, P. (ed) (1987) _Georgetown University Round Table on Languages and Linguistics 1987_. Washington DC: Georgetown University Press.

MacPherson, W. (1999) _The Stephen Lawrence Inquiry_. London: Home Office.

Macpherson, J. A. (Taskforce Chairman). (2000) _Gaelic: Revitalising Gaelic, a National Asset_. Edinburgh: Scottish Executive Publications. Available at www.scotland.gov.uk.

Making it Plain. (1988) _Making it Plain. A Plea for Plain English in the Civil Service_. London: Cabinet Office.

Marenbon, J. (1987) _English, our English: The New Orthodoxy Examined_. London: Centre for Policy Studies.

Marsh, D. & Marshall, N. (2000) _The Guardian Style Guide_. London: The Guardian. Available: www.guardian.co.uk. Consulted: November 2000.

Maurais, J. (ed) (2001) Géostratégies des Langues. _Terminogramme_ 99-100 (special issue).

McArthur, T. (1998) _Living Words. Language, Lexicography and the Knowledge Revolution_. Exeter: University of Exeter Press.

McArthur, T. (1999) On the origin and nature of standard English. _World_

Englishes 18 (2), 161-9.
McArthur, T. (ed) (1992) *The Oxford Companion to the English Language*. Oxford: Oxford University Press.
McCafferty, K. (2001) *Ethnicity and Language Change. English in (London)Derry, Northern Ireland*. Amsterdam: John Benjamin.
McDonald, T. & Boyd, J. (Co-chairmen). (2000) *Languages: the Next Generation. Report of the Nuffield Inquiry into Languages*. London: The English Company.
McKee, V. (1997) *Gaelic Nations. Politics of the Gaelic Language in Scotland and Northern Ireland in the 20th Century*. London: Bluestack Press.
Millwood-Hargrave, A. (2000) *Delete Expletives?* London: Broadcasting Standards Commission.
Milroy, J. (2001) Language ideologies and the consequences of standardization. *Journal of Sociolinguistics* 5 (4), 530-55.
Milroy, L. (1999) Standard English and language ideology. In T. Bex & R. J. Watts (eds) *Standard English: the Widening Debate*. (pp. 173-206). London: Routledge.
Milroy, J. & Milroy, L. (1991) (2nd ed) (1st ed 1985) *Authority in Language. Investigating Language Prescription and Standardisation*. London: Routledge.
Milsted, D. (2001) *Brewer's Anthology of England and the English*. London: Cassell.
Mitford, N. (ed) (1956) *Noblesse Oblige*. Oxford: Oxford University Press
Morris, M. A. (2001) Effets de l'intégration Nord-Américaine sur la diversité linguistique. *Terminogramme* 99-100, 249-64.
Moser, C. (1999) *Improving Literacy and Numeracy: A Fresh Start. Report of a Committee Chaired by Sir Claus Moser*. London: Department of Education and Employment.
NHS Plan. (2000) *National Health Service Plan Summary*. London: Department of Health.
Newbolt, H. (1921) *The Teaching of English in England*. London: HMSO.
Northover, M. & Donnelly, S. (1996) A future for English/Irish bilingualism in Northern Ireland? *Journal of Multilingual and Multicultural Development* 17 (1), 33-48.
ÓhIfearnáin, T (2000) Irish language broadcast media. *Current Issues in Language and Society* 7 (2), 92-116.
Orton, H., Sanderson, S. & Widdowson, H. (1978) *The Linguistic Atlas of England*. London: Croom Helm.
Orwell, G. (1946) Politics and the English language. In S. Orwell & I. Angus (eds). *The Collected Essays, Journalism and Letters of George Orwell. Vol 4*. Harmondsworth: Penguin.
Orwell, G. (1949) *Nineteen Eighty-Four*. London: Secker & Warburg.
Orwell, S. & Angus, I. (eds). (1968) *The Collected Essays, Journalism and Letters of George Orwell*. Harmondsworth: Penguin.
Ozolins, U. (1993) *The Politics of Language in Australia*. Cambridge: Cambridge University Press.
Oxford English Dictionary. (1989) (2nd ed) (1st ed 1933) Oxford: Oxford University Press.
Parekh, B. (2000) *The Future of Multi-ethnic Britain. Report of the Commission into the Future of Multiethnic Britain*. London: Profile Books.
Park, A., Curtice, J., Thomson, K., Jarvis, L. & Bromley, C. (eds) (2002) *British Social Attitudes. The Eighteenth Report*. London: Sage.

Partridge, E. H. (1947) _Usage and Abusage. A Guide to Good English._ London: Hamish Hamilton.

Paxman, J. (1998) _The English. A Portrait of a People._ London: Penguin.

Phillips, L. (1998) Hegemony and political discourse: the lasting impact of Thatcherism. _Sociology_ 32 (4), 847-6.7.

Phillipson, R. (1992) _Linguistic Imperialism._ Oxford: Oxford University Press.

Price, Glanville. (1984) _The Languages of Britain._ London: Edward Arnold. Second edition published as (2000) _Languages in Britain and Ireland._ Oxford: Blackwell.

Quality Schemes. (1999) _A Guide to Quality Schemes for the Public Sector._ available at www.cabinet-office.gov.uk. Consulted 13.12.2001.

Quirk, R. (1990) What is standard English? In R. Quirk & G. Stein. _English in Use._ (pp. 112-25). London: Longman.

Quirk, R., Greenbaum, S., Leech, G. & Svartvik, J. (1985) _Grammar of the English Language._ London: Longman.

Quirk, R. & Stein, G. (1990) _English in Use._ London: Longman.

Rahman, T. (2002) Review of Ricento, T. (ed) Ideology, politics and language policies. _Language in Society,_ 31 (2), 288-90.

Riagáin, P.O. 2001. Irish language production and reproduction 1981-1996. In Fishman, J. (ed) _Can Threatened Languages be Saved?_ (pp. 195-214). Multilingual Matters 116. Clevedon: .Multilingual Matters.

Ricento, T. (2000) Historical and theoretical perspectives in language policy and planning. _Journal of Sociolinguistics_ 4 (2), 196-213.

Richardson, G. (ed) (1983) _Teaching Modern Languages._ London: Croom Helm.

Richardson, J. J. (ed) (1993) _Pressure Groups._ Oxford: Oxford University Press.

Ricks, C. & Michaels, L. (eds) (1990) _The State of the Language._ London: Faber and Faber.

Ruiz, R. (1984) Orientations in language planning. _National Association for Bilingual Education Journal_ 8, 15-34.

Saussure, F. de. (1916) _Cours de Linguistique Générale._ Paris: Payot.

Scottish Office Education Department (1994) _Provision for Gaelic Education in Scotland._ Edinburgh: The Scottish Office.

SEU (2000) _Minority Ethnic Issues in Social Exclusion and Neighbourhood Renewal. Summary Report._ London: Cabinet Office Social Exclusion Unit. Available: www.cabinet-office.gov.uk/seu.

Skeat, W. (1873) _Questions for Examination in English Literature._ Cambridge: Cambridge University Press.

Smith, M. (1993) _Pressure, Power and Policy. State Autonomy and Policy Networks in Britain and the United States._ London: Harvester Wheatsheaf.

Smith, O. (1984) _The Politics of Language 1791-1819._ Oxford: Clarendon Press.

Statistics Canada and Bureau of the Census. 1993. _Challenges of Measuring an Ethnic World: Proceedings of the Joint Canada-United States Conference on the Measurement of Ethnicity. 1992._ Washington, D. C. : US Government Printing Office.

Strevens, P. (1985) Standards and the standard language. _English Today_ 1 (1 (2)), 5.

Stubbs, M. W. (ed) (1985) _The Other Languages of England. Linguistic Minorities Project._ London: Routledge and Kegan Paul.

Sutcliffe, D. (1982) _British Black English._ Oxford: Blackwell.

Swann, M. (1985) _Education for All. Report of the Committee of Inquiry into the_

Education of Children from Ethnic Minority Groups. London: Her Majesty's Stationery Office.

Tannen, D. (1990) *You Just Don't Understand: Men and Women in Conversation*. New York: Morrow.

Thomas, A. (1997) Language policy and nationalism in Wales: a comparative analysis. *Nations and Nationalism* 3 (3), 323-44.

Thomas, D. E. (Lord Dafydd Elis Thomas). (1994). *A Life for the Language*. Annual Radio Lecture. Cardiff: British Broadcasting Corporation Radio Cymru.

Thomas, G. (1991) *Linguistic Purism*. Studies in Language and Linguistics. London: Longman.

Thompson, L., Fleming, M. & Byram, M. (1996) Languages and language policy in Britain. In M. Herriman & B. Burnaby (eds.) *Language Policies in English-dominant Countries* (pp. 99-121). The Language and Education Library 10. Clevedon: Multilingual Matters.

Tollefson, J. (1991) *Planning Language, Planning Inequality*. London: Longman.

Tomlinson, S. (1993) The multicultural task group: the group that never was. In A.S.King & M.J.Reiss (eds) *The Multicultural Dimension of the National Curriculum* (pp. 21-9). London: The Falmer Press.

Trudgill, P. (1974) *The Social Differentiation of English in Norwich*. Cambridge: Cambridge University Press.

Trudgill, P. (1990) *The Dialects of England*. Oxford: Blackwell.

Trudgill, P. (1999) Standard English: what it isn't. In T. Bex & R. J. Watts (eds) *Standard English: the Widening Debate*. (pp. 117-28). London: Routledge.

van Dijk, T. (1998) Principles of critical discourse analysis. Originally in Discourse and Society, 4 (1993), reprinted in J. Cheshire & P. Trudgill (eds) *The Sociolinguistics Reader. Vol 1: Multilingualism and Variation. Vol 2: Gender and Discourse* (pp 367-93). London: Arnold.

Waterhouse, K. (1991) *English, our English (and how to sing it)*. London: Viking Penguin.

Williams, C. H. (1994) *Called unto Liberty! On Language and Nationalism*. Multilingual Matters 97. Clevedon: Multilingual Matters.

Williams, G. (1980) Review of E. Allardt, Implications of the ethnic revival in modern industrial society. *Journal of Multilingual and Multicultural Development* 1, 363-70.

Williams, R. (1976) *Keywords. A Vocabulary of Culture and Society*. Oxford: Oxford University Press.

Williamson, B. (1990) *The Temper of the Times. British Society since World War II*. Oxford: Basil Blackwell.

Your Region, Your Choice. (2002) *Your Region, Your Choice*. White Paper. London: The Stationery Office. available: www.regions.odpm.gov.uk.

Index